The Hitler I Knew

The Hitler I Knew

The Memoirs of the Third Reich's Press Chief

Otto Dietrich

Introduction by
Roger Moorhouse

Greenhill
Books

The Hitler I Knew

This hardback edition published in 2023 by Greenhill Books,
c/o Pen & Swords Books Limited,
George House, Unit 12 & 13, Beevor Street,
Off Pontefract Road, Barnsley, South Yorkshire S71 1HN
www.greenhillbooks.com

ISBN: 978-1-78438-998-7

A CIP data record for this title is available from the British Library

Printed and bound in England by
CPI Group (UK) Ltd, Croydon, CR0 4YY

FSC MIX Paper | Supporting responsible forestry FSC® C013604 www.fsc.org

Contents

Illustrations

*Courtesy of United States Holocaust Memorial Museum. The views or opinions expressed in this book, and the context in which the images are used, do not necessarily reflect the views or policy of, nor imply approval or endorsement by, the United States Holocaust Memorial Museum.

Introduction

OTTO DIETRICH was born in the western German city of Essen in 1897. Resolutely middle-class, he attended a local grammar school before volunteering for service on the Western Front, where he was awarded the Iron Cross, First Class. Returning from the war, he studied at a number of German universities before completing a Doctorate in Political Science in 1921.

Yet, the world that Dietrich saw in the early years of the Weimar Republic did not correspond to that of his studies. Though he soon found employment; first with the Essen Chamber of Commerce, and later as a journalist, he was not unaffected by the intellectual and political ferment of the times. Joining the Nazi Party in 1929, he quickly rose through the ranks, editing a Nazi newspaper and then being appointed Party press chief in 1931. The following year he joined the SS.

By the time that Hitler came to power in 1933, therefore, Dietrich was already well established within the Party hierarchy. In the years that followed, he advanced still further. As a prolific writer and pamphleteer, he produced a number of works through the 1930s that recalled the "heroic" phase of the Party struggle, outlined Nazism's philosophical underpinning or contributed to the growing deification of Hitler.[1] Yet, for all his publications, Dietrich's main

[1] For instance *Mit Hitler an die Macht*, (1933), *Die philosophischen Grundlagen des Nationalsozialismus*, (1935) and *Der Führer und das deutsche Volk*, (1936).

responsibility was as a controller of his fellow journalists. Appointed Reich Press Chief in 1937, he spearheaded the "co-ordination" of the German Press and quickly emerged as a rival to Propaganda Minister Josef Goebbels.

Despite his importance, however, and unlike his diminutive master, Dietrich remained in comparative obscurity and came to public attention rather infrequently. One of the latter instances was in the autumn of 1941, when he was instructed by Hitler to announce to the world that the war in the East against the Soviet Union was "as good as won." This he did, but when the onset of the harsh Russian winter, some days later, brought an end to the German advance, his announcement appeared embarrassingly premature. In spite of such problems, Dietrich was well regarded by Hitler, who referred to him as an "extremely clever man" and a first-rate speaker. Indeed, Hitler once remarked that he was proud to have collaborators such as Dietrich at his side, and that through their skill, he was able to swing the ship of state through 180 degrees and be confident that the German press would seamlessly follow suit.[2] Dietrich retained this exalted position almost until the very end of the Third Reich. Only a month before Nazism's final demise, on 30 March 1945, did he finally fall foul of Hitler. Accused of defeatism during a heated exchange over propaganda tactics, he was sent on indefinite leave.

Dietrich re-emerged in the chaos of the post-war period. Arrested by the British, he was accused of crimes against humanity and membership of the SS. Tried in the so-called "Wilhelmstrasse Trial" of 1949, he was found guilty and sentenced to seven years, but was released after barely eighteen months due to his good behavior. In truth, he had apparently undergone something of a Damascene conversion by this point and had used the comparatively brief period of his imprisonment in Landsberg jail to write this book, which was published in 1955 after his death three years earlier.

[2] See *Hitler's Table Talk, 1941–1944*, (London, 2000), p. 332.

Dietrich had much to contribute. Though he had not been a member of the Führer's household or of his intimate inner circle, he had nonetheless had constant contact with Hitler for over a decade and had been a regular visitor to the Reich Chancellery, to the Berghof, or to Hitler's eastern headquarters, the "Wolf's Lair," so was well-placed to pass comment on his former master. But, unlike many eyewitnesses of the period, his book was not constructed as an affectionate memoir, or as the reminiscences of one "once mighty, now fallen". Rather, Dietrich adopted a rather different tack. Harnessing all the anger and disillusionment of the former disciple, he attempted a political dissection of Hitler, so as to explain to the German people the methods by which they had been seduced, and thereby to warn against future seducers.

One might imagine that—as a former senior official of Goebbels' Propaganda Ministry and a one-time cheerleader in the cult of the Führer—Dietrich would have had much to say on the subject of Hitler's seduction of the German people. However, he concentrates his attentions squarely on Hitler himself, suggesting that "only a thorough and uncompromising knowledge of Hitler's personality, of his innermost nature and his true character, can explain the inexplicable." Though this approach is more than a little simplistic—and ignores the not inconsiderable role played by propaganda—Dietrich's musings on Hitler are still of substantial interest to the modern reader.

The book is divided into two parts: the first addressing specific themes, and the second containing a miscellaneous series of anecdotes and observations. It paints a fascinating picture of the German dictator, as very few would have seen him. Dietrich's thesis is a simple one. Hitler, he says, had a dual nature. To the broad mass of the German people, he showed his benign face—the avuncular father of the nation, the kisser of hands, the lover of children and animals. Only those with a more privileged perspective saw the other side—the diabolical megalomaniac, the psychopath, the dilettante. Those that knew the former, Dietrich averred, would scarcely have recognised the latter.

Dietrich's broadside against Hitler is measured, considered and sustained. He spans the spectrum; presenting the reader with a rich tableau of anecdotes and observations. Much of the book concentrates on the shortcomings and peculiarities of Hitler's personality: from his dismissive attitude to sport to his profound anti-intellectual prejudice. Hitler, he says, was "unteachable", a bohemian and a bigot; a man who would brook no criticism, contradiction or interruption, and for whom any social gathering was simply an excuse to give forth, at length, regardless of who his audience happened to be.

Yet, Dietrich also ventures much deeper to address more serious abuses and failings within the Nazi state. Hitler, he observes, systematically betrayed the trust of the German people by taking them into a war that they did not want. He was a gambler so intoxicated by his successes that he risked all, convinced that he could beat the odds. In addition, Dietrich identified the dark chaotic heart of the Third Reich —the deliberately overlapping fiefdoms and competences, the "dog eat dog" world of what might be called "administrative Darwinism." Indeed, after his own long-standing tripartite struggle with Max Amman and with Goebbels himself, Dietrich was perhaps uniquely well placed to diagnose the condition.

He goes further; suggesting that the lack of any coherent policy to meet the needs and aspirations of conquered peoples during the war—a decision that, he says, came from the very top—meant that all German victories in the field were rendered hollow. Moreover, he argues that for all Hitler's brilliance in military matters, he knew only offensive strategies and was utterly lost when more flexible, defensive modes needed to be employed. Hitler's failings became Germany's downfall.

Dietrich's book is a searing condemnation of the regime that he had so assiduously served and, throughout, he is critical both of the German people and of himself. But his real ire is clearly reserved for the person of Hitler; a man "unparalleled in history," a "schizophrenic… of unique intensity," whose "inhuman and insatiable will shattered the edifice of contemporary life."

His insights are sound and sincere, but the obvious question that arises is when did they first occur to him? Were his criticisms a direct consequence of the defeat of the Third Reich, or did they emerge more gradually, perhaps even during the time that he spent aiding and abetting the man that he would later deride as a psychopath and a monster? Sadly, this crucial question remains unanswered.

There are other notable lacunae. For one thing, Dietrich makes no mention of the Holocaust and only refers to Hitler's anti-Semitism in passing. In part, perhaps, this is a product of the passage of time. The tendency to view the Third Reich almost exclusively through the prism of its persecution of the Jews is of rather modern provenance and would have been alien to many in the 1940s. Yet, even bearing this in mind, Dietrich's omission of Hitler's greatest crime from his account is astonishing. More seriously, perhaps, he fails entirely to examine his own role, and that of his fellow pressmen and propagandists, in assisting Hitler's rise. Though he makes much of Hitler as the "seducer" of the German people, he is strangely silent on his own complicity in the seduction.

Otto Dietrich was an important eyewitness from the period of the Third Reich. Representative of the middle-class, intellectual wing of Nazism, he was highly educated and politically aware, yet also one who clearly suffered from a profound moral myopia. His book is as fascinating for its observations, as it is for its omissions.

Roger Moorhouse, 2010

Part One

Hitler as Leader of "Party, State and Armed Forces"

Chapter 1

Character and Talent

THE CHARACTER and talent of an individual do not change in the course of his life. But what the person's significance to society may be, the sum of his experiences, successes, and achievements, those things which all together constitute his personality—this is the outcome of a process of slow growth. And understanding of a personality, knowledge of a man's true being, is also acquired slowly. We do not gain insight into a man's real nature if we only see him or talk to him now and then, or if we have only heard or read about him. We must study him for many years in his daily life; we must observe his habits. Only then can we, at the end, estimate the success or failure of his existence in terms of his ideas and desires.

Hitler was a demonic personality obsessed by racial delusions. Physical disease is not the explanation for the weird tensions in his mind and the sudden freaks of his will. If any medical term applies to his mental state at all, it would undoubtedly be "megalomania." But he was in no sense mentally ill; rather he was mentally abnormal, a person who stood on the broad threshold between genius and madness. It is not the first time in world history that such a figure has come to the fore. In mind and soul Hitler was a hybrid creature—double-faced. Ambivalence is often the concomitant of genius; inner stresses can strengthen the entire personality. But in Hitler the inner contradictions had got out of hand; the split in his nature had become the determinant of his whole being. For that reason his essential nature cannot be understood in simple and natural terms; it can be grasped only as a union of opposites. Therein lies the secret of his unfathomability. It is this that makes it so difficult to explain the gulf between his outward show of being a selfless servant of the nation and the monstrousness of his actions, which became obvious only in the latter part of his rule.

This fundamental dichotomy in Hitler's nature was apparent in the intellectual realm also. Hitler had extraordinary intellectual gifts—in some fields undoubted genius. He had an eye for essentials, an astonishing memory, a remarkable imagination, and a bold decisiveness that made for unusual success in his social undertakings and his other peaceful works. On the other hand, in many other respects—such as his treatment of the racial question, his attitude toward religious matters, and his astonishing underestimation of all the moral forces in life—his thinking was both primitive and cranky. These intellectual failings resulted in a frightful blindness, a fateful incapacity to deal with foreign policy or to make the proper military decisions. In many situations he could act logically. He was sensitive to nuances. He had the intelligence and boldness to restore seven million unemployed to places in industry. Yet at the decisive moment this same man did not have the spark of understanding to realize that an attack on Poland would necessarily touch off the world war which would ultimately lead to the destruction both of himself and of Germany. Creative intelligence and blind stupidity—these two aspects of his mind, which emerged again and again throughout his life, were the outcome of a basic abnormality.

In Hitler's soul, sincere warmth and icy heartlessness, love of his fellow-creatures and ruthless harshness, dwelt side by side. We have seen him as a kindly person, the enthusiastic patron of artists, affectionate toward children, always considerate of his guests, and gallant toward women, sympathizing with the sufferings and sharing the joys of others. But—as we know today—there raged in that same person the primitive forces of inhumanity. His decisions were based on utter mercilessness. Today, when the frightful facts have been made known and some of the victims have come forward to tell their story, we can only shudder at such repulsive lack of all human feeling. The very same Hitler whom we saw so frequently in newspaper photographs looking into the faces of delighted children gave the order for the imprisonment of innocent wives and children who happened to be related to wanted men. For decades he strongly promoted humane treatment for animals; in conversation he repeatedly stressed his love of animals. And this same man, given the comprehensive powers that were his, must have known of, tolerated, and ordered the horrible cruelties which have been inflicted on men.

To what extent was Hitler aware of his own duality? This question is of crucial importance in any estimate of him. Was he conscious that his actions were monstrous, or was he so caught up in his delusions that he thought them inescapable necessities justified by lofty ends? As I see it, his fantastically exaggerated nationalism—his deification of the nation—was the key to his demonic character. Hitler's unrealistic concept of the nation sprang from his racial delusions. It is the explanation for his passionate ambitions for Germany and for the inhuman crimes he did not hesitate to commit.

Hitler considered himself a very great genius, but not a superhuman, supernatural being. However, he viewed the nation as supernatural, as a god whose prophetic high priest he felt himself to be. He was ready to lay even the most frightful sacrifices upon the altar of the Fatherland in order to preserve the immortality of the nation. When he acted as "Supreme Judge of the Nation," deciding the destinies of human beings, he felt himself raised to a higher level of dignity. Whatever he did for the "higher good of the nation" was exempted from the ordinary strictures of conscience. In all his actions he practiced the notorious principle that the end justifies the means. He did not consider the weal or woe of the people who were actually alive in the present; he thought only of the abstract concept of an unending succession of future generations. His concept of "nation" was something quite different from the people who composed it. That alone explains the frightful tragedy—that in the name of the "nation" he destroyed the actual nation of which he was part.

This unrealistic, this almost transcendental idea of the nation, was expressed in Hitler's Nuremberg speeches. He thought of the nation in terms of thousands of years. He reveled in nationalism when he sat in Bayreuth listening with passionate reverence to Richard Wagner's *Twilight of the Gods*, or when he strode through the mad King Ludwig's "Valhalla" at Regensburg.

There can be no doubt that Hitler had no selfish desires for private riches or superficial comforts. In his whole mode of life he remained amazingly modest and undemanding. He had no taste for pomp; in his manner he remained simple and close to the common people. Nevertheless, at bottom, he exemplified a particular kind of selfishness. He possessed a hunger for power that had nothing to do with cold egotism; his impulse to dominate was a consuming fire. Now that his life stands before me in its completeness, I cannot escape the impression that Hitler's own imagination unconsciously created a vast delusional world in order to give his egotism room to hold sway. Nationalistic megalomania and personal passion for power made him the great, unselfish leader of his people—and made for his tragic failure.

Hitler's dominant characteristic was his extraordinary will power. Jokingly describing in conversation how strong willed he had been even as a boy, Hitler mentioned that he had fallen to the ground, faint from rage, when he could not have the last word in an altercation with his father over some gardening task. He always had to have the last word. So choleric was his disposition that the slightest contradiction would infuriate him. In later years his will became an absolute tyrant, utterly uncontrollable. As long as there was a spark of life left in him, he never yielded. His powerful will could be inspiring and constructive, or it could be depressing and destructive. His will united the people, but his immoderateness tore the nation to pieces again. There was no way of influencing that will of his. That is to say, he allowed himself to be influenced only along the lines he was already impetuously following. Contradiction and resistance only fortified his obstinacy, as friction produces sparks of electricity. This will of his blocked off all attempts to affect it; he enclosed himself in his own authority. And as his power grew, his arbitrariness became more and more absolute. We must understand this in order to put the "influences" upon him into their proper place.

As far as I know, no one influenced Hitler's important decisions. He made them by himself, in retirement, and considered them intuitive inspirations. When he appeared among his close associates around noon I heard him time and again use the phrase: "I thought about that last night and have come to the following decision . . ." Sometimes he would temporarily shelve such decisions, but he never abandoned them. There were occasions when he would refrain from answering pertinent objections right off in his usual domineering fashion because at the moment he had no counterarguments. But in such eases he would return to the subject again and again, with incredible stubbornness, until he had his way. His decision would be proclaimed in the form of an even more insistent order. That was his pattern in the case of less important decisions, with which I was familiar; his behavior in the more important, secret matters was probably the same.

These decisions were not reached in conference; they were handed down. There simply were no meetings of leading members of the government or Party at which decisions were taken. All such supposed conferences belong to the realm of fable. Today we know that the Cabinet of the Reich did not meet at all for many years before the war, and throughout the entire war Hitler never called a meeting. The Party Senate, which Hitler had promised to form and for which the Senate Hall in the Brown House at Munich had been completely furnished, never came into existence. Decisions were made by Hitler alone, then passed on to the government and the Party as accomplished facts. Having announced his decrees, Hitler declared that they were essential to the "welfare of the nation."

He was unteachable. I shall have more to say later about the amazing amount of information he had at his finger tips, and about how enormously well-read he was. On the basis of this he simply insisted that he knew better than anyone else. With unparalleled intellectual arrogance and biting irony he dismissed anything that did not fit in with his own ideas. He spoke with contempt of the "intellectuals." Alas, if only he had had a little more of their despised intelligence and circumspection, what frightful experiences might have been spared the German people. His intellectual arrogance was expressed with an egotism which was often embarrassing. In conversation at table, for example, I have sometimes heard one of his associates correct him on some point of fact in any one of a number of fields of knowledge. No matter how valid the correction, Hitler would not admit his mistake; he would insist upon his version of the thing until the objector would drop the argument from tact and a sense of propriety.

Hitler had a method of impressing foreigners and strangers and preventing them from bringing up any issue. He immediately took control of the conversation, kept the floor uninterruptedly, and talked so long and so vehemently that the interview was over before the visitor had a chance to reply—if he had any desire left to do so. Only once did I see a foreign visitor spoil this trick of Hitler's. He was the Norwegian writer Knut Hamsun. Eighty years old at the time, he was hard of hearing and therefore, consciously or unconsciously, interrupted Hitler repeatedly. He took occasion to voice his complaints about the behavior of the German civil government in Norway with such coolness, and in such drastic terms, that Hitler cut the interview short. After the old gentleman left, Hitler vented his fury in no uncertain terms. Days passed before he succeeded in living down that conversation.

At one and the same time Hitler possessed the power of suggestion and the power to paralyze opposition. By oratory he was able to transmit the suggestive power of his will to the masses, so long as he personally confronted them. It may seem strange today that a very large majority of the Germans voted for Hitler in peacetime, thereby confirming his right to hold the power which old President von Hindenburg had handed to him. But we must realize that over the years Hitler spoke directly to some thirty-five million Germans—aside from the many millions who thronged to see him whenever he rode through the streets of towns and villages. Most of these people were caught and carried away by the suggestive power of his will. We must recall the economic misery of those early days. Hitler had pledged himself to realize the social, economic, and national aims of the people. He had preached to the people in the moving terms of morality and national purity. It is not strange, therefore, that Germans were spellbound by his personality, that they placed their trust in him. His initial successes justified that trust, strengthened it. Even in his later years his followers remained under his influence. For that influence operated on an emotional plane; the intellect could not shake it off, even when doubts arose. His personality acted upon the emotions of the masses in such a way as to paralyze their reasoning processes. That fact explains many things that otherwise appear incomprehensible today.

Hitler had the capacity to fend off any attempt by others to influence him. This I know from many important persons who came to confer with him, each time firmly resolved to put forward certain arguments in opposition to his decisions. Hitler would listen only to their first sentences. Then for an hour he would knead and pound the subject with all the rhetoric at his command, would irradiate it with the peculiar light of his own system of thought. In the end his listeners were in a state of intellectual narcosis, incapable of urging their own point of view—even if they had been given the opportunity to do so. Some knew this method of Hitler's and thought they were immune to it. Some dared to disregard his eloquence and insist on their point. Whereupon Hitler would curtly fall back upon his authority as the Führer. And if the other persisted in holding his ground, an outburst of hysterical rage would freeze the words in the unlucky man's mouth and the blood in his veins.

Hitler's arrogance was founded upon his imagined intellectual superiority. With the growth of his power during the war years it grew to be open megalomania, until ultimately the violence of his will was expressed in outright tyranny. Invoking the laws of war, he made himself master over the life and death of all. Anyone who did not obey his orders without question was branded a defeatist or saboteur.

A pathological restlessness was one of the keynotes to Hitler's character. He never slackened his drive. There was no checking the dynamic thrust of his will. So long as Hitler continued to pursue a policy of peace, such as he had promised and preached, the people still had a choice. But when on his own decision alone he abandoned that policy, the people were left with no choice. It was as if they were in a racing express train with Hitler at the throttle. You cannot get off a moving train; you are on it for good or ill, and must go where it takes you.

Why, we may well ask, was not this dangerous engineer put out of the way in order to bring the train to a stop? But we must remember that this engineer had proved his skill all along, that he assured everybody he would bring the train to its destination. In such an unclarified situation who could take upon himself the tremendous responsibility of depriving the train of its driver, thereby certainly endangering the lives of all? Anyone who had got rid of Hitler would have been branded for all time as the accursed destroyer of the German nation. Since the people still put their belief in Hitler, his death would forever have seemed the cause of the inevitable collapse. The man who killed Hitler would stand before history burdened with the terrible guilt which we now know was Hitler's own. In retrospect the elimination of such a dangerous despot appears to have been necessary and possible; we may even accuse those who were in a position to carry it out of a grave dereliction. But at the time such an act should have been carried out; it seemed disastrous and impossible.

From the time Hitler took power the German people were subjugated by the dynamism of his will. Later the people could not break the chains of violence which Hitler had bound around them.

Among Hitler's own justifications for his actions was his privative philosophy of nature. Both in public speeches and private conversation he would repeatedly refer to this philosophy, his purpose being to convince his listeners that this philosophy represented the final truth about life. He took such principles as the struggle for existence, the survival of the fittest and strongest, for the law of nature, and considered them a "higher imperative" which should also rule in the community life of men. It followed for him that might was right, that his own violent methods were therefore absolutely in keeping with the laws of nature.

In this respect Hitler was thoroughly old-fashioned, a hangover from the nineteenth century. He had no insight into the deep power of spiritual forces; he believed in violence alone. He considered toughness the supreme virtue of a man and interpreted emotion as weakness. He held it to be more correct in principle to inspire fear than to arouse sympathy. Underlying his acts of violence was always the deliberate intention to intimidate. Brutal intimidation was for him the highest political wisdom, the supreme principle of government in politics, in justice, and in war. He would hear no objections and fell into a fury against anyone who recommended consideration and common sense. "Hard" men enjoyed his respect; humane, "soft" people were never in his favor. Characteristically, he made favorites of the very men who were hated by the people; these he would hold up as models to those other of his associates who were popular. And it is typical of Hitler's double-faced nature that the very measures which the people found especially oppressive, the ones that gave rise to the phrase, "If the Führer only knew . . ." were those that Hitler had personally ordered.

Hitler deliberately trampled upon the feelings of humanity; that is the ultimate reason for his fall. Feelings are a tremendous force in the life of nations and in the existence of individual men. Injured, they give rise to passion and fanaticism. Whoever violates them will in the end be defeated by them. Hitler was a master at mobilizing the feelings of other nations against himself. He did everything he could to repel them, nothing to win their liking. His complete lack of sensitivity to the psychology of other nations was always incomprehensible to me. By appealing to the emotions he won over the German people in peacetime; by violating the feelings of humanity he destroyed the German people in wartime.

The tragedy was there from the start. The people had chosen for their leader a man of remarkable intellect and powerful will; but they had not suspected that he contained within himself the demonic forces of a grotesque and frenetic netherworld. In the face that Hitler presented to the people, they saw a brilliant and superior man whose leadership they trusted; in his other, hidden face was reflected the diabolism of his soul, which led them to destruction.

Chapter 2

From Popular Leader to Gambler with Destiny

IN THE FALL of 1931, at the suggestion of Hitler's secretary, Rudolf Hess, who knew me as a journalist, I became a member of Hitler's circle. At that time there was one thing about him that struck me as utterly amazing. He spoke of his coming to power as if there could be not the slightest question about it—although to many persons at this time such a thing seemed impossible, and to me it certainly seemed doubtful. For Hitler, eventual assumption of power was a simple matter of fact. For example, he had for many years been drafting monumental city plans for Berlin, Munich, Nuremberg, and other cities. These were worked out down to the smallest detail and were, later, either begun or actually carried out by him. The building of the *autobahnen* and the elimination of unemployment had been settled policies for more than a decade. The projects he talked about were works of peace and progress, not of war and conquest. In the days when he was still going about from town to town, from whistle-stop to whistle-stop, like an itinerant preacher, he already saw himself taking over the government and carrying out his plans.

Undoubtedly he managed to communicate much of this faith in himself and his mission to the millions who heard him speak at his meetings. At a time of economic collapse and national hopelessness the masses found these new ideas particularly inspiring. As a newspaperman I was present at a great many of those public meetings. As

I recall today what elements in Hitler's thinking had the greatest effect upon his audiences, it seems to me that the following ideas received the greatest applause.

Hitler told the people that national recovery would be achieved only by social measures, and that socialist aims could be attained only upon a nationalistic basis. The national concept he preached was the creation of the classless state by establishing a *Volksgemeinschaft*, a racial community of the people, by eliminating the evils of the party system, and by solving the Jewish problem. The governing principle of this national folk community was to be: "The common good comes before the good of the individual." In foreign policy its aim was revision of the Versailles Treaty.

The socialistic concept developed by Hitler started from the question: By what principle can social justice and harmony of economic interests best be achieved, given the natural differences among men? Hitler's answer was: The socialist efficiency principle, by establishing equality of conditions in economic competition, will produce the most just and at the same time the most successful solution. Consequently he demanded equal opportunities for all, abolition of all privileges of birth and class, breaking the educational monopoly of the propertied class, elimination of unearned income, the "smashing of bondage to interest," and the dethronement of gold since gold is a "nonproductive economic factor." In his economic thinking, work, which creates more work, replaced gold; instead of capitalistic interest he urged economic productivity by the people. Hitler also presented the solution of the Jewish question on a humanitarian basis. There was no talk at all of extermination of the Jewish race. Although he demanded the curbing of their "excessive" influence upon the government and the economy, the Jews were still to be allowed to lead their own lives. I need only mention the Reich Chamber of Culture's department for Jewish cultural affairs, which legally guaranteed to them many cultural opportunities. I may also recall the directives to the Reich Minister of Economics which were issued in 1934 and made public by Propaganda Minister Goebbels. These directives forbade any interference with the economic activities of the Jews so long as they observed the laws of the state.

Many Germans who voted for Hitler in those days did not approve of all his ideas or all the points in his program. Many rejected anti-Semitism; many others considered his economic projects unsound; but they agreed with his other national and social policies and, in view of the situation in Germany, gave his program as a whole their approval. The great majority of them favored the national community and the socialist "folk state" that Hitler proposed. Hitler declared at the time that this socialist folk state was concerned with the inward development of German "folkdom," by which he meant the racial essence of the German people; it was not interested in imperialistic expansionism. He proclaimed National Socialism's desire for peace and made it clear that the revision of the Versailles Treaty was to be achieved by negotiation.

On January 30, 1933 Hitler's appointment as chancellor by President von Hindenburg brought him to one of the crossroads on his path of destiny. Once before fate had given him an unmistakable sign—on November 9, 1923 when his attempt to take power in Munich by force was bloodily smashed. He learned his lesson and straightway made the decision to use legal methods henceforth. After a nine-year struggle those methods led him to his goal. In 1933 Hitler began a new phase; for the first time he came into contact with the world in a responsible position. Once National Socialism came to power the German people had every interest in living at peace with the world, in order to use and develop the positive, peacetime elements of the new ideology Hitler had expounded to them.

At that time I was firmly convinced that a National Socialist Germany would be able to live peacefully with the rest of the world. And so it might have, if Hitler had practiced moderation from the start; if he had checked radicalism at home and if his propaganda for foreign consumption had been objective and had shown some understanding of the interests of other nations. The needlessly provocative demonstrations in Nuremberg and elsewhere, the initiation and toleration of anti-Semitic excesses, and the tone and content of Goebbel's "world propaganda" as shown in his demagogic demonstrations at the Sportpalast, could not possibly win friends abroad for National Socialist Germany. Such behavior inevitably prejudiced other nations against even the good side of National Socialism. Tactless insults decisively influenced world opinion against Germany in the early years following 1933.

From the moment Hitler moved into the Chancellery in Wilhelmstrasse and stepped for the first time upon the international stage, he was faced with an inner decision. I do not know whether he was aware of this. Perhaps at the bottom of his soul he had already made it and was willing to follow it through, come what might. Today, after events have taken their fateful course, we know for certain that during those first years Hitler should have switched to another track if National Socialist Germany was to live at peace with the world. At the time I thought his failure to do so was a concession to the revolutionary enthusiasm of his followers. Today I am aware that the rhythm of his own demonic nature drove him to excesses. When he did rise up in wrath against radical elements—as in the case of Röhm—it was because those elements did not bow to his will and thus represented a danger to him.

There was little change in Hitler's manner and habits upon first becoming chancellor. The Presidential Palace was being rebuilt at this time, for which reason Hindenburg was occupying the chancellor's house. Hitler accordingly moved temporarily into an apartment on the fourth floor of the Chancellery office building. It is worth noting that during his first months Hitler appeared in his office punctually at ten o'clock in the morning. Later on, when he took to going to bed between three and five o'clock in the morning, this ceased to be the case. I shall speak of these personal habits of his in the second part of this book.

In 1933 Hitler's energies were taken up by his struggle with the other parties and by his efforts to solidify his power. The Enabling Act, giving the cabinet legislative powers, and the abolition of other parties ended this stage. The Reichstag fire which he made an occasion for political arrests and for the use of force, came as a surprise to Hitler—contrary to the belief in many quarters. But he regarded it as a gift from destiny and instantly exploited the situation, as he was so adept at doing. He first received word of the Reichstag fire late in the evening. Accompanied by Goebbels, he went to the Berlin offices of the *Völkischer Beobachter* and had the presses stopped. The leading article was thrown out and he himself dictated a new editorial demanding speedy and vigorous measures.

Once Hitler had established himself in an unassailable position of power, he set about with great zeal keeping his promises in the economic and social spheres. The people were deeply interested in these recovery measures, all the more so since after Hitler's radical settlement with his domestic opponents he initiated a policy of wooing the good will of the people. He repeatedly expressed his distaste for acts of revenge on the part of the SA; in an order issued to Röhm he forbade excesses. To former members of opposition parties he opened the doors of the National Socialist Party and the new government, so long as they declared themselves in favor of the "folk community." He allowed almost all of the leaders of these parties to remain at liberty.

Until the late summer of 1933 Hitler had the authority of the aged President above him, and Hindenburg exerted a moderating effect. I believe that old Field Marshal von Hindenburg was the only person in Hitler's career who ever had an effective influence over him. Hindenburg had had something definite in mind when he had obliged Hitler, before appointing him, to retain von Neurath as Minister of Foreign Affairs. When Hindenburg closed his eyes forever on August 2, 1934 he left von Neurath as a kind of political testament. The actual written testament which was published by Herr von Papen after Hindenburg's death has since been repeatedly called a forgery. I personally believe that there is no truth to this rumor. In the circles around Hitler no one ever breathed a word to this effect. I recall that immediately after Hindenburg's death there was talk of certain precautions that ought to be taken in order to secure any posthumous papers of the President's. But Hindenburg had already entrusted his sealed testament to Herr von Papen. Given von Papen's whole attitude toward Hindenburg, it is inconceivable that he would have forged the testament or lent a hand to Hitler in publishing a forgery.

Hitler himself described Hindenburg's relationship with him as at first cool and tentative, later distinctly cordial. During the early months Hindenburg made use of almost every conference between them to bring forward wishes of his own or complaints of other persons who felt they had been treated unjustly by the Party and had petitioned him to intervene. Unless he could show Hindenburg that the complaints were without foundation, Hitler always went along with the president's desires. But in the course of their association Hindenburg's attitude changed so much that he came round to vehemently defending "his Chancellor" against hostile members of the Conservative Party, Hugenberg and Oldenburg-Januschau. Hitler venerated the aged Field Marshal of the First World War. He repeatedly declared that he was very fond of the "old gentleman" who always addressed him as "my dear Chancellor."

Two political events of great importance took place during the eighteen months in which Hindenburg and Hitler guided the destinies of the Reich together. These two events, of great significance in view of later developments, created worldwide tension. They were Germany's withdrawal from the League of Nations, and the case of Röhm.

From remarks Hitler made at the time it is clear that Hindenburg approved of Germany's withdrawal from the League. He agreed that the Reich should be free to make her own decisions—it was in this light that Hitler represented the step. When German delegates to the League and German journalists who had been stationed in Geneva expressed their doubts at the wisdom of Germany's stepping out of the League, Hitler abused them violently and charged that they had been corrupted by the atmosphere of Geneva. Undoubtedly Hitler was already thinking of rearming Germany, but this by no means implies that he was planning war.

Given Hitler's soldierly attitude, only the German army could be considered as the vehicle of rearmament. Here was where Hitler differed sharply with Röhm, and this was the reason for the bloody suppression of Röhm's SA. Röhm felt that he and his storm troopers were being passed over, were being cheated of the fruits of the revolution. But Hitler at that time viewed an attack upon the army as endangering Germany's entire military future. What Röhm was actually planning, I have never been able to find out precisely. Hitler claimed he had proof that Röhm and his immediate subordinates intended to carry out a putsch against the army, and that along with Gregor Strasser and Streicher they were conducting negotiations with foreign powers to muster forces against Hitler. From my observation of the whole course of the purge in Wiessee am Tegernsee and Munich I do not believe Hitler's charges were true, at least not to the degree he asserted. Rather I am today of the opinion that on June 30, 1934 the monstrous side of Hitler's nature for the first time broke loose and showed itself for what it was. On behalf of the nation's future and in order, as Hitler himself expressed it, "to make the army inviolate" and not to compromise its secret plans, Hitler demanded bloody sacrifices. At the time the people were gratified; they considered Hitler's vigorous intervention a repudiation of violence and lawlessness, and thus the definitive end of revolution.

To legalize his actions Hitler had himself proclaimed the "Supreme Judge of the Nation." I can still see him as he entered the house in Wiessee where he arrested Röhm on the morning of June 30. He paced up and down before the storm troop leader with huge strides, fiery as some higher being, the very personification of justice. A few days later Hindenburg called him to Neudeck for a report on the Röhm affair and expressed his appreciation of the swift suppression of these "rebels against the army," as the old president termed them. In later years—and this throws a sidelight on Hitler's own psychological attitude toward political situations—Hitler repeatedly remarked that he was firmly convinced France had not occupied the Rhineland in the months after Germany's withdrawal from the League of Nations only because the French government was well informed and was counting on the Röhm putsch to "extinguish the Hitler regime anyhow."

After Hindenburg's death the Saar plebiscite became the prime issue for Hitler. The peaceful and, for Germany, happy outcome of the plebiscite calmed the political atmosphere again. Then came the concluding of the ten-year non-aggression treaty with Poland, dramatic evidence of Hitler's love of peace. During this whole period his energies were absorbed by the problems of re-employment, of reviving industry, of improving labor conditions and the general welfare. Hitherto he had had little experience with economic problems. But as he plunged deeper into them in practice and achieved tangible results, his self-assurance visibly increased. The title *Der Führer*, The Leader, now seemed to him to designate properly the uniqueness of his mission. At first he adopted as official title Führer and Chancellor. The first symptoms of his development were already beginning to manifest themselves; it is significant that at his own instigation the title of Chancellor was gradually dropped from official use and he was presented to the public solely as Der Führer. At this time the principle of absolute obedience of Party members was introduced, and all members were required to take an oath of loyalty to Hitler personally.

The years 1935 and 1936 were of the utmost importance for the development of Hitler from a domestic reformer and socialist leader to the international desperado and gambler with the destinies of the nations that he later became. During those years he brought his regime through its early insecure stages, successfully carried off the withdrawal from the League of Nations, solidified his absolutist rule, and began looking for new worlds to conquer. With those successes his adventurer's temperament broke through his inner defenses and began operating in the sensitive field of international relationships. During those years he started large-scale rearmament. He also began his intimate collaboration with the "Plenipotentiary of the Reich for Disarmament Questions," Ribbentrop—an association that was later to produce the direst consequences.

Whether Hitler already had well-defined political plans that went beyond mere rearmament is not definitely known. At any rate, if he had any such plans he carefully concealed them even from his closest associates. I learned about the remilitarization of the Rhineland in March 1936 as a great surprise on the morning after it had begun. All that day Hitler waited tensely to see what the reaction of Paris and London would be. He waited twenty-four, forty-eight hours. When there was no intervention, he breathed a sigh of relief. He himself later declared that this step had been proof of his courage. He had played for the highest stakes, and had won. The political future looked rosy.

A change began to be apparent in Hitler's personal manner. He became markedly less ready to receive political visitors unless he had expressly sent for them. At the same time he contrived to erect barriers between himself and his associates. Before he took power they had had the opportunity to air their differences with his political opinions. Now he strictly insisted on the respect due him as head of state and deliberately brought about a state of affairs in which the very persons who saw him most frequently and therefore had opportunities to influence him were unable to talk about political matters. Hitler could no longer tolerate objections to his ideas, or in fact anything which cast doubt on his infallibility. He shied away from any attempts to affect his sovereign will. He wanted to talk, but not to listen; to be the hammer but not the anvil.

From this time on, Hitler also began paying less attention to the Party. His personal participation in Party affairs was limited to his appearance at the big public rallies in Munich, Nuremberg, and so on, and to the speeches he regularly delivered in November and February to his "Old Guard." Chided for this by the Party leadership, he maintained that he was too busy with the affairs of state to give them any more time. That argument seemed reasonable enough—but there was more to it than he admitted. In all his political and military actions henceforth he never took the Party into his confidence, let alone gave the Party leaders an opportunity to state their opinions. Decisions on Party matters were handed down by him through Hess and later through Bormann. Beginning with the withdrawal from the League of Nations, and right down to the bitter end of the war, the entire Party leadership—except for individuals who happened to occupy high posts in the government—learned about all the great and fateful events through the radio and press, like every ordinary German.

The so-called conferences which Hitler held with the leadership of the Party two or three times a year were without exception postscript affairs. At such meetings Hitler either boasted of his triumphs or—especially in the last years—after severe military defeats he inspired his followers with fresh courage by presenting the situation optimistically and hinting of sensational successes to come. Except for a few words of formal greeting or expressions of thanks, none of the other Party leaders ever held the floor. Hitler regularly spoke for several hours. In the course of such speeches he would take occasion to reprimand Party leaders about whose public conduct or private lives he had heard complaints. Overcome with admiration for his victories, filled with new hopes after his defeats, the participants in the conferences would then return to their various posts. Hitler influenced them, but they were unable to exert any influence at all upon him.

As a matter of fact Hitler regarded the Party only as a means to an end, the end being those supreme nationalistic goals he sought to realize. He used the Party when he needed it, neglected it when he did not need it, thrust it aside when it became a nuisance to him. In the early days he often spoke of setting up a Party Senate to advise him; but this whole question was dropped. It may be that even in these early years Hitler's vision had already thrust beyond the narrow confines of the Party; probably he was already looking toward distant goals. Whatever these were, he kept them secret from the Party and the German people. The people hailed the peaceful victory by which Germany was again free to build her defenses as she saw fit; they were convinced that Hitler meant the anti-imperialistic doctrines he proclaimed. They were pleased by the conclusion of the Anglo-German Naval Treaty and spontaneously applauded the French contingents at the Olympic Games held in Berlin in 1936.

In July 1936, while Hitler was attending the Bayreuth Festival, representatives of General Franco flew in from Spanish Morocco bearing a letter from Franco asking for armed aid. Hitler telephoned Göring and forthwith promised volunteer troops. The request provided him with an opportunity to try out his new weapons. And in 1937 he began to show in military parades the arms he had hitherto concealed. Relationships with Fascist Italy, which had been tense since the July 1934 uprising in Austria and Mussolini's threat to send troops across the Brenner Pass, took a turn for the better in 1937.

The year passed quietly. Germany worked. In 1933 Hitler had said, "Give me four years." Since then he had provided millions with work and bread, had raised the living standard throughout Germany. Why should the people distrust him? The people were, of course, aware that Hitler was vigorously rearming Germany. They saw that the preponderant reason for reemployment was armament contracts. But they also believed that the growing domestic strength of the Reich brought with it external dangers; they took it for granted that this rearmament was for defense. Moreover, their physical well-being was dependent upon the new developments. Only a small group of specialists were troubled by German's economic and financial policies.

Hitler's theory of an autarchic national economy was based on the idea that employment creates more employment. A revived economy creates new markets for itself because its demand increases and the employed workers consume more, which tendency in turn stimulates more production, further employment, and further consumption until maximum production had been attained. For this system of pump-priming to work properly, the plants which have been constructed must be productive, thereby assuring repayment of the state subsidies which financed them. Hitler did create employment; he did get the economy started again; it began running at full speed and all the branches of industry were caught up in the rhythm of the humming motors. But the armaments plants swallowed many billions which in spite of prosperity and high taxes did not return to the state treasury. To a certain extent armaments, too, can be economically productive in a larger sense, insofar as they guarantee the country security and the opportunity to develop peacefully. But if armaments are too large in proportion to other production, and if in peacetime the government debt rises so high as a result of military expenditures that a normal reflux from the economy to the state is no longer possible even over long periods, there is good cause for anxiety. In the years before the war it was difficult to judge whether such fears were really justified or whether the rapidly expanding internal economy of Germany could legitimately sustain the increase in debt. Today we know that Hitler purchased economic prosperity with billions in government debt—a debt so staggering that the overloaded credit structure would have made enormous difficulties for him in future years of peace.

Was it this situation, then, that later forced him into war? Nowadays many persons, judging by the logic of the course of later events, would answer that question in the affirmative. I cannot go so far. Economic thinking was basically foreign to Hitler. He was a political figure, not an economist. At the time his primary task seemed to him to "shake off the fetters of the Versailles Treaty." For this purpose he wanted to build up an army which would command respect; the full force of his will was exerted toward this single aim. The aim seemed to him worth all financial sacrifices, and he was too contemptuous of the problems of money to fear the economic consequences.

It is my firm conviction that he was not at that time planning an imperialistic war against any foreign nation. He was driven ahead by the forces within himself, not by any fixed plans. His essays in foreign policy were undertaken without program, in obedience to the virtually pathological rhythm of his aggressive nature. Each thrust was started at haphazard, success accelerating the rhythm and fury of those thrusts. At the end, when he attacked Poland, he staked everything on a single card.

At the beginning of 1938 Hitler suddenly made sensational changes in the leadership of the Army and the conduct of foreign policy. The whole business was cloaked in secrecy. As I saw it, what happened was this. Reichswehr Minister von Blomberg, whom Hitler thought highly of, had remarried. Hitler was a witness at the wedding. For reasons of a private nature Blomberg was shortly afterwards confronted with the alternatives of obtaining a divorce or resigning.* Blomberg refused a divorce, and his resignation became inevitable. Hitler, feeling that he had been placed in a highly embarrassing position vis-à-vis the Army, hit on the idea of settling the Blomberg case discreetly by including Blomberg's resignation in a large-scale shake-up. Numerous district commanders and generals in leading positions were to be replaced by younger officers. The Reichswehr Ministry was eliminated and replaced by the Oberkommando der Wehrmacht (OKW), the High Command of the Armed Forces, headed by Keitel. Keitel's chief qualification was that he could get along with Hitler.

* The "private reasons" that Dietrich does not choose to reveal consisted in the discovery that Blomberg's wife had been a prostitute. Hermann Göring is said to have known of the lady's past all along and to have furthered Blomberg's affair with her in order to force Blomberg's resignation. According to most other testimony, the shifts in the Army High Command, which are pictured here as an incidental outcome of Blomberg case, were the point of the whole affair. Hitler, Göring, and Himmler used the Blomberg case as a lever to pry loose the old Army leadership.—The Translators.

To the surprise of his close associates, Hitler suddenly declared that he was going to include in the shake-up a shift in foreign ministers, in order to cover up the Blomberg case as completely as possible. Casually he dropped the remark that in this way he could kill two birds with one stone. Foreign Minister von Neurath's rival, Ribbentrop, had long been one of Hitler's close associates and had worked with him on all rearmament questions. It was Ribbentrop who had arranged the naval pact with England. He was now recalled from his post as ambassador to London and appointed Minister of Foreign Affairs. Neurath was made president of the "Privy Cabinet Council." Later on I learned to my amazement that this Privy Cabinet Council did not exist and never was set up. It consisted only of a sign on the door of a room in the New Chancellery; I doubt if Neurath ever set foot in that room.

Later on it became apparent that Hitler had, within three and a half years, thrown overboard Hindenburg's political testament.

Among his associates Hitler himself always maintained that this drastic shake-up in the Army and the Foreign Ministry was only for the purpose of throwing dust in everyone's eyes and concealing the real reason for Blomberg's resignation. Today there can no longer be any doubt that the Blomberg case was one of those famous opportunities that Hitler promptly seized in order to achieve his secret ends. He probably felt the time approaching when he would have to guide foreign policy toward the "supreme mission of the nation." Blomberg's withdrawal was for him a sign from destiny. He took advantage of it to create the Oberkommando der Wehrmacht, shaping it into the impersonal military instrument he needed to carry out his orders in blind obedience. At the same time he declared himself Supreme Commander of the Armed Forces and called to his side a man who, as Foreign Minister, would carry out his Master's foreign policy without a qualm.

At the end of February 1938 Hitler felt strong enough to force a change in conditions in Austria. Since 1934 Austrian National

Socialists had been in jail or living as exiles in the Reich. Austria was Hitler's native land and he felt deep obligations toward it. He wanted at last—after having been compelled to hold his hand for so long—to make Schuschnigg "talk German," as he put it. I do not know for certain whether at the time he invited Schuschnigg to Berchtesgaden he already had in mind sending troops into Austria. His express purpose in making the invitation was, at any rate, to impress Schuschnigg with Germany's military strength and persuade him to switch his political course to coincide with that of the Reich. To my mind, if Hitler had intended from the first to march, such a visit would have been superfluous. The order for the troops to march was issued only—according to Hitler's story—after Schuschnigg failed to keep his promises. My first knowledge of Hitler's serious intention to enter Austria came when I was sitting in a car and learned for the first time where our automobile column was heading for.

In the course of the years I have seen Hitler the recipient of a great deal of popular enthusiasm. But the demonstrations when he entered Linz and Vienna were, I believe, the most genuine I have ever witnessed. If before his entry into Austria Hitler had not had a conviction of his supreme destiny to act the savior of the nation, he would have had to acquire such a conviction after experiencing such a wild welcome.

In the first twenty-four hours after his invasion of Austria Hitler was not yet thinking of *Anschluss.* Fearing intervention by the other Powers, he wanted Austrian President Miklas to appoint a National Socialist government. At noon the following day, in the Weinzinger Hotel in Linz, Hitler read the reports I handed to him on the reaction of the foreign press. All the newspapers abroad represented Anschluss with Austria as already a *fait accompli*, and the way they fumed about it made him take a fancy to the idea. He asked himself why he should not carry out an annexation which was already being charged to him. After several hours of vacillation he finally decided in favor of Anschluss, called in his administrative specialists, and ordered them to work out the legal details for incorporation of Austria into the Reich. This almost incredible but historical incident is not the only one of its kind in Hitler's career. More than once Hitler would read an inaccurate assertion and be prompted to do something which until then he had not intended to do. Since I so often handed him the news summaries, I had ample opportunity to observe the psychological development of such cases. Newspaper allegations about his intentions often gave him ideas. Strange as that may seem, it is the fact.

When Hitler spoke over the radio and announced to the German people "the greatest accomplishment of my life, the return of my homeland to the Reich," he was altogether intoxicated with success. That feeling remained with him all during the next several years and was one of the significant motivations of his future actions.

Immediately after the Anschluss, in April 1938, Hitler held elections throughout the Reich. These were the last elections. Approval or disapproval of the "return of German Austria to the Reich" was linked with acceptance or rejection of the regime. Thus Hitler again skillfully exploited the situation to take German nationalism and German feelings of patriotism and link them with his own person. The people's emotional approval of the solution of an historic question that had been unsettled for centuries should not have given him the right to claim the consent of the people for his later political gambles, for his violent methods and their terrible consequences. The popular joy over Anschluss seemed to him a mandate to go ahead with his plans. A year later, he proceeded against foreign nations. That was the betrayal of the good faith of the German people; even if we assume that he himself sincerely believed such actions were national necessities, he stands guilty of betrayal.

The events surrounding the Sudeten crisis in the late summer and fall of 1938 can now be viewed as a determined effort by the other Powers to check the impetus of Hitler's forward march by negotiation and to guide the unleashed forces of his will into peaceful channels.

In Breslau in July 1938 Hitler attended a great German sports festival. The indescribable scenes which took place when men and women from the Sudetenland marched past the reviewing stand and literally cried out to Hitler to bring them liberation made a tremendous impression upon him. Under the sway of that impression he felt that he was carrying out the will of the people when he made his demands on Prague, underlining them with the threat of armed intervention.

Before Mussolini intervened at the critical moment, before Chamberlain and Daladier came to Munich, von Neurath, Göring, and others tried to exert a moderating influence upon Hitler. Ribbentrop alone supported Hitler's position. Ribbentrop, although already Foreign Minister, had stayed in London during the march into Austria. It was plain that he wanted to use the Sudeten crisis to buy favor in the eyes of the Führer. The German people unmistakably sided with those who were trying to preserve peace and smooth things over. The people were moved by Chamberlain's three flights to Berchtesgaden, Godesberg, and Munich. In Munich Daladier was given spontaneous ovations.

Hitler celebrated his triumph as liberator of the Sudeten Germans. For the time being he was content. An hour before his departure for London, Chamberlain paid a surprise visit to Hitler's private apartment on the second floor of the house on Prinzregentenstrasse and asked for Hitler's signature to a declaration that England and Germany would keep the peace. Hitler signed, but with great reluctance. A few minutes later, after Chamberlain had left, he made remarks bitterly accusing the British Prime Minister of having come only "in order to trick and cheat" him.

Since Ribbentrop's return from London Hitler had displayed intense distrust of England—in marked contrast to his former attitude. It is true that I recall conversations in which Hitler commented sarcastically upon Ribbentrop's exaggerated hatred for England. But Ribbentrop's one-sided appraisals soon began to have their effect. As Hitler became aware of England's stiffening attitude toward him, he fell more and more under the sway of Ribbentrop's Anglophobia. All along Hitler had stood for a purely constructive, peaceful policy drawn along racial lines. But instead of using the resources at his command for developing that policy, instead of appreciating the gift of peace given him by the Prime Minister of the British Empire, Hitler succumbed to the intoxication of success. He gave way to the wild impulse to play power-politics; this impulse had grown stronger within him than the politico-moral forces of his ego.

Early in November 1938 there took place in the Reich an event which aroused powerful emotions and which the overwhelming majority of the German people considered disgusting and shameful. This was the burning of synagogues and the smashing of Jewish shops on the night of November 9–10, in retaliation for the assassination of Embassy Counselor vom Rath in Paris. These demonstrations were supposed to have been spontaneous; as I learned the following day, they were staged. The inspiration for them was attributed to Goebbels. In reality they had been instigated by Hitler himself—they were *his* spontaneous reaction to the murder. Hitler ordered Goebbels to carry out the action, and Goebbels passed the instructions on to the SA, who were by no means delighted with this assignment from the top level. The ugly order, which aroused grave doubts in the Party itself, was transmitted to Goebbels on the night of November 9 in Hitler's apartment in Munich. As I learned from an absolutely reliable source, it was accompanied by an outburst of rage on the part of Hitler when the leaders who were to be entrusted with the execution of the orders showed signs of disinclination. Here, as in so many other cases, the people did not consider Hitler personally to blame. In reality Hitler was the sole instigator of that orgy of destruction; it was he who urged the savage violence with which it was carried out—though many others acquired a share in the guilt in the course of the action.

This incident is typical of Hitler's double face. Up to this time he had posed as a man intent only on the good of the nation; now he suddenly revealed the destructive instincts which he had hitherto managed to hide. This man who in so many speeches appealed to Providence for aid in the achievement of the highest national aims was acting as the apt pupil of the Fiend. There is no other way to put the matter. Hitler personally was the sponsor of anti-Semitism. At any and all occasions he alluded to the national necessity for an anti-Semitic program, or harangued those among his associates who drew back from the idea. Though his experts in press matters advised him otherwise, he banned hundreds of newspapers including, finally, the famous *Frankfurter Zeitung*—but although I frequently pleaded with him to suppress the *Stürmer*, which I called a disgrace to German culture, this newspaper continued to be published on his personal orders—although he himself hardly ever read it.

In the late fall and winter of 1938–39 Hitler devoted himself to the building of the West Wall, which was his original creation and which he himself planned down to the smallest detail. Whether at this time, after the international settlement of the Sudeten question and the guarantee of the territorial inviolability of Czechoslovakia, he already had in mind further action against Prague, I was not informed at the time. But in Hitler's public and private statements certain ideas came to the fore which were a far cry from his earlier more modest national and racial goals. He began talking in terms of strategy and geopolitics. The image of Czechoslovakia pointed like a spear into the heart of Germany, and the idea of a "power making for European order" cropped up in his thinking and his arguments. Hitler was moving away from his former anti-imperialist point of view, but he was still held fast by the inner forces of his ambivalent nature.

The destruction of Czechoslovakia was the fatal step that plunged Hitler on to the road to war. By forcing President Hacha's acquiescence, Hitler managed to give the military occupation the appearance of legality, so that intervention by the guaranteeing Powers could be averted. But it is clear to-day that in his heart Hitler had already made the decision; the drive to power within himself had won the upper hand. Hitler had overcome all his inhibitions; he had crossed the Rubicon. When he entered the Hradschin, the castle at Prague where German emperors had once ruled, he was overwhelmed by those impulses that were driving him ever more tempestuously from goal to goal—until the point was reached when he could no longer call a halt before total ruin.*

The tempo of events during those years, one thing following another in such rapid succession, caused grave concern among the members of Hitler's following. They were expecting a far more moderate and tranquil development. After every action, after Austria, after the Sudetenland, after Prague, and after Memel, Hitler swore to high heaven that from now on there would be five years of tranquility. Each time he conveyed the impression that he really meant it, that the pace was getting to be too much for him. But each time, before many weeks or months had passed, his political neurasthenia came to the fore again and he served up new surprises. He committed the rash and fateful step of denouncing the Anglo-German Naval Treaty and the German-Polish Non-Aggression Pact in public Reichstag speeches.

Like a high-tension condenser that slowly recharges after each discharge until it has built up again to the point where a sudden flash leaps the gap—that was Hitler in the crucial year of 1939. He was like a winning roulette player who cannot quit the tables because he thinks he has hit on the system which will break the bank. When the negotiations with Poland had come to an impasse and England had

* At this point I should like to dispose of a legend that has arisen in connection with Hacha's trip to Berlin. It is said that during a pause in the conferences at the Chancellery Hitler's doctor gave the Czech President an injection of a drug which broke down his psychological defenses and made him the helpless victim of Hitler's will. In reality Hacha submitted only under pressure of military threats. The story of the injection arose from the following incident: During a break in the conference Hacha—so I have been told—suffered from an attack of his cardiac trouble and asked for a heart stimulant. Hitler's personal physician was called in and gave him an injection which in fact had a reviving effect upon Hacha. Next day in Prague I myself heard the Czech President thanking Hitler's doctor for the treatment and asking the name of the medicine.

declared her intention of guaranteeing Poland's security, reason should have stopped Hitler. Everyone expected him to make some sort of compromise. In Germany hardly anyone thought it possible that Hitler, who enjoyed the confidence of the people because he had so often proved his political adroitness, would fail to control this situation. No one believed that he would push things to the point of war with England—especially since collaboration with England had been one of the major points in his program from the start of his political career. Everyone attributed to his clever statesmanship the gains that he had won by boldness and good luck. Even now, when we are beginning to understand Hitler's character, it remains incredible that he should have been so struck by political blindness as to incur the probability of war with England and France. Any ordinary German at the time could have told him that a clash with the British Empire would inevitably bring about a second world war which would spell the end of Germany. It is one of the great riddles of history—and one which reveals the abnormal split in Hitler's mind—that, faced with a decision in which his own fate, the fate of his racial nation, Europe and the whole world were involved, a man of his stature could not summon up the logic to recognize what was what. But Hitler called no one in when he risked the life of the German nation; alone and autocratically be took the decisive step and confronted the German people with accomplished facts.

I do not know much about the details of the diplomatic negotiations in Berlin and Warsaw before the outbreak of the war. I was able to follow the course of events only from the sidelines. In May, Hitler spent a week inspecting the underground defenses of the West Wall. In July, after his visit to Memel, he went to Bayreuth for the festival. Here I arranged a meeting between him and the British newspaper owner Lord Kemsley.

Kemsley had come to Germany at my invitation to discuss arrangements for a large-scale exchange of articles between German and British newspapers. According to this agreement, I would have articles from England reprinted in the entire German press, while Kemsley undertook a similar obligation for the newspapers in his chain. My idea in launching such a project was to lessen the existing tension. I thought it would bring about a better understanding between the two nations, and Kemsley had been sympathetic to this idea. He and his wife came to Germany, where we quickly settled details. I had, however, not yet informed Hitler of this project. Shortly before his interview with Lord Kemsley I told him about it. The conversation with Kemsley took place in my presence in the Wagner House where Hitler generally stayed when he was in Bayreuth. In the course of their talk, which lasted for about an hour, Kemsley took occasion to speak of his concern for the maintenance of peace in Europe. I was struck by Hitler's marked reserve throughout the talk. When Kemsley offered objections to something the Führer had said, he replied with monotonous insistence that everything depended upon England. At the time I thought his behavior a tactic aimed at influencing negotiations with the British. But since I had expected the interview to be a vigorous step toward the preservation of peace, I was disappointed by Hitler's attitude. I believe Lord Kemsley's feelings were the same. The events of a few short weeks later provided me with the explanation for Hitler's extraordinary reserve. I am now certain that Hitler was being deliberately non-cooperative. In accordance with my agreement with Lord Kemsley, I wrote the first article for his newspaper. Hitler asked to see it before it went out and made numerous changes in the interests of a "firmer line." I sent the article to Lord Kemsley and waited for his contribution to the German press. The outbreak of the war put an end to our collaborations.

At the time I did not know Hitler's intentions toward Poland. If Poland refused to yield to his demands and cease her aggression toward those of German race living within her borders, Hitler planned to strike. England, however, was not to be brought into the fight. On August 28 a decisive conversation between Hitler and British Ambassador Henderson was to take place.

That afternoon as I watched Henderson's car drive through the great bronze portal into the New Chancellery, I had a clear conception of the gravity of the hour. I was of the firm opinion that an attack upon Poland would be the spark in the powder barrel which would ignite the world conflagration; I saw the terrors of a second, still more terrible world war descending upon humanity before the wounds of the first were entirely healed. And I saw in my mind's eye the massive round table along the short wall of the huge room in the New Chancellery where Hitler and England's ambassador sat facing one another. Hitler could look out into the garden where Bismarck, his "model," had so often walked, lost in thoughts about the future of the Reich. If Hitler is ever to receive an inspiration from on high, I thought at the time, let it come to him at this moment for the sake of our nation and all humanity.

After about an hour and a quarter Henderson's car left the Chancellery. I went inside in order to listen around and find out what had occurred. People were saying that the upshot of the talk had been unsatisfactory. Obviously England had reiterated that she would fulfill her obligations toward Poland.

The general impression was that von Ribbentrop encouraged Hitler to believe that England was not now in a position to wage war, that she was only bluffing in order to frighten Hitler out of his plans to attack Poland. In the course of the discussion Hitler threw in the possibility of compromising by creating a corridor to Danzig through the Polish corridor. This proposal, however, was not submitted to the British ambassador in writing. England did not reply since, as Henderson later explained, there had been no written offer. Hitler was now in a dilemma. He obviously could not make up his mind to reverse his course. And so, in spite of continuing negotiations, on September 1 he gave the troops the order to march.

Fortune had smiled upon him. This time he again took a chance and leaped. Forty-eight hours later he had England's declaration of war. The dice had been cast—against him. From now on destiny took its inexorable course over mountain and plain and into the abyss.

Hitler had not expected England and France to enter the war on behalf of Poland. It was plain to see how stunned he was by the declarations of war. He thought the Western Powers were not yet sufficiently rearmed and believed the West Wall also constituted a political shield against them. This miscalculation on Hitler's part was ultimately rooted in his complete lack of understanding of moral factors in international politics, his exclusive faith in force. But Ribbentrop undoubtedly also played a fateful part. It is true that Hitler could not be swayed once he had made a decision, but without Ribbentrop he would not have come to such perverse conclusions about England. Hitler had never been abroad, except for his brief visits to Fascist Italy. Although ordinarily unteachable, he depended upon his foreign minister for the facts of life about foreign countries and diplomatic relations. If Ribbentrop had advised against it, he would scarcely have undertaken the attack upon Poland, with all the consequences that inevitably flowed out of it, given the political situation of the time. That is my firm conviction. I still cannot decide whether Hitler appointed Ribbentrop foreign minster in February 1938 because he knew in advance that Ribbentrop would abet his reckless political and military enterprises, or whether Ribbentrop on his own so strongly influenced Hitler's view of England that the Führer took such a frightful and incomprehensible risk. I recall a remark that Ribbentrop made to Hitler in the middle of the Polish campaign, just after he had persuaded the Führer to turn all foreign propaganda over to his ministry. He and Hitler were standing in front of the special train in which Hitler's headquarters had been installed. What Ribbentrop said I never forgot: "My propaganda will so disgrace England in the eyes of the world that no dog will accept a piece of bread from her." And in discussions of Germany's military capabilities I frequently heard Ribbentrop make the dangerous statement: "We are much stronger than we ourselves believe."

Hitler later repeatedly blamed Italy's attitude for the fiasco of his own policies. He asserted that an Italian Crown Council had secretly decided not to enter the war on Germany's side, and that during those crucial days this decision had been flashed to Chamberlain by the Italian ambassador in London, Signor Grandi. Believing that Germany would be standing alone, he argued, Chamberlain had then been willing to risk a declaration of war.

Before Hitler left Berlin to lead the Polish campaign personally, he gave strict instructions to the propaganda ministry and the press to maintain extreme restraint in dealing with England and France. Over the radio and in the press all attacks upon these nations were to be avoided, even in cases of justified self-defense. He was still hoping for a compromise before open hostilities with the West began.

At four o'clock one morning I learned that Russia was marching into Eastern Poland. I rushed to Hitler with this surprising news, which he received with feelings of relief. However, this act of Russia's put an end to all thought of leaving a remnant of Poland independent, an idea that Hitler had at least entertained, in the hope of placating England and France. His observations in Galicia led—as he later admitted—to his deceiving himself about the strength of the Russian army.

His offer of peace to the Western Powers after the completion of the Polish campaign was honestly intended. Because I considered this offer a last chance to avert a global conflagration and spare the nations of the world untold suffering, I acted on my own initiative and passionately urged this solution upon the representatives of the foreign press in Berlin. Before Hitler made the announcement of his peace offer in the Reichstag, I called a special conference of foreign correspondents, appealed to the solidarity of journalists of all countries, and asked them to put their united influence to work for the salvation of world peace. I promised that I would do my part in Germany. I told the correspondents that it is given to few men in their lifetime to affect directly by their personal acts the course of world history. Those assembled here in Berlin had that rare opportunity. "If all of us at this moment," I said, "work passionately for peace; if out of our deepest sense of responsibility we write in the cause of peace; if the newspapers and press agencies you represent print your call to peace, and if you can persuade them to advocate with the same fervor the peaceful interests of mankind, no government in the world will be able to oppose such a phalanx of public opinion. . . . I do not know whether you will succeed in persuading your newspapers to act in this way. I, at any rate, should not like to have to reproach myself in the future for not having pointed out to you this possibility at a moment so crucial for the peace of the world."

The strength of the press response was insufficient to halt the impending catastrophe. From London and Paris Hitler received no reply to his offer. It was obviously too late. Only then did he decide to get set for the blow against the West.

In the course of the war there were frequent reports abroad about alleged peace feelers on the part of Hitler. Every few months some such rumor sprang up, always accompanied by a spate of accusations or more or less serious commentary. From my knowledge of what went on I can say that Hitler himself, aside from his public statements, never made the slightest effort to end the war by negotiation. On the contrary, whenever he heard of such rumors or read any of these hoaxes in the press, he gave orders that they be emphatically denied. He feared that such stories, even though they were false, would be interpreted by his enemies as weakness. There was only one single case, at the very end, in March 1945, when he gave his tacit consent to a genuine peace feeler. That was when Ribbentrop in Stockholm sent up a trial balloon through Dr. Hesse—an inappropriate attempt at an unsuitable moment to deal with an unsuitable person.

On the day the war began Hitler donned the gray uniform and declared that he would wear it until the end of the war. When he put off his civilian clothes, he also stripped himself of the political skill he had possessed up to then. Throughout the war until the day of his death he displayed not a single impulse toward political activity, no ambition to employ statesmanship in foreign affairs. All his fire, his hardness, his savagery, and his passion which had failed him in foreign politics he now poured into the role of soldier and Supreme Commander. The fact that he led the war not as a statesman, but as a commander obsessed with military ambitions, was the crowning misfortune that his demonic personality brought to the German nation.

Chapter 3

Hitler's Foreign Policy During the War

HISTORY SHOWS that wars fought on a military plane alone seldom come to a good end. And heads of state who during a war have done nothing but lead campaigns and have failed to consolidate their victories politically—have failed to shape successful battles into a new order—resemble rockets that shoot flaring into the sky and fall, burnt out, as fast as they rose. In this sense Hitler was a shooting star that glowed only briefly and in its fall shattered the German Reich and shook the entire world.

This dichotomy between the political and the military ran through the whole of Hitler's career. A simple soldier, he "decided in November 1918 to go into politics" because he believed the Germans had lost the First World War politically, not militarily. In his role as politician he gave the German people a new order on the domestic front, only to drop the Second World War into their laps. When his political strategy of force in peacetime ceased to produce results, he would not admit that this line of approach had been pursued as far as it should be. Instead he pushed on further, practicing his unrestrained excesses, his rash adventures, and his suicidal methods upon the German people in wartime. Twenty years after his first switching of roles the politician again became a soldier—and lost the Second World War by military catastrophes of almost unparalleled magnitude.

At first he seemed the very personification of daring and success, energy, and good luck. His generalship seemed altogether inspired. In less than two years he had secured military control of almost the entire European continent. Allies flocked to his victorious standard; new alliances and pacts followed hard upon the brilliant military advance. Hitler, carried away by the intoxication of victory, made frequent use of a significant comparison. He would declare that something of the spirit of Napoleon's revolutionary armies had flown before the marching feet of the National Socialist army in Europe, that the new ideas had opened the way for the tanks and prepared the way for the Wehrmacht. But his lack of moderation and his political irrationality were to change all this so utterly!

What chances a great, farsighted, and moderate statesman would have had during those years. Such a statesman would have resisted all temptations to convert the military successes of the war into permanent territorial conquests. He would have given the defeated nations peace, and for his own nation, aside from temporary military guarantees, would have sought no other political ends than those he had announced when he took up arms in September 1939.

From 1939 to 1941, what could Hitler not have done on the European continent, provided he had clear aims, a program of foreign policy, and a rational concept of how Europe was be shaped; if he had shown the other peoples of Europe new ways to progressive evolution and peaceful cooperation; if, respecting the native traditions and problems of other nations, he had left them their independence, or restored that independence; if he had not, by his everlasting suspicion, poisoned all relationships with the other nations of Europe. Comparisons have often been drawn between the German political mentality on the one hand, and the mentality of the English on the other. The unsentimental English have been highly successful in their government of other people. It has been said of the Germans that they have a soft heart but a hard hand. But with Hitler even the soft heart was lacking, while the hard hand was only too evident. He added to this a large measure of psychological incompetence. By his ignorance of foreign countries, his inability to grasp the psychology of other nations, his violent methods, and his attitude that he was master, by his stubbornness and his unteachable arrogance, by his exaggerated prizing of Mussolini on the one hand and his corroding suspicion of all other political friends and allies on the other, he threw away enormous political capital. He occupied countries but conquered no hearts. He promised liberties, and forged new fetters. He had unique opportunities to shape constructively the future of Europe—and muffed every one of them. A whole continent that the soldier had won was, during those years, at the disposal of the politician; he might have done glorious things with it. Instead he converted it into a political rubble heap.

This estimate of Hitler's foreign policies is not my personal one alone. In recent years many Germans, politicians and military men both, have made substantially similar remarks to me in more or less blunt terms. Most of them, it should be added, thought Hitler was not responsible for these misguided policies; they blamed his advisers, his military or civilian governors in the occupied territories. Hitler himself supposedly did not know what these officials of his were doing.

After the successful campaign in Poland the victor might have contented himself with Danzig, the Polish Corridor, and the areas inhabited by German elements. To have done so would have been to convince the world of the morality of his action. He would also have gained prestige and won respect for the principles of a meaningful and constructive nationality policy in Europe—a policy which had an important place in his doctrines. The Poles enjoyed the sympathies of the world as a "poor, homeless people" of twenty millions. A generous peace leaving part of Poland independent would have been the mark of a genuine statesman, although such an attempt at a magnanimous solution would have been somewhat nullified by the Russian occupation of East Poland. But Hitler manifested not the slightest trace of any such farsighted attitude; in fact the grave psychological errors of six years of rule in Poland showed how far he was from any such attitude. On his instructions the Government General of Poland established its capital at Cracow, the former residence of Polish kings. From many remarks I heard Hitler drop in the course of years there can be no doubt that he himself constantly urged the German military authorities and the Governor General to institute harsh measures. He ironically referred to the Governor as "Stanislaus," and for years treated him with rude contempt because he tried to administer his territory temperately and to establish conditions of occupation suitable to the Polish racial character. The iron fist over Poland was Hitler's hand, and the will that clenched that fist was the pitiless law of his nature.

An equally glaring example of Hitler's lack of talent for statesmanship was his occupation of Norway and the crassness of his administration in that country. Norway had taken no part at all in the war. She was the innocent victim of alleged strategic necessity. If Hitler believed he had to occupy this northern land temporarily in order to safeguard the vital Baltic for the Reich, if he felt that necessity drove him to impose upon the Norwegians this monstrous sacrifice of their sovereignty, then he had every reason to make the occupation more tolerable to them by offering every possible concession in domestic affairs. Instead he appointed a Norwegian government that had virtually no backing by the people. He instituted the cruel system of hostages. The German civil administration committed economic crimes against the Norwegians. Clearly, Hitler was in no way attempting to reconcile the Norwegians to the occupation. In spite of all of Hitler's initial illusions, the Quisling government struck no roots in the country. It was inacceptable to the cosmopolitan spirit of the people. And the German civil administration under Terboven was a fundamental political blunder that made the Germans hated throughout the greater part of the Nordic world. The arrest of the best-known Norwegian bishops and of the students of Oslo University who staged patriotic demonstrations destroyed whatever sympathies for Germany still remained in the international academic world. These severities also lost Germany the sympathy of Norway's Swedish brothers. Terboven's actions were in the spirit of Hitler who had appointed him, who kept him at his post in spite of protests from German as well as Norwegian sources, and who constantly encouraged him on his visits to Berlin or the Führer's headquarters.

Hitler's mad foreign policy was equally catastrophic in Denmark. In contrast to Norway, the Danish government had remained in the country, so that at the beginning all remained calm. But in the course of time the same political blunders were committed there, producing the same reactions, until the country was ultimately in open rebellion.

Vacillating aims, half-measures, suspicion, and ambiguity—these were the characteristics of Hitler's policies in Europe. The peoples of Europe saw in these policies a lack of sincerity. By Hitler's own conduct the very foundation stones of the New Europe whose advocate he had been, crumbled as soon as they were laid. Hitler's policy toward France is a striking example of that.

Theoretically Hitler intended to build the New Europe with the aid of the French people. To impose upon the whole French nation the burdens, tensions, insecurity, and humiliation of a five-year armistice and at the same time to expect the Pétain government to win the confidence of the country and the consent of the people to a revolutionary change in spiritual attitudes, was not policy—it was foolishness. No one with common sense could believe that pure and honest intentions lay behind such behavior. Hitler's meeting with Pétain in Montoire was the moment for a resounding signal for peace. That meeting should have been the starting point for the creation of the "New Order", which he supposedly intended to base upon equal rights for all and a harmony of interests. Peace concluded at this time, with a France whose honor and sovereignty were left unimpaired, might have opened the way for a general compromise and so averted the frightful bloodletting still to come. As I watched the aged Marshal of France step out of his automobile in front of the railroad station of that small French town and walk down the red-carpeted platform to Hitler's salon car, I thought that he, too, may have had some such hope in mind. Certainly many Germans of foresight were hoping for such a settlement. When Pétain returned to his car, Hitler walked back with him. But as we soon learned this was only a political gesture on Hitler's part. His sly smile was that of a victor who could not rise to the opportunity, who had missed his chance for a great, liberating political act.

The only consistency noticeable in Hitler's unfortunate policy toward France was its distinctive rhythm of one step forward and two steps back. In the course of almost five years he destroyed by his own hand all elements making for fruitful collaboration. Soon after the meeting at Montoire he himself—not some subleader or administrator gone wild—ordered Bürckel and Wagner to tear down signs in French in Alsace and Lorraine. He himself ordered the expulsion of tens of thousands of Frenchmen from those areas—an act that inevitably mortally offended the feelings of all Frenchmen. It was he who instructed the commanders in France to answer every attack upon German soldiers by terroristic reprisals and the shooting of hostages many times the number of Germans killed. He issued these orders although he certainly knew the cruelty involved, and although he could learn from his regular reading of translations from the foreign press how these acts outraged the conscience of the world.

He had the bones of the Duke of Reichstadt, Napoleon's son, brought from Vienna to Paris as a cheap gift to the French. But he personally always blocked Pétain's return to the French capital—although establishment of the French government in Paris was a prerequisite for practical cooperation between Germany and France. He always distrusted the French politicians who were willing to shape the future of France on the basis of collaboration with Germany; in every step of theirs which was intended to engender confidence and peace he scented mischief and treachery. It was a typical trick of Hitler's to reject those who approached him in a cooperative temper; then, when they in their disappointment took another road, he would point out how right he had been all along to be wary of them.

Hitler's excessive partiality for Mussolini's Italy was criminal folly, especially as it affected his policy toward France. He catered to Mussolini until it was too late, until the Allied invasion of French North Africa created changed conditions and forced him to violate the armistice he himself had dictated to France.

His policy toward France was not liked at all in Germany. Even Ribbentrop, whose diplomatic conduct was ordinarily tactless in the extreme, who invariably offended the sensibilities of other nations, often dissociated himself from Hitler's policy in France. In all probability he tried to change Hitler's mind, but Hitler remained unteachable, stubborn, inaccessible to reason. Once he had been defeated in the political theater by England's strong stand, the statesman in him was snuffed out. Once he began seeking fame as a military commander, his gaze remained fixed upon the success of his arms and his faith in victory grounded solely in military power. He was no longer capable of solving political questions on a political basis.

That fact was demonstrated once more in Belgium and Holland throughout the entire occupation of those countries. He had promised these countries that he would restore their sovereignty as soon as possible after the victorious end of the campaign in France, when military necessity would no longer require occupation. He did not keep that promise. Instead, for five years he had Belgium and Holland administered by a Reich Commissioner and a military commander, with all the burdens and humiliations that such occupation meant for these nations. He held out to them no prospect of improvement in their conditions. Here again we are struck by the complete absence of any plan which would allow Belgian and Dutch people to live their own lives freely and independently. What, in Hitler's concept of the New Europe, was this corner of the continent to look like? Hitler gave no answer.

His system of pacts with the Balkan states might have seemed, to a superficial observer, a grand endeavor to work out a general European commonwealth. But in truth there was no constructive idea behind these pacts. They were a screen hiding the fact that Hitler had no political program in the event of military victory. The Three Powers policy in Southeast Europe was a more or less routine affair arranged by the foreign office; Hitler himself was in the field and took only casual interest in it. At the ceremonies held in Berlin and Vienna to celebrate the signing of each pact great stress was laid upon the friendship and harmony of interests of the signatory states within the framework of an imaginary New Order in Europe. But all this was mere rhetoric. To Hitler the true significance of these pacts was that—in the cases of Hungary, Rumania, and Bulgaria—they provided for the right of transit for German troops. In the case of Yugoslavia, where this right was not included in the treaty, Hitler immediately took advantage of the fall of the Cvetkovic regime to assure his influence upon this country by invading it.

For the rest, Hitler's actions in the Balkans can only be considered in connection with Mussolini's previous attack upon Greece. Hitler had not been informed beforehand about Italy's intentions in Greece and—as he often remarked to his aides—disapproved. He first learned about it via radio reports while he was in his special train on the way to Italy for a conference with Mussolini. When they met in Florence Mussolini greeted Hitler with the words, "I have decided to march against Greece in order to suppress once and for all this threat to Italy!"

After his military victory in the Balkans, Hitler attacked the difficult problems of this storm-center of Europe with the same ignorance, amateurishness, and lack of success that he had displayed everywhere else on the continent. He would take up the idea of the first person who suggested a solution to some administrative problem which happened to accord with his own mentality and follow it through in the most liberal fashion. In the course of years he assigned mutually contradictory powers to ambassadors, special envoys, army commanders, police commissioners, and so on, in the Balkans. This confusion, combined with Italian ambitions in the area, created absolute chaos. One diplomatic expert characterized the situation in these words: "In the Balkans twenty-five German authorities are operating alongside of and against one another, all assigned overriding powers by Hitler. Opposed to them is only a single authority: Tito."

It is revealing of the internal hollowness of Hitler's entire system of pacts in the Balkan states that the whole thing collapsed like a house of cards the moment his military power was shaken.

During the period between the Balkan and the Russian campaigns there came the flight of Rudolf Hess to England. It was widely considered a serious peace overture on the part of Hitler. But Hess's flight was just as much of a surprise for Hitler as it was a sensation for the German people and the rest of the world.

At the time Hitler was at Berchtesgaden. The morning following the night Hess parachuted down over northern England, Hess's personal adjutant came to Hitler's house in the Berghof to deliver an urgent letter from Hess. He had to wait until noon before Hitler would see him. As Hitler read the letter he was overcome by tremendous agitation which in a few minutes spread through the ordinarily quiet Sunday atmosphere of the house, though none of the others present had any idea of the reason for Hitler's excitement. Hitler sent for Hess's staff chief, Martin Bormann, had the bearer of the letter put under arrest, then sent for Göring, Ribbentrop, and Keitel, who were in the vicinity. There followed hours of conferences which continued until late in the afternoon and were suspended only because a reception for Darlan, the French admiral, happened to be scheduled for that afternoon.

In the course of the day the general outlines of what had taken place gradually trickled out of the conference room. In his letter to Hitler, Hess had described his intention and explained the motives for his action. A few days later an adjutant showed me the letter. The greater part of it—a fact that seemed very odd to me—was devoted to a precise description of the technical aspects of the flight, which he had attempted without success once before. Hess emphasized that his intention did not arise from cowardice or weakness, nor should it be interpreted as an escape, since it required more courage to undertake this dangerous air venture than to remain in Germany.

Only after all this preliminary did Hess come to the political essence of his plan. His goal, he said, was to establish contact between England and Germany by getting in touch personally with certain distinguished men in England whom he knew. In the interests of both nations, he maintained, such contact was necessary; a serious attempt must be made to end the war by negotiation. He pointed out that in a recent conversation with Hitler he had convinced himself, by asking a pointblank question, that at the bottom of his heart Hitler still desired an Anglo-German understanding. He had not said a word to Hitler about his intention of flying to England because he knew the Führer would have forbidden it. Since he had been born and brought up in an English environment [Alexandria, Egypt], he considered himself the right sort of man for this mission. He would emphasize in England that his action must not be interpreted as a sign of German weakness; on the contrary, he would lay stress upon the military invincibility of his country and point out that Germany did not have to ask for peace.

After reading this letter Hitler knew where Hess had set out for, but he did not know whether he had arrived. In order to obtain professional advice on Hess's chances, Hitler sent for Air General Ernst Udet. Udet thought it highly improbable that an amateur pilot flying a single-motored Messerschmitt 109 would be able to reach a particular destination after a long night flight. He thought it more likely that Hess had crashed either over the North Sea or over England, or while attempting a landing in the dark. In view of this opinion Hitler decided to withhold any statement in order to await a possible announcement by the British. But when no such report came from England by the next day, Hitler decided after all to make the announcement himself; Ribbentrop argued that it would be wiser for the German version to be presented to the world first, for the sake of Germany's own allies.

Hitler had already stated his conviction that Hess was not motivated by treason, but by an obsessional idea which had been further intensified by his association with soothsayers and groups of dabblers in the supernatural. He therefore dictated the report stating that Hess had not been in full possession of his mental faculties. Today I see clearly—although at the time I could not guess this—that Hitler laid special stress on Hess's insanity in order to prevent the British from crediting anything Hess might say about Hitler's intention to attack Russia. Hess was one of the few who knew about this plan, and Hitler feared he might have betrayed it.

The evening of that same day the British communiqué confirmed the fact that Hess had landed in England.

Two days later Hitler assembled the Party leaders at his home on the Obersalzberg to brief them on the Hess case. He took occasion to mention that cases of mental illness had already occurred in the Hess family. In this connection it is politically significant and a typical example of Hitler's secrecy about his own intentions that he did not so much as hint at the possibility of an imminent military clash with Russia. Yet this meeting in the middle of May was the last conference of Party leaders before the beginning of the campaign against Russia.

At the beginning of March 1941 one of my aides informed me that rumors were circulating among the war correspondents to the effect that some action against Russia was in the air. I was shocked to hear this and convinced that the reports were erroneous. I promptly branded such dangerous rumormongering as a political crime designed to undermine German–Russian relations, which had been put on a satisfactory footing by the pact. Sternly, I forbade all my colleagues to pass on such rumors. I thought such talk the wild fancy of political madmen, if not deliberate political sabotage. My feelings about this were all the stronger because I kept constantly in mind the importance of good German–Russian relations. I recalled the incident at Berchtesgaden in August 1939 when Hitler received the telephone call from Ribbentrop in Moscow reporting the conclusion of the Russo-German economic pact. Hitler, who was dining at the time, jumped up from the table exclaiming, "We've won!" I recalled also Hitler's convincing explanations of the nonaggression and consultation pact which was concluded between Germany and Russia at the end of September 1939, during Ribbentrop's second visit to Moscow. At the time Hitler praised Stalin as an "extraordinarily realistic and constructive statesman." He spoke of how pleased he was to be able to resume the Bismarckian tradition of friendship with Russia, declared that henceforth the peril of a two-front war was banished forever, and hailed the common interests between Germany and Russia as a tie fraught with blessings. That tie had existed throughout history, he said, and had been broken during the past world war only as the result of intrigues by other countries. Goebbels was accordingly given directives for revising our propaganda; the line was to be that the differences in ideologies and domestic systems would not affect Russo-German relationships. Recalling all this, I remembered also the formal correctness of Russo-German relations in the past eighteen months. To be sure, during that time Russia had pushed forward her western border as the result of her winter's war against Finland, her actions against the Baltic States and the repossession of Bessarabia. But the published communiqués on Molotov's visit to Berlin in November 1940 seemed to me to indicate no lessening in mutual harmony.

Later, in the spring of 1941, rumors of an alleged impending clash between Germany and Russia began appearing in the international press also. Most Germans, including myself, saw such talk as stemming from the customary and indispensable military precautions being taken by the German High Command to guard against a supposed concentration of Russian troops on the Russian western frontier. But the flood of rumors continued to influence public opinion; all sorts of wildly contradictory suppositions were put forward, none of them backed by facts. The atmosphere was one of extreme confusion. The arrest of an official in the Propaganda Ministry created an international sensation. At a diplomatic tea given by a foreign embassy this official, allegedly having drunk too much of something other than tea, had dropped hints of an imminent clash between Russia and Germany. Hitler, urged on by Ribbentrop, gave orders for severe punishment of the man. At the time I attributed this severity to his fear that the spreading of such rumors would damage German–Russian relations.

After a conference with Rumanian Premier Antonescu in Munich around the middle of June, Hitler returned to Berlin. I was struck by the atmosphere of doubt and tension that now gripped international and political circles in Berlin, as if they were affected by the contagion of the foreign press. But in spite of the thickening rumors I still believed, on the basis of all that Hitler had said in speeches and private statements, that Germany would never undertake aggressive action against Russia. Not until the night of June 21–22 did I realize the frightful truth. Even then the words were not spoken; up to the very eve of the invasion the few persons who were in the know dutifully kept the secret. But the unusual bustle in the Chancellery that evening, all the coming and going and the excitement in every face, made it impossible to doubt any longer that some tremendous action against Russia was in progress. At four o'clock in the morning I received a telephone call requesting me to take part in a press conference of the German and foreign press at the Foreign Office. Ribbentrop, I was informed, would then issue an important government statement. At the same time it was announced that Goebbels would speak over the radio at six o'clock in the morning. The incredible had happened. At dawn Hitler launched the attack on Russia.

With his invasion of Russia Hitler had attained the climax of his intoxication with power, the ultimate phase of his political delirium and the highest peak of his self-devouring, demonic possession. He imagined that his preventive war against Russia would enable him to subjugate this land of infinite space within a few months, thereby becoming master of the continent. Running amok against all reason, he believed he could throw overboard all the laws of political logic and all the lessons of history. Here the fateful dichotomy of his dark nature emerged into the light, was revealed in its true form. Hitler was playing a double game of truly sinister proportions. Impelled by his conviction of carrying out a supreme racial mission, he saw glimmering before him the chance to secure his nation for the entire future against any possibility of a threat from the East. For this he was ready to practice an incredible deceit. His megalomania had overcome the political good sense he had formerly possessed.

In the very hour that German troops marched forward at his command from the Baltic to the Black Sea, Hitler was overcome by his first gloomy premonitions. He listened to the official proclamation of the Russian campaign and to a newly-composed arrangement of fanfares (based on Franz Liszt's "Prelude") which was to precede radio announcements of the expected victories. Then, I was told, about three o'clock in the morning he remarked to some of his intimates, "I feel as if I have opened a door into a dark, unseen room—without knowing what lies behind the door."

The same troubled atmosphere prevailed during Ribbentrop's press conference at the Foreign Office, which I attended about five o'clock in the morning. The journalists present were sleepy-eyed and depressed. Hitler must have sensed this mood, for a few days afterwards he remarked to me that the press had not supported his assault upon Russia in a sufficiently effective and convincing manner. But then new intoxicating reports of military victories banished Hitler's anxious premonitions and put to flight his doubts.

The advancing German armies occupied vast territories in the East—the Baltic states, White Russia, and the Ukraine. And once again Hitler showed that he knew no better methods of administering conquered territories than those that had already failed in the rest of Europe. How could he have succeeded, given his absolute contempt for the feelings of others and for the ways of life of other peoples? Whatever his motives, he had brought war upon a country of 180 million people. In Russian eyes he would therefore remain forever an usurper and foreigner, even had he had the desire to give them an ideal form of government. But he had neither the desire nor the ability to do so.

He established a Ministry for the East to rule this broad land by red tape and conferences, without any reference to its traditions or its national needs. In the country itself, meanwhile, Reich commissioners who felt themselves independent reigned more or less harshly. Once again Hitler was demonstrating his ruinous lack of understanding of foreign races; his administrative decisions for Russia were political dilettantism of the worst sort. The force behind the Eastern policy of suffocating and oppressing a foreign people was Hitler himself. He personally wanted the government to be exactly what the Russians felt it to be. The strongest exponent of such a policy was Reich Commissioner Koch, and Hitler himself constantly backed Koch in spite of criticisms. Instead of checking the man, he held him up to others as a fine example of uncompromising hardness. Hitler himself remained deaf to all advice; in his arrogance he declared that he understood the mentality of the East better than those who thought to counsel him.

And yet, in the end Hitler was defeated in Russia, not only by the great spaces, but by the spirit of the people. When the German fronts reeled and broke under the reviving power of Russia's will to live, which Hitler had so gravely underestimated, the German armies found no support in their rear. Behind their lines were only partisans who hated the Germans with all their hearts.

What political outcome did Hitler imagine the Russian adventure could possibly have? That will always remain an enigma. The only idea he ever expressed—that was at the height of his military triumphs in the East—was the vague hope that perhaps Stalin would realize the hopelessness of further resistance, would abandon large parts of European Russia to Germany, and would content himself with building up the strength of his country in Asia. What wild wishful thinking!

Another striking example of the terrible world-wide effects of Hitler the soldier's governing the decisions of Hitler the statesman may be seen in the circumstances surrounding the declaration of war against the United States.

From the beginning of the war in Europe Hitler had, for reasons of practical good sense, taken pains to avoid giving the United States a strong pretext for entering the war. From the experience of the First World War he had a vivid conception of what the participation of that country, with its mighty potentials in men and materials, would mean for the prospects of Germany. He feared the arsenal of armaments, the political and moral power of America, and wanted to spare the German people America's throwing her full weight into the scales of war against Germany. But he also had a wholly exaggerated estimate of Japan's military strength. The thought of having Japan for an ally overshadowed all considerations of political rationale. The power-obsession of the soldier in Hitler thrust aside all his statesman's caution and he involved the German people in the war with America.

Hitler often told of his enthusiasm as a boy when he read newspaper stories and saw pictures of the Russo-Japanese war. He had admired the Japanese victories at Port Arthur and Tsushima. Ever since that time, an excessive admiration for the strict discipline and soldierly spirit of the Japanese had remained with him. It had become an established part of his thinking. Having made a cult of the island kingdom, Hitler disregarded the advice of specialists on East Asia and sacrificed Germany's amicable relations with China. In the Anti-Comintern Pact of 1936 he, together with Italy, drew Germany close to Japan. These ties were developed into an alliance in the Three

Powers Pact of the fall of 1940. Finally Hitler personally pledged himself to declare war on the United States if Japan and America became involved in an armed conflict.

That Japan would first strike the United States at Pearl Harbor was, however, something Hitler never suspected. I believe I have good evidence for this statement. On that dull Sunday afternoon of December 7 or 8 I was at Hitler's headquarters, which at the time was located in a forest in East Prussia, near Rastenburg. In my small office I was the first to receive the Reuters report on Pearl Harbor. I promptly went to Hitler's bunker and sent in word that I was bringing an extremely important message. That very day Hitler had received depressing reports from Russia. He received me with an unfriendly question; he obviously feared more bad news. When I made haste to read the flash, his look of surprise was unmistakable. His face cleared; his expression became one of extreme excitement and he asked quickly, "Is this report correct?" I said it definitely was, for a minute before, while I was waiting in his anteroom, I had received a telephone message from my office to the effect that confirmation from another source had come in. Hitler snatched the sheet of paper from my hand, strode out of the room, and walked unaccompanied, without cap or coat, the hundred yards to the bunker of the Chief of the High Command of the Armed Forces. He was the first to bring the news there.

I do not doubt that Japan's entry into the war was completely unexpected by him. He had hoped for it, but not counted on it. However, the Japanese action automatically brought in its train Germany's declaration of war against the United States. Once again in a question of fateful importance for the German nation Hitler had acted alone, made the decision alone. In his overestimation of Japan Hitler committed a blunder similar to his sacrifice of German interests in France to Mussolini's Italy.

In his political role Hitler was a figure out of the past, not the future. He was enamored of medieval conceptions of heroism and lordly behavior, and the power-political outlook of the German

Imperial Age. He dwelt in history; the future was closed to his mind. He had no grasp of political evolution and the spiritual progress of man. Therefore he was without any vision of a new Europe such as others had who were capable of looking into the future. He used to say that even he had been somewhat infected by democratic notions, but in fact he had no feeling whatsoever for the great binding ideas that unite nations; these were utterly alien to his mind. By main force he united the nations of Europe and in so doing laid the foundations for a future commonwealth of the European peoples. But he also raised a host of new problems; and in the solution of these problems he never took the slightest interest.

Again and again in the course of the years earnest-minded Germans and non-Germans urged him to proclaim his conception of Europe, at last to provide the nations of the continent with a "European Charter" which would point new ways for future development. Year in and year out he refused to do anything of the sort. When he was requested at least to announce certain principles and concessions, he would also refuse, giving a reason that sounded very strange in the light of his customary political amorality: "I am no politician; rather, I have a historic mission to fulfill." What he meant by this was that he would not make political promises which he would later be unable to keep because of the demands of his so-called historic mission.

Wherein lay this historic mission, in his mind? What distant goal hovered before his eyes since he had gone to war, since he had smashed all the old forms of society and was necessarily confronted with the question of establishing new ones? Beyond the general expression of his determination to lead the German people to victory, he never offered a concrete definition of his mission. What he really had in mind can only be judged in retrospect by his actions.

It has been said that Hitler strove to dominate the world. I do not believe that his goal was that unlimited, for all the elementary force of his will to power. How could a man who had never been outside of Central Europe, who had no knowledge of foreign lands and overseas territories, who was not even ambitious for colonies, who altogether lacked anything resembling a cosmopolitan horizon—how could such a man conquer a world of which he had no conception? His field of vision was too narrow for such a goal. More within his mental sphere was the concept of an imperial Germany as the supreme arbiter in Europe. He did not want to be the creator of a new Europe in an age of united nations; rather his dream was to be master of an old, isolated, conservative continent. Militarily he would be the protector, politically the governor, economically the administrator of a Continental *Lebensraum*; in opposition to all tendencies toward progressive, universal cooperation, he would maintain Europe in a state of limited, narrow-minded isolation from the rest of the world.

This, I believe, was the goal he had in mind after he had begun his struggle against the Old Order in Europe. These were the perspectives that guided his actions during the war. But he kept them concealed. When he spoke, it was always of justice, peace, and the welfare of the nations. Anyone listening to him—the German people, many of them sincerely striving to find a constructive conception, and numerous non-German Europeans who hopefully and trustfully looked to him for leadership—could not but believe that he intended to solve the European problem on the basis of equal rights for the cooperating nations. How could they assume that he who stood for such progressive ideas on the domestic scene, in order to consolidate his rule within his own country, could harbor such reactionary ideas with regard to relations among the countries of Europe?

And so he deceived everyone—the German people and all the others who, believing in his good will and in his idealistic intentions, were therefore willing to shape the destinies of their own nations by collaborating with him. His dual nature deceived them all and plunged them into misfortune.

As the war went on and took its unhappy course, the German people themselves gradually realized that Hitler was anything but a great statesman. Not for him the solution a farsighted and realistic statesman would have chosen under any circumstances—to attempt to end the war before it was too late by a passable compromise peace, or at least to save his people the last horrors by capitulating. Up to the very last minute he remained a gambler determined to have everything or nothing.

During all the years, when he certainly must have known that nemesis was approaching, he nourished himself on false hopes and remained completely passive in foreign policy. His sole political activity consisted in empty polemics. His sole political vision was the wish-dream that the coalition of his enemies would fall apart, although reason should have told him that the alliance would last at least until the total military defeat of Germany. In order to support this unrealistic hypothesis, which was the sum and substance of his statesman's wisdom during the last year of the war, he constantly attributed exaggerated importance to the most trivial diplomatic reports and the most insignificant items in the foreign press. These he constantly put forward as proofs of his mad theory.

To this one hope he clung to the last days of his life. As a last desperate and naive gesture he even stripped the western front along the Elbe of troops, the idea being that this would bring about a situation which would make his enemies quarrel among themselves at the last moment.

Thus Hitler as a statesman lacked truly great stature. As a political man he did not see beyond his nation—and supra-national vision is the mark of the true great statesman, for it alone opens the way for progress for humanity. While Hitler conquered great spaces as a soldier, as a politician he remained pent up in his nationalistic narrowness. His limited mind could not control those spaces. Where he should have been creative on the international plane, where he should have harmonized and shaped constructively the relationships among the nations of Europe, he instead acted in terms of a wild supernationalism that led inevitably to grim disaster.

Chapter 4

Hitler the Soldier

MY MILITARY KNOWLEDGE is based solely upon my experiences at the front during the First World War. I therefore lack the qualifications to judge Hitler's abilities as a general and to pass definitive judgments upon his tactics and strategy during the war. Moreover, my knowledge of the relationships among Hitler as Supreme Commander, the Oberkommando der Wehrmacht (OKW-Supreme Command of the Armed Forces) and the three services, is limited to what I learned later from public sources, since I was not present at secret military conferences. But my personal observations of what went on at Hitler's various headquarters may, by their very military innocence, have some value. What details I can supply and what light I can throw on the connections between events may make it easier for the public to form its own opinion about Hitler's military capabilities. To start with, there is the question most often asked about Hitler as general. What military equipment did Hitler bring to his task? Here was a former enlisted man who became Supreme Commander and took over the direct leadership of the German armies in the field. How well fitted was he for this role?

During the war of 1914–1918 Hitler had been a courier between various front-line staffs. He was a passionate soldier. He often recounted how happy he had been in August 1914 when he read the bulletin announcing the outbreak of the war. He had felt the war a personal opportunity. He saw it as opening the gateway to the world of great adventure. The fixed forms of the bourgeois life he hated would break up and in the anarchy which would ensue he hoped to fulfill his craving for greatness. He was then twenty-five years old and hailed the war as the arena for the display of his love of combat and his hope for fame.

It has often been said that every soldier carries a marshal's baton in his knapsack. Hitler not only strove toward such advancement; he achieved it. His path was very different from the slow rising in the ranks of a soldier. He went to war with a pocket edition of Schopenhauer's works in his pack. In the war he was promoted from private to corporal and won the Iron Cross, First Class. Later he declared that in November 1918 he had dreamed of being at the head of a division. He could then have "established order" in Germany and inspired a "total resistance" which would have turned the tide of the war. The dénouement of the war which he did lead from 1939–45 gives little grounds for the supposition that he would performed this miracle in 1918.

The fact is that from his early youth Hitler displayed a degree of interest in military affairs wholly astonishing in an artistic nature such as his. Long before he took power he possessed a very wide knowledge of military matters and the technology of armaments. He had read a great deal of military history; he was familiar with the technical literature on warfare, both that of Germany and of foreign countries. And he would sit up late carefully reading all new publications. In this field he was truly a phenomenon; even in peacetime his theoretical knowledge put many a general and admiral in the shade. Hitler possessed an incredible memory for military history, for the course of battles and of entire campaigns. He had an extraordinary knowledge of weapons. For example, he knew all the warships in the world, insofar as they were listed in Weyher's *Handbook of Navies* or other such reference books. He could recite from memory the age, displacement, speed, strength of armor, turrets, and other armament of every ship. There was little missing in his knowledge of the most modern tanks and guns of all the countries in the world. He frequently visited the big arms factories and shipyards of the Reich in order to keep a personal check on the progress being made; on such visits he planned and probed, discussed technical matters with engineers, considered and made decisions. He made a point of being supplied with photographs of the various stages of construction of big guns and ships and was constantly concerned with such problems. The building of the West Wall was directed by him down to the smallest detail, in accordance with the actualities of front-line fighting.

During the winter of 1938 he once sent for me and told me, to my amazement, that he had heard I had been a front-line artillery observer in the World War. He wanted, he said, to devise the simplest, safest, and most practical artillery observation post for the standard bunkers of the West Wall, but he was making a point of not asking armchair theoreticians how they thought these bunkers should be constructed; he wanted the design based upon direct practical experience. After he had taken possession of the Sudetenland, he promptly visited the lines of Czech bunkers in that territory in order to study their construction. Similarly, after the invasions of Austria and Czechoslovakia he checked personally on the military setup and fortifications in those countries.

To sum up, Hitler possessed an extraordinarily comprehensive theoretical knowledge of warfare, and had in addition the practical experience of four years of soldiering as a front-line corporal. The building of the German Wehrmacht that went to war in 1939 was his work. He had created it, and it was his ambition to lead it. Motorizing it and equipping it with large, swift, independently operating tank formations modeled on those the British had developed toward the close of the First World War, was his idea. The tanks, he believed, had been the decisive weapon in that war. The strategy and tactics of bold tank breakthroughs to completely disorganize the enemy front from the rear was his conception. He was the father of Blitzkrieg armies and he wanted personally to harvest the glory he expected them to win.

When he set up his headquarters in a train and arranged for it to start rolling eastward as soon as the war began, so that he would be able to intervene directly in military operations, he never guessed that he would reside for six years in that mobile headquarters. During all that time, shifting constantly from place to place, he lived with the Oberkommando der Wehrmacht, planned all the campaigns of the war personally, and directed the execution of those plans. His view of the government of his country was restricted to its military operations; his functions as chancellor became subsidiary. As leader of the nation, of course, his place was at the seat of the government; there he should have been holding all the threads in his hand and supervising the armed forces along with other departments of the government. But he was too selfishly arrogant to see this; he lacked the wisdom to recognize the limits of one man's abilities; he wanted to know and to do everything himself.

As it was, he conducted the war, but not the nation. The eighteen-day campaign in Poland increased Hitler's self-assurance in military matters, although the far superior forces of the Germans made the outcome a sure thing. He accepted the plaudits, but at the same time ordered the press to keep silence about his tank tactics in the battles in Poland, because he intended to launch further surprises against his adversaries. During the Polish campaign Hitler's headquarters was in his special train. He took frequent trips by automobile to the combat areas, visited the advancing troops, and personally directed the movements of front-line divisions. He drove up to Warsaw, flew over the city, and participated in the victory parade through its streets.

The invasion of Scandinavia was Hitler's idea. During the winter of 1939–40 he drafted the first plan for the seizing of Norway and Denmark. He was afraid that England would use Scandinavia to create a bridgehead on the Baltic Sea, thus threatening the long, unprotected northern coastline of Germany. This he wanted to anticipate. The attack upon Norway Hitler always considered his riskiest campaign. To load German battalions on frail torpedo boats in waters always dangerous at the end of winter, to expose them to the storms of the sea and the British navy, to send them to Narvik and numerous other coastal points where they would have to capture the batteries they needed for their defense, since supply lines could not be maintained—this was an operation whose daring was unequaled in military history. Hitler himself said that afterwards, when he recollected the dangers, those days and nights of terrible suspense, he had to shudder. For all the splendid efficiency of the officers and soldiers who participated in this undertaking it was purely a gamble that luckily succeeded. His plan to occupy Iceland also and build a bastion there had to be abandoned; here England got in first.

From a purely military point of view the French campaign of 1940 was Hitler's greatest achievement in strategy. This successful offensive against the West, in the course of which Belgium and Holland were ruthlessly overrun, bears all the marks of a Hitlerian plan—although, as in the Polish campaign, the German forces had all the advantages in the matter of armaments.

The sketch of this campaign, determining the direction each army was to take and the strength of each—all this was Hitler's intellectual property, although the preliminary draft was apparently supplied to him by General von Manstein. I can assert this definitely because the matter was the subject of many lively discussions during the campaign and long afterwards. In opposition to the German General Staff, Hitler rejected the "Schlieffen plan." Schlieffen had always called for encircling the enemy by strengthening and extending the right wing. Hitler characterized this scheme as absolutely mistaken, since the German right wing, if extended to the coast, would come to a dead halt at the Channel and be unable to encircle anything. The Channel formed an insurmountable obstacle and the enemy would always be able, by retreating, to present an unbroken front to the German assault. Again and again Hitler dropped contemptuous remarks about the "petrified strategy of the General Staff" and the "Schlieffen worshippers" on it. He declared that in a modern war of movement only a frontal breakthrough along a narrow line would make it possible for the attacker to take the enemy in the rear. The advantage of surprise would then always be on the side of the attacker in choosing the point for the breakthrough. With this in mind he himself drafted the main plan of attack for the West and picked the Ardennes-Sedan-Channel direction as the point of breakthrough.

Later on there was a great deal of talk about an incident which caused Hitler extreme agitation a few weeks before the starting date of the offensive. A German major who had been sent as a courier to take the secret plan of the offensive to western Germany had disregarded orders and used a plane. Flying in fog, he had overshot his destination and made an emergency landing some ten kilometers over the border, in Belgian territory. It was therefore taken for granted that the plan of attack would be in the enemy's hands. Hitler had to decide whether to throw everything over, or to risk going ahead with the existing plan. He counted on the enemy's suspicion, reasoned that they would take the major's emergency landing for a staged trick and the deployment plans in his briefcase as fakes. They would believe all the more firmly that the Schlieffen plan was going to be used, would send their main forces to the north where they would be trapped in the proposed encirclement. Consequently, Hitler did not change one jot of his plan, although he took it for granted that the enemy now knew all about it.

On the morning of May 9 it was announced that Hitler and his entourage would take a special train that evening to Hamburg, to inspect a shipyard there. Everything was made ready for this journey. After the train had covered about two thirds of the way to Hamburg, it was suddenly switched to the West, toward Cologne. On May 10, about six o'clock in the morning we left the train at the

Euskirchen station to proceed by automobile. As we did so, the first squadrons of planes flew overhead in the cloudless sky, their direction toward the west. Without asking I realized at once that the great offensive had begun.

An hour later Hitler stood upon a solitary hill near Muenstereifel in front of his small, camouflaged bunker, waiting impatiently for the first reports of the glider plane attack upon the Belgian fort of Eben Emael, and for news of the parachute drops upon the bridge of Moerdijk and the Dutch forts. From this "eyrie," the first of his headquarters posts, Hitler directed the first part of the campaign in the West. From here he took his first trip to the front, visiting a corps staff in the Belgian town of Bastogne where, four and a half years later, his attempt at a breakthrough to the Meuse was to fail; and here he received his reports of the battles at Brussels, Ghent, Lille, and Dunkirk. The news of the taking of Paris and the French army's request for an armistice reached him in the "Wolf's Ravine," his second headquarters in the West, near Rocroy.

Early in the morning of June 23 he visited Paris for two hours. Virtually unrecognized, he made a brief tour of the city, with a special stop at Napoleon's grave. He directed the end of the campaign in the West from one of the peaks of the Black Forest, his "Pineland" retreat—a small group of bunkers in a clearing among pines to the west of Freudenstadt. From there, following the movements of the troops, he crossed the Rhine to Strassburg and drove on into the Vosges. On June 27 the armistice with France was signed, in his presence, in the forest of Compiègne.

Hitler was now beginning to feel himself the master of Europe. However, after the air battle over England he did not dare to venture the leap across the Channel. Other reasons may have entered his mind, but I do not believe these played a part in his final decision not to invade England. The surprising swiftness of events in France had not given him enough time to make the comprehensive preparations which would have been necessary for so decisive a step. Success,

Hitler thought, was highly improbable. The difficulties of maintaining a frail "bridge of ships" against England's naval power and the perils of the sea were far too great. He did not want to gamble with his victory on the continent.

He spent New Year's Eve of 1940 on the Obersalzberg in Berchtesgaden, and there he raised his glass at midnight to Final Victory in the coming year.

Hitler the soldier had reached the top of the ladder which he himself had set up. In three victorious campaigns he had won the reputation of a military genius as well as a successful leader of battles. Even if we discount good luck and the technical advantages in armament that the German army then held, there remains enough real achievement to justify this reputation. His technique depended on lightning-like armored breakthroughs, followed up by the encirclement and annihilation of the enemy. This same strategic and tactical principle which established his fame as a soldier also destroyed it. For as a commander Hitler knew no other strategy; it was the only way he knew to overcome the enemy. For three years he employed it profitably until, at the climactic point which was Stalingrad, he was driven to the defensive. Then, once he had lost his superiority in arms on land and in the air, he lost the initiative also.

Hitler's strategy was good only for offensive warfare. But he clung to it on the defensive also and repeatedly tried to put it to use under reversed conditions. In this he was following a habit of his in many other fields: Whenever he had succeeded in doing something one way, he would repeat the same maneuver again and again. This man who always wanted to talk and never to listen, who was given always to outbursts of temper and to imposing his will upon others, who as dictator crushed all dissenting opinions, inevitably revealed—once he no longer possessed absolute power and physical superiority—all the weaknesses of his nature. He was incapable of adjustment, unable to adapt to changed circumstances. The successful strategist on the offensive was utterly at a loss when he was forced on to the defensive.

Hitler had not mastered the general's art of conducting an elastic defense in order, once the enemy had exhausted himself on the attack, to come up with a successful counteroffensive. That is what Foch had done in the summer of 1918; that was what the Russians would do so effectively at Stalingrad. But Hitler remained rigid on the defensive; he clung desperately to his positions, no matter how insecure they had become. Instead of withdrawing his forces in time, regrouping them in order to save them so that he might prepare new surprises for the enemy by emerging suddenly from newly-occupied defensive positions, he ordered the "hedgehogging" of outflanked positions. Then he would leave the hopelessly encircled troops behind in the vague hope that later he might be able to relieve them or use them as a bridgehead for a new offensive.

On the basis of his successes during the first three years of the war he always, in the last three years when the tables were turned, overestimated his own forces and underestimated those of his enemies. And because he did not know how to yield the smallest territory, in the end he lost everything.

Hitler directed the Balkan campaign of April 1941 from his headquarters in the special train at the railroad station of Mönichkirchen, south of Wienerneustadt. Crete, and the offensive against Russia in the summer of that year, seemed at first to increase his reputation as a military genius.

I do not know who drafted the plans for the summer campaign in Russia, or whether the execution of the campaign corresponded to the original plan. From conversations I happened to hear on this subject I gathered only that Hitler was discontented with the shifting of the center of gravity from the southern sector, which he considered by far the most important, to the central and northern sectors. I know he blamed the General Staff for this shift. At any rate, soon after the start of this adventure he realized that the advance was proceeding far less swiftly than he had originally hoped. He had expected a blitzkrieg across the Russian steppes; nothing of the kind took place. In subsequent post-mortems Hitler often declared that the beginning of the campaign against Russia had been delayed for six weeks because of the intervening Balkan War. It was just these six weeks, he later maintained, that he had lacked in the autumn; otherwise he would have defeated Russia before the severe winter descended.

After the two great encirclement battles of Viasma and Briansk he believed he had destroyed the bulk of the Russian armies in the field. This was a fantastic underestimation of the strength and tenacity of the foe, as well as a complete misunderstanding of the territorial and climatic situation. He was convinced that the road to Moscow lay open to his panzer corps, and that the real decisive stroke of the campaign had already been delivered. The military men in his entourage supported him in this view. In passing on this information at a press conference in Berlin I committed a blunder that seriously diminished my journalistic reputation. But the statement I gave to the press had come directly from Hitler as Supreme Commander of the Armed Forces. In view of the sensation this affair aroused I shall tell the story in full.

In giving information to the public on offensives in progress, Hitler was often excessively restrained, so long as there was the slightest chance that he might give the enemy any hint of the extent, direction, and aims of his operations. Many Germans did not understand this at the time. But this, for example, was the policy he observed in the early part of October 1941, although great battles had long been in progress. On October 9—his headquarters during this period was in a forest near the Masurian Lakes—as he was coming from the room where he held his situation conferences, he called out to me in passing. The time had come, he said, to make up for all the restrictions that had been placed on information to the press. The public could now be informed about the latest operations, which had been kept under wraps. I was to come to see him in half an hour.

When half an hour later I reported to him, accompanied by my secretary, he received me in his study in the bunker. He was in high spirits. Pacing the room with vigorous strides, he dictated to me word for word the statement I was to give to the press in Berlin next day. My secretary took down every syllable he spoke. Hitler said to me—to sum up once more the message that created such a stir—that after all the preceding battles, these two last great battles of annihilation had taken such a toll of the enemy in respect of men and war materials that he no longer had the strength to resist the victorious German panzer armies with any prospect of success. Although a number of more or less major battles might be necessary before the enemy was completely defeated, the German armies were now over the hill; for all practical purposes the campaign in the East was as good as decided. Our foes' dream of a two-front war had already burst like a bubble.

At this moment Hitler was firmly convinced that the war was as good as over, and he expressed this conviction to me in an emotional outburst—although in my press conference I did not go so far as to quote him in this. But I had no reason to doubt what the supreme commander spontaneously told me about the events in the East. Moreover I was specifically ordered to publish this statement. Nevertheless, in order to make sure, I personally submitted my secretary's stenographic copy, in the form I intended to use for publication, to General Jodl, chief of the Army Liaison Staff, so that he might check it over.

Shortly afterwards the unexpectedly sudden, premature, and extraordinarily bitter winter set in. The German armies, which had counted on at least four weeks more of mobility, were instantly brought to a halt and their vehicles literally frozen into the mud. At one blow a higher power had altered the whole situation. The frightful difficulties to which the German troops before Moscow were exposed during the following weeks belied the statement I had issued in good faith. Nonplussed, Hitler said nothing about it, and I had no choice but to take the blame of false prophecy upon myself, in order to spare the German head of state. As a matter of fact, before the beginning of this battle for Moscow, which he considered so decisive, Hitler issued a printed proclamation to the troops expressing the same ideas. This proclamation was signed by Hitler himself. But after the winter disaster no one seemed to remember it.

It is true that a higher power had taken the field during those October days in Russia. Napoleon had once said, "I can fight men, but not the elements." Nevertheless, this wrong prediction of Hitler's in this early part of the Russian campaign showed for the first time his fatal inclination to overestimate enormously his own military strength. He was trapped by his own unbroken chain of previous successes and his sovereign contempt for the abilities of the enemy. Later this tendency developed into that unreasonable optimism which he displayed publicly on all occasions, thus reviving the hopes of all those who believed in him and looked up to him. By his iron energy and convincing outbursts of temperament he was able to encourage the strong and revive the spirits of the weak.

In order to clarify Hitler's general attitude toward public relations I shall add another incident, of lesser importance than the above, which took place at an earlier time. On the last Sunday in June of 1941—many Germans will remember it still—ten "special communiqués" were announced over the radio at intervals of about an hour. This strange method of supplying the public with information by storing up communiqués, and then issuing them in rapid succession in order to make an impression, was both foolish and unsuccessful. It aroused great resentment. Hitler himself had personally prepared these ten special communiqués. He had kept back military successes for several days and then ordered the propaganda minister, in spite of the latter's objections, to make them public in this unusual form. Hitler thought the idea brilliant. Then criticisms from an irritated public began pouring in. These criticisms were reported to Hitler, who ignored them and responded with violent fury to all recommendations that the practice be discontinued. When I brought him the reports of dissatisfaction, I too seized the opportunity to inform him in a calmly objective manner that Sunday radio listeners were thoroughly annoyed at having to keep to their apartments on such a fine day. He snapped at me that I did not know anything about propaganda; he knew the mentality and the feelings of the broad masses of the people better than I and all the other intellectuals put together. Embittered over his unreasonableness and self-righteousness, I said that if such was his opinion of my abilities I should like to request that he employ me rather as a soldier in the field. Brusquely, he cut me off, ordering me to be still, obey, and do my duty in this war. There were things he, too, did not like, but he was not able to throw everything up and quit.

With Hitler there was no such thing as handing in your resignation. He recognized only complete subservience to his orders, or "desertion." He, on the other hand, claimed for himself the right to dismiss an official arbitrarily, without giving any reasons.

On December 15, 1941 Field Marshal von Brauchitsch was relieved of his command. Hitler personally assumed supreme command of the army. This represented the formalization of the role he had in practice long played. But Brauchitsch's dismissal at this moment meant far more than the elimination of an intermediary between leader and army who had become superfluous to Hitler. The lack of proper winter equipment for the soldiers in the East had deeply shocked the German people. Brauchitsch was the scapegoat. Hitler wanted to pose before the German people as the righteous one, who was coming down hard on those responsible for the mess in the army supply system. But in order to understand the situation aright it is necessary to know something that was later credibly reported to me. Brauchitsch, and precisely Brauchitsch, had from the first advised against continuation of the German offensive against Moscow that winter and had recommended that it be resumed only after the capture of Leningrad and thorough new preparations. Thus he was opposing Hitler's own view, and it is clear why Hitler wanted him to go. But for Hitler on top of that to dismiss Brauchitsch so ostentatiously in December, thereby branding him with the blame for the fiasco of the winter's campaign and all its dreadful concomitants, when Brauchitsch himself had warned against the campaign—that was a piece of monstrous unfairness.

In this incident Hitler was displaying a highly inglorious trait which was to become more and more prominent in his character. He put the blame for all his own mistakes on others. To witness his bursts of indignation, his denunciations of "these scourges of the people" when he heard of any grievous piece of news, one could well believe in his deep sincerity and responsibility at any given moment. But when afterwards the true facts came to light, and the trouble was traced to a quite different source, he refused to recognize it. He never accepted correction and never admitted to having been wrong. This absence of self-criticism and this tendency always to put the blame on others was all the more serious because Hitler knew that, since he was absolute dictator, the accused had no chance to justify himself. It was this trait which developed into his mania for discarding deserving army commanders right and left after every defeat. In such cases he was deaf to their protest that they had not acted freely, but had simply followed his own orders. Whenever anything failed, he regularly hurled charges of "treason and sabotage." Consequently, toward the climax of the drama, when the number of his defeats and blunders mounted, he began running amok against everyone and everything.

Undoubtedly there was resistance, treason, and sabotage during those many years of bitter history. The lack of resolution within the German officer corps during this war undoubtedly weakened the striking power and the capacity for resistance of the German armed forces in those last decisive years. Many people thought this weakening came from Hitler's own inadequacy, that it was caused by his exaggeration and lack of measure, his free throwing around of insults, his arbitrariness and injustice—whereas Hitler thought it was the officers' lack of spunk that provoked him to this conduct. By his own behavior, Hitler alienated the army men. His hasty, ill-considered, often contemptuous judgment of the officers of his army produced the mood which he then—rightly or wrongly—so often ranted against and which at the end he blamed for the collapse of the army's resistance.

With the best of military intentions he set up the élite divisions of the *Waffen-SS.* But the creation of this service produced a spirit of mistrust in the German officers corps. So much internal friction resulted that in some it took up more of the strength of the German army than could possibly have been compensated for by the SS formations' military efficiency, splendid as this was.

Hitler overburdened himself, and after five years of warfare he made demands upon the troops which they were simply no longer able to meet. With such self-deception he made matters harder for himself. And since he threateningly insisted that the impossible should be made possible, he could only blame himself for a large part of the lack of honesty in the reports from the lower levels of the army leadership—about which he often complained so bitterly.

Thus he himself conjured up the spirits he could no longer shake off. By his own uncontrolled temperament, his arrogant superiority, and his insulting distrust, he converted the initial coherent harmony and fraternity into confusion and hostility, a whirlpool from which there was then no escaping—in spite of the almost superhuman resistance of his will to being sucked in by that dread current.

In the inferno of the mighty struggle this will of his manifested again and again remarkable surges, a pitching of his psychic energies to the highest levels. How compellingly evident that was during that Russian winter of 1941–42, when Hitler's will was laid down before the German armies, an immovable barrier preventing them from pouring back in wild retreat.

On New Year's Eve of 1941 Hitler's power of will and steadfastness won their greatest victory. Field Marshal von Kluge wanted to withdraw the Central Army Group. He was firmly resolved upon the retreat. At midnight Hitler spoke to him over the telephone from his headquarters to persuade him to hold, for otherwise he feared that the entire eastern front would collapse. The fierce battle over the telephone, while his associates waited to bring him their New Year's greetings, lasted for more than two hours. Kluge warned and pleaded; he appealed to reason and declared that he would not take the responsibility for the abysmal dangers he foresaw. He spoke in the names of the hundreds of thousands of German soldiers who were waiting during those freezing days and nights for the word to retreat to better positions, the word that would release them from their agony. He gave the best of reasons for his resolve, and swore that it was his plain duty to order a retreat.

But in spite of everything, Hitler was fighting for the future of the army, for the foundation upon which the whole war in the East rested. He shattered Kluge's arguments. The supposedly prepared positions in the rear did not exist. Why should the army be better off moving backwards than holding where it was? The climatic conditions were the same anyhow. Hitler argued and soft-soaped, raged and shouted, kept at it and at it, insisted and commanded, and won his point. The center remained where it was and held. The eastern front escaped a great peril. Its positions and basis of deployment for the next year's fighting remained. By the end of the spring of 1942 the army was again ready to take the offensive.

Napoleon had said in 1812: "The cold destroyed me." Hitler's will mastered the situation; his steadfastness held off catastrophe. To be sure, the question remains whether the German people would have been better served, ultimately, by a retreat rather than an advance into the endless spaces that a year later brought about collapse and started Germany on the road to defeat.

Steadfastness is a great virtue in a soldier, but it is not the specific quality that makes a great commander. Steadfastness and impelling energy were Hitler's great traits as a military leader. He was the revolutionizing spirit of the German Wehrmacht; he was its motive force. He sparked its organizational machinery, which even the enemy recognized as magnificent. He was aware of its tendency toward overthoroughness and bureaucratic rigidity and he fought untiringly against that tendency. Wherever he found instances of clever improvisation by the enemy, he held them up as examples to be followed. For he knew that the German talent for organization should be supplemented by flexibility. Ultimately this concern led him to interfere so far down the line of command that he was constantly meddling with the lower levels of army leadership. This gave offense to many, besides being inconsistent with his ambition to be a commander operating on the highest plane. He quite rightly reproved many of the lower levels of command for lacking the spirit of improvisation. But as a commander, Hitler himself, with his intellectual rigidity and monotonous repetition of previous patterns, lacked originality just as much as the lowliest lieutenant.

From 1942 on, none of Hitler's offensives produced a successful encirclement. On the contrary, from the end of that year on he was the one whose troops were encircled. The Russians had learned from the experiences of the past year and retreated when necessary. But Hitler could learn nothing and would take no advice. Since he was unable to yield in anything, the thought of moving back, of withdrawing before forces temporarily stronger than his own, was unendurable. Such an idea had no place in the dictatorial structure of his mind. Once the possibilities for taking the offensive vanished, the fire of his spirit went out. Stalingrad proved to be the grave of the Sixth Army and the turning point in the fate of Germany. There Hitler's will, the dynamic basic element of his existence, was broken—and along with it Germany's fighting spirit.

The commander in chief's genius was a spark that flashed only when he took the initiative, only when he followed where his own will led him. That spark died the moment he had to yield, the moment he had to master obstacles imposed upon him by the actions of others.

From the middle of August 1942 on, there lay upon Hitler's desk, polished and ready for the press, the special communiqué which was to be issued upon the fall of Stalingrad. That event was expected to occur hourly. Hitler's headquarters had by then been moved forward into the Ukraine and were now in a small pine wood near Vinnitsa. Three months later, at the traditional meeting in the Munich Bürgerbräukeller on November 8, he defiantly told his Old Guard, "I am in Stalingrad and I shall remain in Stalingrad." A little earlier, at three o'clock in the morning of that same day, while his train was at the Calau station on the way to Munich, he had received the report of the Allied landing in French North Africa. Hard though this is to comprehend, the landing struck him as a complete surprise. He was now harvesting the fruits of his policy in France.

On November 20 Stalingrad was cut off. On February 1, 1943 the city, along with 80,000 German soldiers, fell into the hands of the Russians. During those six months from August to February there took place the decisive crisis which shattered Hitler's spirit.

After this collapse of his far-reaching hopes for conquest of the Caucasus, he had a violent disagreement with the generals of the Oberkommando der Wehrmacht. He stopped eating with them at the headquarters casino; from then on, until the end of the war, he dined alone most of the time. He maintained that his orders, which he delivered orally during the daily discussion of the situation, were not transmitted at all, or transmitted wrongly. He ordered Bormann to set up a special stenographic staff. Henceforth every word he spoke during these hours-long conferences had to be taken down and filed; this was done right up to the end of the war. He dismissed his Chief of the General Staff, Colonel General Halder, replacing him with Colonel General Zeitzler. He made his principal military adjutant, Colonel Schmundt (who was later killed in the assassination attempt of July 20, 1944), chief of the Army Personnel Office. Thereafter all appointments to army posts were directed, through Schmundt, by Hitler personally. In consequence, stability in the army leadership became the exception, and constant change became the system.

Meanwhile the Russians had broken through on both sides of Stalingrad and had overrun the Rumanian and Italian armies. Then Hitler made his ghastly decision, strategically a monstrous piece of folly. As yet the encirclement around the Sixth Army was only a thin belt; there was still a chance for this army to break through to the west. Instead Hitler ordered it to dig in and wait until it was relieved by a counterattack. This counteroffensive, undertaken with utterly inadequate preparation, was smashed by the Russians, who continued their advance.

This suicidal ostrich policy was born of inner uncertainty, insufficient political clarity, and a passion for gambling. But from then on it became Hitler's invariable pattern; intoxicated by his own "fanatical steadfastness," despising all the rules of mobile warfare, he ordered his troops to dig in whenever the enemy achieved a breakthrough.

The reconquest of Kharkov by the commander of the Adolf Hitler Division of the SS was one of Hitler's last successes; he postponed the Memorial Day for National Socialist Heroes to March 15 so as to have this triumph included in his speech. But his last great offensive in the East was a dismal failure. This "Operation Citadel" at the end of June 1943 was supposed to break through between Belgorod and Orel, but after ten days the attack had to be called off without the public's ever hearing that it had been begun.

Hitler refused to build an East Wall, say along the Dnieper. On principle he would not permit the construction of fixed positions in the rear of the German fronts. The knowledge that there were better positions behind them would, he maintained, undermine the fighting spirit of the front-line troops. Then, when the initiative passed to his enemies, he habitually belittled all their armored breakthroughs as small raids; the enemy must be punished for his "impudence" and "shamelessness" by being cut off and "starved to death" behind the

German lines. Therefore, when big breakthroughs took place he ordered whole armies, corps, and divisions to remain behind as isolated islands. Supposedly these groups were to close gaps by executing flanking movements—when in fact those gaps had already become gigantic holes through which a flood of enemy troops was pouring to form new fronts in the rear of the encircled German units. These units, after heroically holding out, would eventually be crushed by superior forces.

From the Volga to the Oder, Hitler sacrificed the German army by this strategy in a vacuum. The same story was repeated during the great Russian offensives in the Central Sector, at Vitebsk and Orsha Bobruisk, later from the Baranov bridgehead and on both sides of Warsaw into East Prussia, Poland, and Pomerania; it was repeated all the way to Cracow and the Neisse River.

In the days of his successes Hitler had often gone to visit the troops, to inspire them and strengthen their morale by his presence. But after the disasters began he visited the fighting troops only a single time.

That was in February 1943 when the fall of Stalingrad and the dangerous concomitant retreat threatened to carry along the entire German southern sector. Hitler flew to join Manstein at Zaporozhe, and by his personal appearance and intervention succeeded, after a three-day stay at the Dnieper front, in bringing the withdrawal to a halt. Thereafter he never again, throughout the remaining years of the war, took the road to the front to join his soldiers. Although in critical situations he was urged to do so countless times, nothing could persuade him to repeat the experience. In defeat he lacked the vigor and faith which he should have had to radiate to the fighting men. Formerly the direct influence of his personality upon the masses had been his great strength; now he could no longer throw that influence into the scales. Inwardly, he was no longer what he had once been; for that reason he kept away from the front, and for that reason he became alienated from reality. He, too, became an armchair general; he issued his orders without consideration for the limitations of his own forces and without regard for the real strength of the enemy.

I recall with what contempt and misunderstanding of the situation he criticized Patton's decisive breakthrough in Normandy. In all seriousness he expressed the hope that "the more Americans the better" would pour through the gap almost ten kilometers wide, so that the German troops would then be able to "close the trap." He kept on saying this until the German army—which had been ordered to carry out this mission—was itself entrapped and only remnants of it succeeded in escaping across the Seine. Then he blamed the army commanders in the West for the fiasco and put through one of his usual shake-ups. He charged the command in the West with having begun the attack prematurely, thus squandering its effectiveness before strong German forces could combine.

During the Ardennes offensive of December 15, 1944 he once more seized the initiative. He had begun planning this offensive right after the attempted assassination of July 20. His greatest problem, one he discussed for weeks, was whether the point of the attacking army ought to reach the sea to the north or to the south of Antwerp; that the offensive would succeed he did not for a moment question. He counted on cutting off the entire British army from its base of supplies and wiping it out. The certainty he publicly displayed once more revived the hopes of the German people. But this fantastic hope was buried in the bottomless mud of the roads in the Ardennes, and the simultaneous attack across the Vosges also failed. Thereupon Hitler made a decision which even he characterized as reckless and dangerous, in view of the Allied crossing of the Rhine and the Russian breakthrough toward the Oder. While the enemy was approaching the vital heart of the Reich, he sent the Sixth Panzer Army from the Rhine to Budapest where at his command several German divisions had allowed themselves to be encircled. Instead of protecting the Ruhr or Berlin, he spent weeks planning another grand counteroffensive. The attacking troops were to cross the Danube south of Budapest, take the city from the rear, and, if opportunity offered, advance eastward into the vacuum left by the advancing Russians. In support of this idea he declared that the vital oilfields west of Budapest must be saved. Transportation and deployment of the Sixth Panzer Army consumed six precious weeks; but after a few days the Russians broke through elsewhere and the planned offensive was converted into a disastrous retreat which resulted in the loss of Vienna and large parts of Austria. Around the same time, between February and March, Hitler ordered Field Marshal Model to hold his positions in the Ruhr, which the Allies had meanwhile bypassed. The Ruhr, Hitler averred, would later be relieved by an attack from the south. Once more he was hoping to turn the spearhead of the enemy's offensive the other way and cut off the encircling troops.

One last time, in the midst of the death agony, Hitler bounded to his feet again. And again his new resolve sprang from delusory hopes—that he might save Berlin and avert the fate which had already descended upon Germany. On April 22, 1945 the Russians unexpectedly pushed forward into the northeastern suburbs of Berlin. At first Hitler gave everything up for lost and prepared to put an end to his life. But on the night of April 22–23 he gathered his energies once more. Previously he had issued the watchword: "Berlin will be defended on the Oder." Now—at five minutes before midnight—he ordered all army groups which still remained to come to the relief of Berlin. He wanted to strip his western front completely, gather all his forces in Berlin, and defeat the Russians there. Then, having won one final victory, he hoped to negotiate an armistice with the supreme commanders of the Western Powers—for he expected them to stop at the Elbe. In line with this fantastic plan he ordered Wenck's army to march toward Berlin from the Elbe, Steiner's and Holste's corps to approach from the north. But although time was pressing, he ordered Busse's army in the east to wait in order to join later with Schörner's army group, which would be moving up from the southeast, thus forming a pincers around the east of Berlin. In this way he expected to cut off and annihilate the Russians fighting inside the capital. His Chief of the General Staff and the other generals implored him to allow Busse, who was close to Berlin, to go into action at once; otherwise all would he lost. There simply were not enough troops to hold back the Russians. Hitler refused to listen; in defiance of all advice he clung to his plan. To the end he carried out his suicidal strategy. He wanted all or nothing, gambled to the last. And for the last time he overestimated himself. The superior forces of the Russians smothered all movements in the bud and crushed Berlin.

On the night of April 23–24, 1945 the Oberkommando der *Wehrmacht* moved out of Berlin, shifting its headquarters to North Germany. Hitler remained behind in Berlin, accompanied by Goebbels and Bormann and a few others. Here he was to meet his destiny. On the afternoon of April 30, 1945 he put an end to his life.

I had been dismissed by Hitler on March 30, 1945. The events which took place thereafter at the headquarters I learned later, from eyewitnesses whom I have known for years. Hitler had relieved me of my post because I refused to have any part in the "atrocity propaganda" against the Allied troops, which Goebbels had started on orders from Hitler in order to incite the German civilian populace to carry on senseless guerilla warfare. I had also spoken against the insane "werewolf program"; and had earlier argued against Hitler's intention of declaring Germany's non-recognition of the Geneva Convention.

Any picture of Hitler's total personality as a military man would be incomplete without an account of his relationship to the navy and his attitude toward the conduct of the war in the air.

Hitler loved big ships. From boyhood on he had been enthusiastic about them; the sight of ships delighted him, and as head of state he wasted a great deal of time and money on naval vessels. But it was an unrequited love. Hitler's fondness elicited no response and his hopes in the navy were not fulfilled, so that later he turned away in disillusionment. One after the other, those masterpieces of German shipbuilding sank beneath the waves—not because they were poorly handled or fought badly, but because Hitler recognized too late that success in modern naval warfare requires, first, the closest co-operation with a well-developed air force and, secondly, the use of the latest techniques in shortwave radio. When the English navy was driven off from the coast of Norway by the then superior German Luftwaffe, Hitler realized that the age of the battleship's independent supremacy was gone forever. But he did not fully grasp the significance of this new development in naval warfare until that wakeful night when the Bismarck went down on the high seas, after a brave, solitary struggle. From then on he damned the German navy, which he had formerly adored. The big ships which had not yet been sunk he had laid up. All his efforts and hopes in the maritime sphere were now given over to the rapid expansion and development of the submarine arm of the navy. For a long time he overestimated the ratio of sinkings to new construction and therefore concluded that the U-boats would ultimately have a decisive effect upon the whole war.

For years he deceived himself and others by his estimates of the productive capacities of the United States and Great Britain. The boasts that later proved to be cruel reality, Hitler called bluffs. In 1813 Napoleon remarked to Prince Metternich that he possessed a sure means of determining the military strength of his enemies: mathematics. By figuring the natural wealth in men and raw materials of a country he could determine the maximum military effort of which it was capable. It is curious that Hitler employed the same method to convince his associates that the "mammoth figures" of his enemies were not to be believed. On the basis of the Allies' coal production he calculated their maximum possible steel production; from the available supplies of rubber and metals he arrived at statistics for the maximum possible production of arms and other war materials. Production is the same everywhere, he declared with assurance, and therefore his foes' potential was in reality far smaller than their exaggerated figures would indicate. As a result, he constantly promoted an optimism that proved false.

The barometer of his expectations in the submarine war rose and fell as Germany got ahead or fell behind in the technological race. The magnetic mine gave her a brief lead, which was soon overcome. In the field of ultrashort waves the Allies came out far ahead. The use of radar for locating submarines from airplanes initially inflicted such enormous losses that U-boat activities virtually came to a halt. German submarines were forced to remain almost constantly under water; for a time they were practically eliminated from the war. Then the U-boats were equipped with "snorkel" for obtaining air while under water; this permitted them to move about again. Mass production methods were building a series of sensational new U-boats of great speed intended for use completely under water. But there was time to get only a few of these into action before the war ended. The loss of the Baltic ports put a sudden end to this one great and well-founded hope. The new submarine undoubtedly would soon have given an entirely new turn to the U-boat war.

Hitler's position on air warfare can only be called tragic—from the military point of view. He himself had no feeling for planes; he did not like flying and had a psychological aversion to the whole idea of aviation. This revolutionary in military matters had no sympathy for the most revolutionary weapon of the century. From remarks he dropped now and then one gathered the impression that he felt rather uncomfortable at the prospect of future developments that were alien to his nature. There may well be some connection between this feeling and his offers to discuss air disarmament. The creation of the German Luftwaffe was Göring's work. Deeply concerned as he was with the other arms of the service, Hitler at first scarcely bothered about the aircraft construction program. He entrusted it completely to Göring. When the war began and he recognized the value of the air force in his campaigns, he gave full praise to Göring's work, and saw to it that the Luftwaffe was used with great vigor. It is one of the great mysteries of Hitler's military thinking that he did not draw the obvious conclusions from his own illuminating experiences with the air arm. He was the first in the war to possess a strategic air force—but he recognized too late the importance of air strategy for the war as a whole. He put through intensive production programs for the most modern tanks, cannon, and warships, but did little to further technical progress in the air. He lacked the farsightedness to push the development of an efficient big bomber—the weapon which in the later phases of the air war was to give our enemies such a decisive advantage. No one can say what a turn the war might have taken if in 1940, with the advantage he already possessed in the air, he had also possessed a model of a big bomber and had given priority to its mass production. Instead he depended completely upon Göring whose so-called experts experimented for years on dozens of different types of planes—until it was too late, until the Allies dominated the air and forced him on the defensive.

The fighter plane program went even more badly. Toward the end of 1942 Hitler finally recognized the extreme peril; he wanted—as he said—to clear the skies above Germany and save the Reich from destruction. In 1944 mass production of fighters was pushed with all the energy of Germany's industry above and below ground. A monthly production—so Hitler said—of 4,200 planes had been reached (6,000 was the target). But as soon as the first 300 planes came up against the enemy, the fearful truth was known. Even the improved mass-production fighter was a failure, a "flying coffin" unable to cope with the fire of the enemy bombers and their fighter cover. After this completely unexpected disaster in plane production came the last act in the fearful tragedy of the air war that shattered Germany. The fighter program was halted. The last hope in plane production was the jet alone, capable of a speed of 500 miles per hour. It was one of the best German planes, but there was no time for it to be put into effective mass production. At the time Hitler thought it better to build the first series of 100 planes as bombers to be used against the ships of the coming invasion fleet. Göring was for building fighters; Hitler criticized him for his "fighter obsession."

Hitler deeply shared those last great popular hopes based on the "new weapons." In instinctive harmony with the soul of the people, who were boiling with rage over the enemy bombings, he coined the phrase "Vengeance" weapons, a name he insisted on even when his generals advised against it. Goebbels then proposed the term "V-weapons," having earlier burned his fingers by going too far in his propaganda. Hitler fanned all the hopes. He expected a great deal of the V-1, which could be launched both from the ground and from planes. After long preparation and month-long postponements, the V-1 was put into action at last. After the first week Hitler was so disappointed by the results that he forbade the weapon's being mentioned in the radio and press, although he himself had previously whipped up a great propaganda campaign for it, replete with exaggerations which went far beyond the alarmist foreign descriptions of the observed effects.

Shortly afterwards he had the V-2 announced. He gave express instructions for emphasizing that more powerful and more terrible V-weapons were to follow. But the V-2, though it was later employed on the battlefields of the West and especially against the port of Antwerp, was also a bad disappointment to Hitler.

He frequently talked in general terms about the possibility of unleashing atomic energy for military purposes, but in my presence he never said a word about the prospects for an atomic bomb in the near future for Germany. He knew how to keep great secrets, so that no conclusions could be drawn from his silence. But today we know that Germany did not have the bomb.

In the last year of the war Hitler realized that the ultimate cause of all his defeats lay in his inferiority in the air. He reproached not only Göring, but himself also for not having seen to the development of the Luftwaffe much earlier. But by then it was too late; he had closed his eyes to the idea for too long.

Hitler was aware of the terrible effects of the bombings upon the cities of Germany. He knew the frightful suffering and the heroic endurance, an endurance beyond praise, of the German population. Nevertheless he, who in the years of good fortune, when he was being hailed on all sides, had enjoyed spending much time among the people, did not once in all the long years of misfortune visit a single bombed German city to offer consolation to the suffering people. He was often asked to do so, but he always pretended that such visits were militarily unfeasible. I shall mention one scene that was typical of his behavior on this score.

In 1943, after the first terrible bombing of my birthplace, Essen, I set out for a visit to the population. Before leaving I told Hitler of my plan while we were at table together. I was hoping he would give me some personal greeting to take to the hard-hit inhabitants of the city of Krupp. He ignored my remark, seemingly not hearing it. After returning from Essen I tried to give him a report of my impressions. During our lunch, I was unable to draw him into a conversation on the subject. I therefore followed him into an anteroom, intending to speak of what I had seen and of the reaction of the populace of Essen. As soon as he saw me behind him, he suddenly burst out—before I could say a word—with an almost insulting complaint about some ridiculous, unimportant press item which he had read in some newspaper. Then he hurried off to his rooms. It was obvious that he had thought up this far-fetched complaint on the spur of the moment in order to put me off. He simply did not want to hear my impressions of the terrible effects of the bombings in the cities of the Ruhr.

Hitler did not want to see how the people of Germany were suffering. He could not bear their unspoken reproaches that he had plunged them into unendurable misery. He felt responsible to the people because he was their Leader, but he did not have the power to alter the circumstances. The dark side of his nature, coming more and more to the fore in the horror of obliteration bombings, was alienating him from the people, just as the light side of his dual character had once brought him so close to them.

Hitler's attitude toward aviation was rooted in his character. His mind was restricted to the narrow range of national interests; he lacked all supranational breadth of vision and therefore could not appreciate the international, progressive elements of modern aviation and electronics. This narrowness of his, which I have mentioned so often in other connections, was here ruinous to Germany's military effort. In spite of all his passionate experiments in the national and social fields, he was a figure of the past, not of the future. That, it seems to me, was the deepest cause of his failure in air warfare. Occasionally he would make remarks to the effect that modern developments in aviation—the domination of soulless, inanimate forces—were depersonalizing human life and cheapening life's essential content. In such a world, he would declare, life no longer seemed to him worth living. As a private person he might have had the right to think such thoughts; as a leader he was in duty bound to act otherwise.

We may, then, sum up the picture of Hitler as a soldier winning glory and honor in the beginning, achieving defeat and suicide in the end. As a soldier, as in all his other aspects, Hitler was the victim of the duality of his nature, the ambivalence of his character. In his latter days as a soldier he was precisely as incompetent as he had been brilliant in the earlier days; in the second half of the war he had as much bad luck as he had enjoyed good luck in the first half. His superiority in the air and in military technology, his offensive strategy, his break-through tactics, and his encirclements, passed to his opponents and were used against him.

Hitler was the soul and conscience of the German Wehrmacht. But by the very intemperateness and violence of his passions he was also its ruin. He was a corporal who became a military genius; but in order to win recognition as a great commander he all too frequently showed himself an overweening corporal.

Even war has its laws and its moral limits. These he despised; he made the antediluvian law of violence the sole guide of his military actions. He recognized no code of military fairness; guided only by considerations of military expediency, he introduced savage methods into warfare. During the last months of the war, in spite of all representations by his associates, he resolved to declare Germany's non-adherence to the Geneva Convention, in order to intimidate German soldiers so that they would not allow themselves to be taken prisoners, and in order to frighten them with the prospect of terrible reprisals against their families.

The German people, who approved these methods no more they did the inhumanities of the war in the air, will pronounce a just verdict upon Hitler, once they have come to a clear understanding of his nature. Up to the very end he threw the whole weight of his authority behind the promise of victory, if victory was doubtful, he declared, it was so only if the German people themselves, by their attitude, threw it away. He ordered the people to fight for that victory and branded any questioning of victory as a crime against the state.

Hitler was the standard-bearer throughout the war. He appealed to the patriotism and loyalty of the Germans and declared that no German conscious of his duty might desert the flag. But he himself deserted the flag, shirking his responsibility, and left the people to their fate. His departure from life was in terms of, "After me the Deluge!"

Perhaps history will revise the present generation's judgment of Hitler as a soldier. But so overpowering has been the misfortune he brought down upon the Germans of today, and upon other nations as well, that they cannot possibly respect him for his soldierly achievements. He himself destroyed the foundations of any such respect.

Chapter 5

The Leader State—Chaos in Leadership

HITLER WAS THE victim of his own ideas. His rigid will never bent, even when reality physically overwhelmed him. In the struggle with his enemies he was the first to collapse. He lived entirely in a delusory structure of excessive nationalism, never budged from it as long as he was alive, and even in death offered defiance to reality. There was no room at all in his mind for any thought of the German people's continuing to live without him and the "blessing of his hand." Hitler had the arrogance to tell the Germans that if they did not withstand the trial of this war and come out victorious, they no longer deserved to live upon this earth. He asked the impossible of them, and when they did not meet his standards he said they had no right to life. He who all his life had deified his nation took no part in the dire fate that he had brought upon it.

His death represented the egocentric antipode to that altruism he so often stressed when he declared that he wanted to do "everything for his people and nothing for himself." When his dream of rule went down to dust, Hitler showed that he was not ready to sacrifice himself for the future of his people; on the contrary, he had sacrificed the people to his own hunger for power and the selfishness of his ungoverned imagination.

In theory Hitler had built up an ideal Leader State. But in practice he created utter chaos in the leadership of the state. Before the eyes of his adherents he held up the mirage of a classless Leader State such as Plato had celebrated in his "Laws" as the highest possible form of the state. The Father of Philosophy described such a system as one which automatically brought forth out of the people the wise men to be their leaders, to whom the masses would voluntarily subordinate themselves. After two thousand years of human evolution and political experience the time seemed ripe to Hitler, and the people ready, to bring an experiment of this sort to fruition.

Hitler established his "folk-community" in Germany. At the same time he created a class of leaders who had, he said, risen by natural selection out of the political struggle on the domestic scene. He equipped these leaders with "authority over those below and responsibility to those above." On top of the heap he himself sat enthroned as absolute Leader responsible to no one. According to Hitler's planned "Constitution" the Leader was to be advised by a Senate appointed by himself. This Senate would then choose the Führer's eventual successor.

This "classless race-and-leader state" had been brought into being by revolution. Hitler wanted to ensure its continuance by setting up a functioning, permanent system for the selection of leaders. For this purpose, all barriers of privilege were to be removed; the potential leaders seeking to rise above the broad masses of the people were not to be hampered by birth or economic condition. Competence alone was to be the qualification for leadership in this new state. The best youths of the nation were to be constantly recruited out of the people, were to join the leadership and grow into the pulsating life of the nation. Thus the state would be assured of both stability and progress. It would advance to the highest possible point of evolution. This system of perpetual renewal, of creative forces developing out of the society's own rhythm, was to constitute the best and most modern form of state, the most beneficial to the commonweal and at the same time the most just for each individual.

That was the "idea." In theory it was alluring and attracted many fine minds. But what was it like in practice?

In the twelve years of his rule Hitler created in the political leadership of Germany the greatest confusion that has ever existed in a civilized state. Instead of developing the hierarchy of leaders who were to stand at his side, checking his work, giving advice, and adjusting conflicts, he concentrated the leadership more and more exclusively within his own person. He permitted no other gods besides himself. The cult of personality he fostered was directed solely toward himself. He wanted no suggestions; he wanted only execution of his orders.

For centuries the conduct of government has been based upon the tried and tested principle of independent chiefs of different departments. But Hitler, wherever possible, eliminated this system and set up a series of dependent secretariats without authority. He did not appoint competent persons with independent responsibilities to important posts, persons who would then have borne their full share of the burden in the conduct of war and peace. Instead he set up mere executive arms who had to go to him for their exact instructions, who could do no more than carry out his orders.

For example, throughout the war Hitler never had the aid and support of a war minister or a commander-in-chief of the armed forces. In February 1938 he had dismissed the war minister and assumed those functions. In his place he appointed a chief of the OKW who was directly attached to himself. For the same reason he personally took over, in December 1941, the post of supreme commander of the army, although he certainly could not handle all the details of the commander's tasks. In August 1942 he transferred the leading post in the Army Personnel Office to one of his own adjutants. In this way he held the reins of the entire personnel organization of the army. Similarily, in May 1941 the administration of the Party was taken out of the hands of the independently responsible "Deputy of the Führer." Thereafter party affairs were handled bureaucratically by the "head of the Party Secretariat" (Bormann) who acted directly on Hitler's orders.

The strangest aspect of this leadership policy was the fact that in wartime the Reich had, to all practical purposes, no chief of government. As commander of the armed forces Hitler was unable to keep up with his duties as chancellor. He patently had no intention of submitting to Cabinet decisions. As I have already mentioned, throughout the war he did not call a single meeting of the Cabinet; his ministers therefore served no political functions whatsoever. He repeatedly stated that he was deliberately keeping himself free of all such "hampering" influences. The chancellor's business was conducted for him on a civil-service level by his "Chief of the Reich Chancellery" (Lammers), to whom he assigned the rank of minister in order to facilitate his dealings with the members of the Cabinet. Hitler permitted a degree of independence only to the chiefs of those departments whose operations he did not feel he knew enough about. Among these were the air force (Göring) and the navy (Raeder-Dönitz). He also allowed a certain freedom to the men of whom he felt absolutely sure, men who were completely devoted to him, like Goebbels (Propaganda), Ribbentrop (Foreign Policy), and Himmler (Police).

With his overwhelming need to dominate, Hitler could not permit the development of any other personality besides his. Instead of drawing to himself men of high character, rich experience, and breadth of vision, he gave such persons a wide berth and made sure they had no chance to influence him. A miser unwilling to share his power, he consistently, cunningly, and stubbornly isolated himself from the influence of all those whom he suspected of even the shadow of opposition to his will and his plans. Far from being the prisoner of his advisers, Hitler was rather the jealous guardian of his own rule. He surrounded his own autocratic dominion with impenetrable armor.

In addition, he systematically undermined the authority of all higher political organs in order to increase the absoluteness of his own power. He destroyed all clarity in the administration of government and established an utterly opaque network of overlapping authorities. It was almost a rule with Hitler to set up dual appointments and conflicting agencies.

By making Göring head of the Four Year Plan Authority he gave him control of the entire German planned economy. But then, at the same time, he kept in office a rival minister of the economy (Schacht–Funk) whose functions were practically the same. Later on he added to these a minister for war production (Todt–Speer) who, incidentally, was engaged in a permanent feud with the OKW over problems of armament.

So long as Neurath was foreign minister Hitler handled his most important and most secret foreign affairs through the "Plenipotentiary of the Reich for Disarmament Questions" (Ribbentrop). When the latter became minister of foreign affairs, Neurath was appointed president of the nonexistent Privy Council. But in addition to the Foreign Office there was a "Foreign Policy Office" (Rosenberg) and a "Foreign Organization of the National Socialist Party" (Bohle). No one could possibly unravel their various jurisdictions in foreign affairs.

One day at Hitler's headquarters Ribbentrop persuaded the Führer to commit to him in writing the conduct of all propaganda intended for foreign consumption. Propaganda Minister Goebbels knew nothing at all about this. The morning of the following day movers, sent by the Foreign Office, appeared at Goebbels's various offices in Berlin to remove all the physical apparatus used for foreign propaganda. Goebbels's men barricaded themselves in their rooms, and the propaganda minister himself promptly telephoned to Hitler for help. Hitler, who had actually signed the order to Ribbentrop, ordered Goebbels to come at once by plane. When Goebbels arrived, he told him to sit down with Ribbentrop in a compartment of his special train and not to leave it until they had ironed out their dispute. Three hours later both men emerged redfaced and informed Hitler—as might have been expected—that they could not agree. Furious,

Hitler withdrew and dictated a compromise which largely revoked his previous written order. In practice, however, Ribbentrop never adhered to this latter decision. Holding a facsimile of the first, rescinded order, down to the end of the war he continued to challenge the Propaganda Ministry's jurisdiction in all German missions abroad. Moreover, Ribbentrop had the obsession that all German authorities that had anything at all to do with foreign countries belonged under the Foreign Office. This fixed idea involved him in jurisdictional disputes with virtually all the ministries and *Oberste Reichsbehörden,* those "Supreme Reich Authorities" which existed side by side with the ministries. He even battled with the High Command of the Armed Forces. Hitler knew all about these squabbles. He frequently commented mockingly upon Ribbentrop's morbid ambitions, but in spite of all the complaints about the impossible situation he never intervened.

In 1933 Hitler assigned all press policy to the propaganda minister and appointed Goebbels Chief of the German Press Organization. But this did not stop him from installing a "Reich Head for the Press" (Amann, president of the Reich Press Chamber) under Goebbels and a "Reich Press Chief" (Dietrich). My official high-sounding title was "Press Chief of the Reich Government," but the title did not carry with it corresponding powers. My work was largely publicity and keeping Hitler informed on press matters. Since the Press Division of the Foreign Office dealt with foreign correspondents, and since the OKW during the war also claimed a considerable portion of the functions of the press officials, the jurisdictional disputes in this field were unending.

In the sphere of culture Goebbels and Rosenberg quarreled incessantly; in art Göring and Goebbels were rivals; in the control of German writers Goebbels, Rosenberg, and Bouhler tilted against one another.

In the Party organization Ley and Bormann had the same radius of activities; in Party education Rosenberg and Ley were in competition.

In the armed forces the interests of army, Waffen-SS (SS-in-Arms), and air force field divisions were inextricably confused and incompatible. Hitler had arbitrarily set up these organizations side by side.

Hitler divided the Reich Communications Ministry into Railroad and Post Office departments, thereby creating an inexhaustible source of disputes.

In the sphere of justice he had a Minister of Justice and a Head of the German Legal Front (Gürtner and Frank) who feuded with one another.

He had a Labor Minister (Seldte), a Leader of the German Labor Front (Ley), and a Commissioner General for Manpower (Sauckel). In general education the field was divided between Rust (Minister of Education), Wächtler (National Socialist Teachers' League), and, Axmann (Reich Youth Leader). Even in public health there were similar obscurities and crossing jurisdictions.

This is but a small sample of the utterly wild confusion of leadership. Everywhere in the Reich and in the occupied territories Hitler established the same conditions: dual appointments, special commissioners, a horde of officials with overlapping jurisdictions. I recall the pungent comment of Minister of Economy Funk in 1943, when he arranged a press release regarding a clarification of jurisdiction which Hitler had supposedly ordered. With biting irony he said to me over the telephone: "Consider what that means! Consider that for the first time in the history of the Third Reich we really have clear lines of jurisdiction and a distribution of spheres of operation!"

It was not negligence, not excessive tolerance and consideration which prompted Hitler, ordinarily so ready to cut across complexities, to create a tangle of struggles for position and conflicts of authority among the top men of the National Socialist State. There was a method in the madness. In this way Hitler had at his disposal two or three "chiefs" in every field, each with an extensive apparatus. He could ensure the execution of his plans by playing one man off against the other or showing preference to one rather than another. His method systematically disorganized the objective authority of the higher departments of government—so that he could push the authority of his own will to the point of despotic tyranny.

A further situation resulted from these jurisdictional squabbles. Each of the disputants naturally strove not only to maintain his own sphere of authority, but to enlarge it at the expense of the spheres of rivals. The scene was thus cluttered with numerous staffs and offices, each dependent upon a different chief, each employing large numbers of persons whose sole activity was to straighten out internal jurisdictional conflicts. A large number of persons were thus engaged in totally nonproductive work. The apparatus of government and Party, which has always been the breeding ground of human weaknesses, swelled beyond all proportion.

How fearfully such conditions destroyed that vital intangible, the confidence of the people in their government! It is depressing to consider how these internal conflicts paralyzed energies, hampered performances, and drained the strength of the nation during the war.

Such was Hitler's "brilliant idea" of the Leader State in practice. His megalomania and his lack of talent for leadership killed the idea; it was buried in the sober facts of daily life, bruised and broken by the harshness of reality. Like so many great ideas in the history of mankind it failed miserably in the realm of actuality because of human weakness and inadequacy.

Was the idea in itself invalid, even without these weaknesses? That is a question that must also be answered. Undoubtedly there are Germans who will say that it is an ideal to be striven for irrespective of failures—an ideal which must be striven for even though it may never be fully realized. There is no doubt that even the best idea needs more time for its fulfillment than Hitler, in his hysterical haste, gave it, or than the war gave to the German people. But on the other hand there are sociological aspects of the idea that make it appear highly questionable.

The principle of "selection of leaders" by "achievement," by eliminating privilege and establishing complete equality of opportunity in the struggle for existence, proves to be, if we study the matter more deeply, an ideological concept based upon unrealistic premises. Almost all the privileges of modern life, in those nations recognizing private property, are of economic origin. Education, culture, choice of occupation, the opportunity to set up in business—all these are dependent upon capital. The man who has capital, whether inherited or obtained on credit, always has greater chances for advancement than those who must enter the labor market or the business world without financial backing. Hitler promised categorically to eliminate all privilege, but he did not add that the equality of opportunity cannot be achieved without solving the problems of capital, rent, and interest, and without eliminating the inheritance of property. Had he said anything about that, his fantastic conclusion would have been exposed for what it was.

Hitler accepted private property and the role of capital in modern economic life because he recognized these as the economic foundation of our culture. He opposed capitalism as an "abuse" of capital, but did not attack capitalism in principle. Although "smashing interest-slavery" was one of the points in his program, in practical government he recognized that he could not solve the problem of interest and would not be able to eliminate interest without undermining his own political existence and that of his state. Communism, too, has failed to do away with property, inheritance, and interest in any fully consistent manner, although Communism has rendered these negligible by lowering the entire standard of living. And it has paid for carrying out its economic theories by renouncing a cultural life, without which the peoples of Europe and of the Western Hemisphere would find life poor indeed.

Suppose we think Hitler's idea through to the end. We then see that in a modern civilized state based upon private property the principle of selection of leaders by achievement can be realized only in one way. The state would have to set up a special credit system providing for the support of all the talented and ambitious young people of the nation. Financial aid would be given without tangible security, solely on the basis of ability. These young people would then be free to choose the profession in which they could develop their potentialities to the fullest.

But such government planning would probably produce more dangers, more bureaucracy, more jealousies and difficulties than its advantages warranted. Some of the slumbering talents for leadership among the people might be developed. But the nation as a whole would find itself paying more tuition than could ever be repaid. A significant light is thrown upon what we could expect to happen when we consider the confusion which prevailed in the leadership schools of the Third Reich: the *Ordensburgen* (training schools for National Socialist Party leaders, usually housed in castles), the Adolf Hitler Schools, the National Political Educational Institutions (preparatory schools for civil service careers), and the Training Academies. These schools were entirely lacking in clear principles, experience, and traditions.

Hitler's view was that life and natural selection were the best of schools. But life has in fact taught us otherwise. The idea of rationalizing and developing according to plan the genius of a nation, the idea of selecting the fittest as automatically as a magnet attracts iron filings, will remain utopian so long as the inhabitants of this earth are human beings, so long as endless variety in all the forms of existence constitutes the worth of life.

For who are the best and most competent persons in a nation? What qualities determine their success? By what standards are they to be judged? Are they the tough and the unfeeling, the cunning and unscrupulous, those who know best how to use their elbows? Or are they the wise and gifted, inwardly decent and outwardly retiring, who are energetic but not noisy? Will such prove in the end more capable, fitter than the others? Hitler took it for granted that those who are physically the toughest and psychically the rashest were necessarily strongest. But later his strong men proved to be weak, his selection of the fittest a selection of the wrong persons. His standards were both false and disastrous.

Hitler carried this theory of leadership so far that he wanted to rationalize the thinking of the German people. He conceived of his state as establishing a kind of highly developed division of labor. Only the top leaders needed to think, so to speak; the others were merely to believe. In his arrogant manner he despised those whom he thought too smart to be strong. Of the masses he remarked: the less intellect and the fewer intellectuals among them, the stronger would be their faith and the greater their force.

Hitler flattered the people, flaunting his socialistic intentions before them. There is no denying that he achieved great things in the sphere of public welfare. But he also awakened exaggerated hopes for a still more intensive socialistic program without ever being able to fulfill those hopes by peaceful means. And similarly, he made capitalism serve the ends of his power politics without feeling any twinges of his socialistic conscience. It was one of his unfortunate character traits that he subordinated all his ideas to the ambition for power which so completely dominated him.

Chapter 6

The Führer's Will and the Will of the People

IT WAS HITLER'S nature to carry all things to extremes until they were transformed into their opposites. So was it with all the institutions he attempted to reform. He set out to rid society of pernicious outgrowths, for which reason he made a revolution. But then he tore everything up by the roots. A horrid example of this process is his treatment of the judicial system.

Hitler incessantly attacked the nation's judges for being "remote from life," without links to their race, sticklers to the dead letter of the law, "petrified bureaucrats," and the last pillars of reaction. In his private conversation violent abuse of magistrates was one of his constant themes. He made no bones about his hatred of them. Undoubtedly one of the reasons for this feeling was the sense that judicial independence constituted concealed resistance to his absolutism.

Apparently out of deepest conviction and without ulterior motives he asked for a type of justice which would accord with the "sound instincts of the nation." This slogan was flattering to the masses but had no other validity. He refused to see the other side of the question, in spite of its being often pointed out to him. Otherwise he would have had to realize that judges were not bound to fixed statutes and laws solely because all his predecessors since the beginnings of civilization had suffered from calcification of the brain. He would have had to recognize that the conservative qualities of justice derive from sound experience, from the wisdom of the human race built up over countless generations. Men have recognized that a certain amount of inevitable formalism in justice is the lesser evil, for if justice is left to the discretion of the individual judge, it will be hopelessly at the mercy of human frailty. Such a conception of justice will lead inexorably to the self-destruction of justice, to pure arbitrariness rather than right. In attacking the concomitants of a precious and unalterable principle, Hitler destroyed the very foundations of justice.

He appointed himself a legislator with restrictive powers; he also appointed himself supreme judge of the nation, and made free with the operations of the law. Characteristically, he imagined that he was acting in the name of the nation, that he was fulfilling a noble mission. If his absurd ideas are thought out to the end, it becomes obvious that the "sound instincts of the nation" which he made so much of would be destructive forces rather than constructive ones.

Hitler declared that for him, too, the will of the people was supreme law. In reality he put forward his personal will as that of the people, and he made the people believe that his will was theirs.

An incident of the last year of the war throws much light upon this matter. In a dinner conversation, which centered around the psychology of women and the diplomacy necessary in marriage, Hitler praised the cleverness of women who know how to convince their husbands by suggestion that the male will is dominant in the marriage. The point was that they did not let the husbands realize that it was the wife who actually was holding the reins. With deliberate intent I remarked rather brashly that such women knew the secret which was widely held to be the key to political leadership. In mass psychology also, the leader's formula for dealing with the people might be, "They must want to do what they have to do!"

Hitler repeated the phrase, but did not contest it. I sensed that the discussion made him uncomfortable and pensive; all through the remainder of the meal he was obviously thinking about it. Apparently

I had touched him at the quick of his demagogic soul, the true nature of which I was only then beginning to suspect. If I were now to sum up Hitler's method in a few words, I should say this: The essence of it was to get the people into his grip by cunningly planting false premises into their minds.

Hitler had a technique for presenting false or highly debatable premises at the very start of his argument, giving them the air of being indisputable, obvious facts. Building upon these premises, he could then prove to the listener who accepted the premises whatever he wished to prove. From the untenable base his thesis was built up with unassailable logic and put forward with great force of conviction. Anyone examining the first premises more closely, and challenging them rather than accepting them without question, would soon have recognized the faultiness of his conclusions. But challenging his premises was not so easy. To support his view Hitler would marshal an array of facts that could not be checked by most of his listeners. He would dress up such facts and inflate their importance enormously while he would either belittle or entirely ignore the arguments on the other side.

By means of this trick of his, along with the suggestive force of his oratory and the deep conviction he put behind his words, no matter what he was saying, he was able to reassure and encourage those who had dealings with him. He always sounded as if he were speaking under inspiration from on high. During the last years of the war many persons came to him beset by doubts; they left him inwardly strengthened and in spite of everything filled with new faith. When such visitors emerged from Hitler's study at headquarters, they seemed like new men in their whole expression and attitude. The confidence Hitler himself displayed even in the most desperate situations spread like wildfire on the home and the fighting fronts and was the chief constituent of that faith which the world could not comprehend, that faith which upheld so many Germans to the very end, and which was so sadly betrayed.

Hitler's demagogic passion operated somewhere in between consciousness and imagination; it was a compound of self-deception and remarkable courage, of patriotism and deliberate mendacity.

Hitler was always afraid that prudence would cripple youthful vigor. For that reason he deliberately gathered young people around him, kept aloof from the experience of age, and hated the "intellectual reservations" of the mature. Worried as age crept up on him, constantly fearing that he would be unable to finish his work when his youthful élan gave out, and believing that he alone could finish that work, he drove himself incessantly. Out of that fear sprang his reckless, ill-fated haste and the inorganic, destructive character of his acts. On the one hand, he thought in millennia when decades would have been more to the point; on the other hand, he wanted to achieve in years things that would require centuries. Child of fortune that he was, he lacked all feeling for development and tradition, growth and maturation. On the one hand, he was dazzled by pictures out of Germany's past—electoral princes and imperial glories. These he wanted to revive in new dress—in a modern industrial country! On the other hand, he smashed forms of contemporary life that had developed over the course of generations, and he imagined that by the stroke of a pen he could set up new forms for all eternity.

His political structure had no tradition behind it, no historical foundation in the people. Consequently, as soon as the tower began to sway, it collapsed like a house of cards.

Hitler had created a classless state. But this was not the state of people and leaders painted in his ideology; it was merely a naked dictatorship. Curiously enough, the legal foundations for this state were the emergency clauses of the Weimar Constitution (Article 48, Section 2). Yet the principles by which he acted were diametrically opposed to parliamentary democracy. In a parliamentary democracy the administration is fundamentally responsible to the elected representatives of the people. Responsibility proceeds from the top down; that is, the leadership is responsible to the people and the will of the people is its supreme law. In Hitler's state, however, the responsibility was to proceed from the bottom to the top and authority from superior to subordinate. In other words, the Führer was not to be responsible to the people; on the contrary, the people were responsible to him and he to nobody at all. Hitler himself decided what the will of the people was.

Systematically, he wiped out all control of the leadership by the people. He eliminated all institutions that might have served the ends of such control. He created a party which many thought was fulfilling a great mission, but which was in no way dependent upon the people, though it dwelt among them. The National Socialist Party did not control the Leader; on the contrary, he used the Party to control the people.

Initially, the Party, too, was an institution built up on a democratic foundation. According to the original Party statutes the Party Chairman was to be elected annually by a general convention. Until 1933 Hitler had been elected in this manner. But once he held state power, he dispensed with these democratic rudiments in the Party, just as he did later in the conduct of government.

As Hitler proceeded step-by-step toward usurpation of all power in Party and State, he abandoned his own idea of a new and progressive form of human society—that mirage with which he had dazzled the people. He did not establish an ideal *Volksstaat* with authoritarian leadership, but a full-blown dictatorship—a perfect system for exercising without hindrance the tyranny of his own will. Systematically, he made it impossible for the people to control his actions in any way. By the time they realized what had been done to them, it was already too late for them to change anything. This elimination of all check on his conduct of the government left Hitler free to make the fate of whole nations the plaything of his passions and his megalomania.

The magnitude and frightfulness of the consequences of Hitler's dictatorship have taught the German people a basic lesson in history. The catastrophe is the strongest proof that the democratic form of government is absolutely indispensable. That applies not only to the Germans, but to all nations that have not yet come to this conclusion. The fiasco of the Third Reich appears to have brought the human race to a point in its experience at which the age-old question of democratic versus authoritarian government has at last been answered in favor of the democratic form. All the attacks, doubts, and criticisms heretofore directed against democracy apply only to its deficiencies and excesses. It is clear today that the errors and weaknesses of all the democratic governments in the world do not outweigh the harm that a single man can bring down upon his nation and humanity when that man is not controlled by the people's institutions.

The realization of this comes to us too late, comes when all the weight of disaster is bowing us down. Perhaps it is for this very reason that many Germans rebel, from a sense of national pride, against admitting it to themselves. Nevertheless, the painful experience of the recent past requires us in all conscience to make the admission. Many of us are profoundly bitter over the necessity for humbling ourselves spiritually and intellectually at the same time that we are so humbled by the frightfulness of material defeat. But true understanding must rise above false pride. Even if such understanding runs counter to what we used to believe, the more honorable course is to profess it, rather than to cling to dead ideals out of a mistaken sense of loyalty. The chronicler's obligation requires me, for my part, to make an honest confession that I served a wrong cause. The experiences which have led me to change my mind are today plainly evident to all Germans. All those who in good faith followed Hitler from nationalistic socialism to catastrophe are obligated to reflect and to reform.

Hitler flattered the German nation. In order to win the people over so that he might use them for the purposes of his megalomania, he heaped praise on the Germans' good traits and passed over their bad ones. For the sake of our place in the world it would be better for us to recognize our faults as well as our gifts. The Germans have often presented their consciousness of their own strength all too crudely. Highly intelligent, the Germans give way to arrogance where modesty and a sense of realities would be more appropriate. Foreigners have often expressed admiration for German discipline and the German ability to organize; but when these tendencies are carried too far, they invite ridicule. Uncritical submission to the will of a strong personality is a dangerous trait in the German national character.

Our ability to organize is a splendid characteristic as long as it stays within healthy bounds. But it makes for mischief as soon as we become fanatical about it, as soon as we let it become a rigid pattern that represses the development of individuality. We rightly boast of our industriousness, but we are mistaken when we think that foreigners are merely expressing envy when they criticize our bustling ways and our inability to leave them in peace. Our culture enjoys great prestige throughout the world—but our failures in the art of life are often regretted or despised.

Throughout its history the German nation has never distinguished itself by an overdose of political instinct. Its lack of knowledge of the world and of cosmopolitan ways has adversely affected the life of the nation. It is high time that the "people of poets and thinkers" at last develop into a nation with an international horizon.

Now and henceforth, the prerequisite for international status is a democratic state. Democracy means rule of the people. Rule of the people cannot be attained directly. The people can govern effectively only through forms and institutions which they themselves shape. In Germany, parliamentary democracy was "organized" after the First World War. No national tradition stood behind it; it was not the product of inner growth, of maturity on the part of the people. Consequently, it gave rise to excrescences which did its prestige no good. Focusing attention on these excrescences, Hitler was able to win the people to himself. Other nations, by national education, consciousness of tradition, stability, and political maturity have produced extremely workable political institutions. Such democratic institutions must necessarily be different in every nation, must correspond to the peculiarities of the race, the nature of the land, the character of the people, and their historical origins. But we must recognize that democracy in itself, with all the variety of its forms, has in fact become the dominant political mode of our time. In the present stage of technical, economic, and social progress it has proved to be the historical solution to the problem of human organization, the only possible principle of social order.

The question of the workability of democracy already belongs to the past. The problem of the future is merely one of developing and perfecting democracy. It is up to us to realize that only those nations will participate in culture and progress which organically develop the democratic forms of life, which shape them meaningfully and keep them pure from harmful elements.

We were obviously destined by fate to run a misguided historical course to the very end, to drink the cup of misfortune to the dregs, so that we would at last come to see that our dire way must be abandoned forever.

Part two

Scenes from Hitler's Life

Scenes from Hitler's Life

HITLER came from a petty bourgeois Austrian milieu. In point of fact he never left it all his life, even when he attained the highest point in his political career. That this emphatically southern German adopted the Prussian military tradition in order to attain his political ends is but another sign of his paradoxical personality. In the end he was left without any tradition—neither that of Austrian diplomacy nor that of Prussian militarism—which could help him extricate himself from his gruesome adventure.

Hitler's Austrianism emerged unmistakably in two of his traits. One of these was the persuasive, charming, jovial manner he employed in private life to cover up his basically inflexible political toughness; toward artists and women, particularly, he practiced an almost exaggerated courtesy. And the second was his absolutely astonishing inability to run his life and work according to any kind of schedule.

During his lifetime the public, and journalists particularly, were eager for information on Hitler's personal life, his habits, the pattern of his day, and similar details. People would sometimes apply directly to Hitler for such material. He always put his foot down against any such publicity.

In my opinion he led the strangest private life of any man in a high political office. He seemed unable to distinguish between his official and his private life. He carried on official business in the midst of his private life, and lived a private life in the midst of his public affairs. This was so partly because Hitler reserved virtually all decisions on political, military, cultural, or other matters to himself alone. The inevitable consequence of such absolutism was that problems were incessantly being presented to him for decision all through the day. Since he thus imposed upon himself so enormous a burden of work, he had to handle it after his own fashion, which meant by highly personal methods. That is why he did not—as he so often said of himself—have any private life, why his life was devoted to service to the nation.

By nature Hitler was a bohemian. He allowed himself to be governed almost exclusively by emotional considerations. Regular work and office hours were foreign to his nature. He often said that a single brilliant idea was more valuable than a whole lifetime of conscientious office work. Only diplomatic receptions, which were arranged by the chief of protocol, were held punctually. Most other visitors, whether they had been sent for or had come of their own accord to discuss their various tasks with Hitler, had to wait for hours in anterooms, adjutants' rooms, or similar places until they were admitted to Hitler's presence or promised an interview some other time. Ministers and other holders of high office were often not received for weeks and months, in spite of their persistence. His adjutants had strict orders to admit no one without his express permission. If Hitler did not want to see someone, that person would be kept waiting for years.

On the other hand, Hitler was far from being antisocial. In fact, he could not bear being by himself. His fear of solitude was striking. It often seemed to me that he was afraid of facing himself. For that reason, he made a practice of never retiring until three or four o'clock in the morning, and he expected his entourage to remain with him until he went to bed. He often said that he could not go to sleep before dawn.

Since Hitler literally turned day into night, he could not arise before noon. Generally, he did not leave his bedroom until noon or later. His breakfast consisted of a glass of milk or a cup of tea, taken with a slice or two of zwieback. This he would hastily snatch on his way to his office, because he knew that at this time of day a great many tasks were waiting for him. As a result of this strange schedule, the authoritarian machinery of government regularly did not function during the morning. Anyone who understands the importance of the morning hours for work in government offices and military headquarters will realize what confusion and road-blocks such a routine will produce. Just as an example, there is the recognized practice of a government's stating its position on the important political events of the previous day, news of which is generally published in the morning. Publicity releases, replies, denials, and so on are practically excluded from international discussion unless they are prepared in time for press conferences and the afternoon newspaper deadlines. The daily Armed Forces communiqué, for example, was often delayed so long that it was not ready for the two o'clock radio news broadcast and could not be published by the afternoon papers. The chief of the OKW always had this communiqué by one o'clock, but Hitler insisted on looking it over and correcting it before it was released. The result was that it was usually not ready in time for publication.

The first persons Hitler spoke to were his adjutants, who were generally waiting in the corridor outside his door with the most urgent questions or requests. They would call his attention to the most important matters for the day, and he would instruct them as to the day's visitors. Hitler himself made up his own appointment list, decided whom he would see and whom refuse to see or put off until later. He provided for no special visiting period during his day. Everything depended upon the way he was feeling, his moods, and his attitudes; he never gave any explanation for his decisions in such matters.

There would then follow—regularly but not punctually the report of the chief of the Chancellery during peacetime in Berlin, and during wartime at his headquarters the daily situation conference with the High Command. Since Hitler usually went on talking and talking, sounding off about an endless variety of subjects, these conferences lasted for hours. For many years, consequently, the time for beginning lunch oscillated between two and four o'clock. In Berlin Hitler generally lunched in his apartment with his immediate entourage and casually invited guests; at headquarters he dined in the casino with the officers of the OKW. Since at table, too, Hitler often talked for a long time, these simple lunches extended well into the afternoon, although they could easily have been completed in half an hour. Customarily Hitler did not get up from table for a good two hours. Since the same thing happened at dinner, his table-companions found this almost unendurable; they had, after all, a great deal of pressing work waiting for them. During the last years of the war Hitler introduced a second daily situation conference which was to take place in the evening. Given his habits, it usually began at night, later and later with each passing day. During the last half year of the war Hitler fixed one o'clock in the morning as its starting time. Afterwards, however, Hitler did not go to bed; instead he asked a restricted group, including his female secretaries, to join him in his living room, as his private guests, so to speak. In the special train these little gatherings were held in the small salon adjoining Hitler's bedroom compartment. At Berchtesgaden nightly gatherings around the fireplace served the same purpose of keeping him from being alone until it would be possible for him to fall asleep. I shall have much to say later on about these gatherings.

Hitler did not issue his orders in writing, directed to the proper authorities. Instead he impulsively gave them orally, off the top of his head, to whoever happened to be standing near him, with instructions to pass on the order personally or by telephone to the appropriate official. No special time of the day was fixed for the

A publicity photograph of Otto Dietrich from 1940. He is shown in the uniform of an SS-Obergruppenführer and is wearing the Golden Party Badge and the Iron Cross First Class. (© Corbis)

Adolf Hitler and Prime Minister Neville Chamberlain meet in Bad Godesberg on 24 September 1938 to discuss the Sudeten crisis. In the background stands Otto Dietrich, right, and interpreter Paul Schmidt. The Munich Agreement was signed five days later. (Bundesarchiv Bild 146-1976-063-32)

Adolf Hitler and his entourage visit the Eiffel Tower on 23 June 1940, following the fall of France. Left to right: SS General Karl Wolff, architect Hermann Giesler, followed by Field Marshal Wilhelm Keitel, Hitler's adjutant-Wilhelm Brückner, Reich Minister Albert Speer, Adolf Hitler, followed by Minister Martin Bormann, sculptor Arno Breker, Otto Dietrich. (Bundesarchiv Bild 183-H28708)

In April 1941, Dietrich accompanied Hitler on a visit to Maribor, Slovenia – then known as Marburg an der Drau – which had recently been annexed to Nazi Germany from Yugoslavia.

Top: *From left to right: Reich Governor of Styria Siegfried Uiberreither, Martin Bormann, Adolf Hitler and Otto Dietrich on a bridge overlooking the Drau. (Bundesarchiv Bild 121-0723)*

Bottom: *Front row, from left to right: Dietrich, Hitler, Siegfried Uiberreither, Martin Bormann. (Bundesarchiv Bild 121-0721)*

Hitler and entourage at the Wolfsschanze headquarters in May or June 1940. Front row, from left to right: SA Obergruppenführer Helmut Brückner, Otto Dietrich, head of the OKW Field Marshal Wilhelm Keitel, Hitler, head of the Wehrmacht operations staff at Headquarters General Alfred Jodl, head of the Party Chancellery Martin Bormann, OKW Adjutant Captain von Below and the NSDAP official photographer Heinrich Hoffmann (Bundesarchiv Bild 183-R99057)

Left: *Dietrich in a collection of portraits included in a 1939 calendar of Nazi officials. (United States Holocaust Memorial Museum, courtesy of Geoffrey Giles)*

Below: *Nazi Interior Minister Wilhelm Frick addresses the Reichstag. Dietrich is at his left. Reichsmarschall Hermann Göring, who also served as president of the Reichstag, is seated at the back. (© CORBIS)*

Above: *Hitler, Propaganda Minister Joseph Goebbels, and Dietrich. Dietrich and Goebbels had a very difficult relationship, as their roles frequently overlapped. Goebbels was by far the more public figure, but it could be argued that Dietrich was just as powerful.*

Below: *On the seventeenth anniversary of the Munich Beer hall putsch in November 1940, those involved in Germany's fight for self-sustenance—acquiring food supplies from defeated countries—are presented to the Führer in the Chancellery building in Berlin by Walther Darré, Reich Food and Agriculture Minister (at left). Dietrich and Goebbels stand behind Hitler.*

Above: *On 6 March 1945 in Berlin, the Army Chief of Staff Colonel-General Heinz Guderian speaks to the national and international press about the atrocities allegedly committed by members of the Soviet Army. German officers (on the left) are used as witnesses. Otto Dietrich sits to Guderian's left. (Bundesarchiv Bild 183-J31300)*

Below: *The defendants of the Ministries Trial sit in the dock at Nuremberg in 1947. First row, left to right: State Secretaries Ernst von Weiszäcker, Gustav Adolf Steengracht von Moyland, Wilhelm Keppler and Ernst Wilhelm Bohle. Second row: Dietrich, SS General Gottlob Berger, Intelligence Chief Walter Schellenberg and Reich Finance Minister Lutz Schwerin von Krosigk. (United States Holocaust Memorial Museum, courtesy of Robert Kempner)*

disposition of such matters; he would issue orders at any time, as they happened to occur to him or in response to conversations. This habit did not precisely contribute to clarity. Officers accustomed to receiving written and signed orders ran into difficulties because such casual instructions, given out by Hitler in the course of conversation were not recognized as orders and were consequently not carried out.

Visitors to Hitler would often seize the opportunity offered by the Führer's being in good humor; they would extract some promise from him which they would then pass on independently as a "Führer's order." Many such a "Führer's order" was diametrically opposed to another "Führer's order." So many complaints and so much unpleasantness resulted from this practice that Hitler eventually directed the chief of his chancellery to issue special regulations concerning requests for his personal decision. Henceforth department chiefs were to ask him for orders only after having come to an agreement with their opposite numbers, against whom such orders were usually aimed. Since "agreement" between two rivals whose jurisdiction covered the same field was normally impossible, this Solomon's judgment only relieved Hitler personally of some annoyance; in the administration itself it merely added to the confusion.

All through the day, from noon to past midnight, Hitler insisted on having the latest foreign broadcasts and the most recent items from the foreign press. These reports were delivered in writing to his personal servant, who always remained close by him and kept them ready at hand for him. In the morning they had to be at his bedroom door, in case Hitler awoke early. There has probably never been a head of government who was so swiftly and completely informed on public opinion throughout the world as Hitler.

He did not want summaries; he had to have the original news items, word for word. In addition he was kept posted on the newspaper opinion of almost every country; editorials were telephoned or teletyped to Berlin several times a day, and from Berlin transmitted to wherever Hitler happened to be staying at the moment. Hitler valued this news from the outside world so highly because it gave him a certain check on the reports he received from his own department heads, especially those concerned with foreign and military affairs. Since I was well aware of his dangerous inclination toward one-sidedness and his tendency to exaggerate, I was particularly careful to transmit all reports to him with a precise indication of their source and an estimate of their importance.

Hitler did not work at a desk, although he had many handsome offices whose furnishings he himself had planned. These offices were only stage sets. Hitler could not concentrate sitting down and keeping silent—he had to be moving about and talking.

Almost every German is familiar with Hitler's speeches. In the course of years I heard hundreds of them, and their character is firmly impressed upon my memory. They had a style of their own, their own special form, and unvarying construction. They are, in a sense, the embodiment of Hitler. They were conceived on the grand scale, but were concerned less with actual problems than with emotional effects. Not a single one began by a statement of subject. Instead they started out in a sweeping manner, always invoking the same philosophical ideas and historical examples, repeating the usual social criticisms, and employing the familiar, belligerent Hitleresque language. The audience was being worked on; it was being won over to his general political conceptions. Generally this broad introduction, entirely ideological in outlook, took up the greater part of the speech. Hitler had, as it were, to "idle" for a while in order to warm up and really get going. Once he was properly "warm," he would switch to current political questions. Always he would pick out the weakest points in his political adversaries' argument and attack them from his own point of view, with which his audience had meanwhile been indoctrinated. With sarcasm, biting irony, and often personal vituperation, always brilliantly formulated, he so overwhelmed the audience that serious political controversy and a real clarification of the problem no longer seemed necessary. After these oratorical fireworks came the climaxes that everyone remembers: those prophecies against the effective background of his own fabulous rise and his signal triumphs, those appeals to faith and those solemn vows. In the end the speech would mount to an apotheosis of the nation, which for any patriotic German would put an end to concrete objections—supposing that he had had the impulse to object.

At least 80 percent of Hitler's speeches were delivered extemporaneously. I repeatedly called attention to the dangers—especially for foreign policy—inherent in a responsible statesman's making impromptu declarations which could not be checked beforehand and phrased in a considered fashion. Hitler always disregarded these cautionings; he knew how effective his extemporaneous oratory was for the audience at mass meetings—whose response in turn stirred Hitler to even more passionate flights. These speeches which Hitler delivered without a prepared manuscript had to be revised for style before they were released to the German press. Before release Hitler always demanded to see the press version in order to make final corrections himself. It was often difficult to persuade him to eliminate offensive phraseology. He would flare up at any such objections and insist on keeping the original text. Any criticism of his speeches, of which he was especially proud, was painful to his vanity.

Although Hitler read so many newspapers every day, his hostility toward the press as an institution was well known. He might sometimes make concessions to newspapermen to save face, but among his intimates he stubbornly maintained his animosity toward journalism in general. One of the reasons he gave for this attitude was that newspaper criticism had vilified so many geniuses in their day. For this reason—as an act of compensatory justice, he said—he made the propaganda minister decree a complete ban on all art criticism in the press. Criticism was to be replaced by neutral "observation of art"—simple description. This decree was hardly a service to the artists. Hitler made no attempt to conceal another of his motives: During his struggle for power he had been the object of furious attacks by the press which had left him with an undying hatred of newspaper writers. There was nothing I could do, try as I might, to persuade him to revise this attitude, which certainly did no good for Germany in world public opinion. I several times pointed out to him how inconsistent it was to expect the foreign press to report his speeches favorably and in detail when in these very speeches he sneered at the men responsible for reporting them as "Jewish journaille" (a portmanteau word made up of *journalist* and *canaille*). But Hitler refused to listen to such arguments.

The few important public speeches which Hitler prepared in writing and delivered from manuscript were dictated by him directly to his stenographers, often in one draft and without assistance from anyone. As he spoke he would pace the room rapidly. Usually he did this work the night before the speech was to be delivered, and the manuscript was generally not ready until the last minute before the meeting. No one knew beforehand what he was going to say. In earlier years Hitler had given his associates a chance to look at the text and propose changes. But in later years he allowed less and less interference of this nature. He would lock himself in while dictating.

Sometimes, while the manuscript copy was being proofread and typed clean by the stenographers, I would have an opportunity to get a brief look at it—on the sly, as it were. In such cases I sometimes persuaded Hitler's adjutant or one of the stenographers to call his attention to certain objectionable phrases. The time his last Memorial Day speech was being prepared, he refused to see me although I implored him, through his personal servant, to give me a hearing in the interest of the Cause. Hitler sent back a contemptuous dismissal of my plea. His stenographer finally said to me, her voice heavy with resignation, "Leave it; it's no use. You know how he is." For Hitler, the most important aspect of a speech was its power to ignite the broad masses of his listeners by its simplifications. His appeal was to the people; he believed that the applause of the masses was his justification as a statesman. The intoxication of words mattered more to him than the vital interests of the nation.

I have mentioned Hitler's speeches here because they derived very much from his private life. They were not the spontaneous creations they seemed to be if judged by the fluent manner in which he dictated them. Rather, the ideas in them and their arrangement matured gradually in his mind, within the peculiar rhythm of his daily life. The speech that he dictated directly to the typist in the course of one night contained subject matter he had spoken of for days and weeks before to the people in his entourage. For hours, by day and night, Hitler would pace back and forth in the large rooms he was so fond of, almost always surrounded by his adjutants, orderlies, close associates, or chance visitors, by his doctors and often by dinner guests, officials of the Party or the Government whom he had invited to remain. To this rather haphazard circle, whom Hitler kept about him more out of habit than by choice, and whom he needed solely as listeners, he spoke incessantly, not giving anyone a chance to interject more than a comment now and then. Before such audiences he shaped, in the course of expositions that sometimes ran on for hours and were frequently repeated, the elements of the addresses he would later deliver in public.

Hitler's conversations were monologues. They were characterized by endless digressions and repetitions of the same basic ideas. Even the most edifying patriotic ideas lose force when they are trotted out on all occasions, suitable and unsuitable. For thinking persons in Hitler's entourage, years of listening to those reiterated discourses represented a considerable burden, which led to their absenting themselves as often as they could, or to trying to cut Hitler short—attempts which would rarely succeed. But Hitler was so wrapped up in himself that he was unaware of the strain his egotistic talking imposed upon others. In the course of years Hitler used up a great many listeners. I have seen many guests come enthusiastically and depart burned out, so to speak. The endless conferences by day and night were also physically exhausting. Newcomers to the circle would say how they envied those who were fortunate enough to be in the presence of Hitler all the time. And when, after years or months, they turned up less often, they would let fall some remark to the effect that they pitied those who had to give up their private lives and spend all their time in the nerve-racking atmosphere that Hitler engendered. Göring, Hess later on, and some others had the best of it; they could afford to call on Hitler once every few weeks. They would then be treated as rare and favored guests, while those who were constantly around Hitler were scarcely noticed by him. However, Hitler jealously saw to it that his audience was always sizable and always at his disposal. Chance visitors who were involved by Hitler in a prolonged philosophical or political conversation often took it into their heads that he placed some special value on their opinion. In reality they were merely members of that large body of extras whom Hitler needed as sounding-boards, so that he could intoxicate himself with his own ideas and try out the effect of his words. In talking, Hitler was indefatigable; talk was the very element of his existence.

Hitler's official quarters in Berlin were in the Chancellery. His private residence was in Munich, on the second floor of No. 1 Prinzregentenplatz. In Berchtesgaden he had the *Berghof,* situated on the Obersalzberg at an altitude of 3,300 feet. During the war he lived in his various headquarters, to which the OKW followed him as it did when he went to any of his three residences. In addition to the special train, where he spent much of his time, he also had seven different field headquarters in the course of the war—five in the West and two in the East.

Until the outbreak of the war Hitler spent the greater part of every year traveling. His habit of being almost constantly on the go had developed out of his incessant activity as a speaker at political meetings during the early years. There was no real need for him to move about so. Rather, it was due to his inner restlessness, so that he constantly sought pretexts for moving from place to place. Up to 1939 Hitler was everywhere, and nowhere at home. His adjutants, in addition to working out the itineraries of his official trips and electoral campaigns, were kept constantly busy planning his private journeys. He covered hundreds of thousands of miles by automobile. It may be said that he felt a certain link with highways which later resulted in his vast program of road construction.

During the early years, when Hitler was not so well known in Germany, he often stopped his car on the highway to hand out small sums of money or packs of cigarettes—although later he became a fanatical opponent of smoking—to young hikers. On one of these trips, he encountered a man who was walking along in pouring rain, and stopped his car to give the stranger his own raincoat. Longish stops for picnic lunches amid the beauties of the landscape were a part of the enchantment of travel for Hitler. As his entourage grew in size, he would take along the steward of his Berlin household, who would have a special car equipped as a mobile kitchen. After his assumption of power Hitler's cavalcade would be greeted by the well-known demonstrations of mass enthusiasm. In a Swabian village a butcher's apprentice jumped square in front of the car, crying, "Over my dead body." Hitler's car was barely brought to a halt in front of the boy, whereupon the entire village swarmed around the Führer. In Heilbronn a girl jumped on the running board of the open car to give him a kiss in front of a crowd numbering thousands—a feat, incidentally, that an American girl almost duplicated during the Berlin Olympics.

In his tours through the Reich, Hitler touched at many places. Munich, Berchtesgaden, Berlin, Nuremberg, Weimar, Bayreuth, and Godesberg, and later Linz and Vienna, were his favorite cities, to rank them according to the frequency of his visits. There were years in which he did not remain at any one place or at any one residences longer than three or four days at a time; consequently one could with fair accuracy tell in advance when he would issue the order to his companions to get ready for another move. Sometimes he himself did not know where he was heading for. Sometimes, when his restlessness drove him on, he would decide between two destinations by tossing a coin—leaving the decision to chance or, if you will, to the hand of fate. Once the decision was made it was unalterable. This was, by the way, the only concession Hitler made to superstition. Of course he often expressed supreme belief in himself and his "racial destiny." But contrary to widespread opinion, he would have nothing to do with astrology or any kind of occultism. I have mentioned that he had a low opinion of Hess because he leaned heavily on such mystical business. Because it so happened that the days of his mass demonstrations were for years blessed with fair weather, the people coined the expression "Hitler weather." But Hitler himself was deeply worried at this run of good luck with the weather, fearing that faith in it would become so firmly established among the people that the inevitable reverses would harm his reputation.

Hitler himself once compared his mode of traveling around and stopping at a large number of particular places in Germany with the progress of medieval German emperors from one imperial estate to the next.

Weimar was one of Hitler's regular stopping places. What attracted him to Weimar was the cultural atmosphere of the city, and the fact that it was the home of a group of his early followers. He always stayed in the historic Hotel Elephant, which was later renovated and made into one of the finest hotels in Germany. When in Weimar he regularly attended the performance at the German National Theater, and would afterwards invite the actors and actresses to join him at social gatherings in the lobby of the hotel. Such parties often lasted until nearly dawn.

In contrast to his pronounced fondness for things artistic, Hitler had amazingly little inclination toward the things of the mind. He saw all intellectual matters only through the spectrum of his nationalism. Not once was I ever able to involve him in a serious conversation about such matters. Science he respected and regarded only if he needed it immediately for military or other utilitarian purposes. Otherwise "professors" were for him an object of good-natured mockery, although as head of state he himself was often cast into a professorial role.

Hitler read a great deal, usually late at night after he had retired and was unable to fall asleep. His personal reading consisted of technological matter, biographies of all sorts, and studies of his favorite arts: architecture, painting, sculpture, music, the theater, and the cinema. But he ignored on principle theoretical or belletristic works. He had a special antipathy for novels, which he never read, and for poetry; poems were an abomination to him. In the earlier years of his reign he once more read through all the volumes of Karl May's Indian tales, which had been his favorite boyhood reading. Bernard Shaw's social and socialist satire aroused his enthusiasm both in print and on the stage.

He felt no kinship at all with the titans of German literature. From his nationalistic point of view Schiller was much to be preferred to the universalist and cosmopolitan Goethe. I never heard Hitler say a word about Goethe.

On his visit to Weimar Hitler almost always paid a brief call upon Frau Foerster-Nietzsche, the sister of Nietzsche. But from the works of Nietzsche Hitler culled only the cult of personality and the doctrine of the superman; he was not interested in other aspects of the philosopher's writings. He presented Mussolini, on the latter's birthday in 1944, with a fabulously expensively bound edition of Nietzsche's collected works. Aside from Nietzsche the only philosopher I ever heard Hitler mention was Schopenhauer. When he went to war in 1914, he used to say, he carried a paperback "Reclam" edition of Schopenhauer's works in his pack. But what interested him in Schopenhauer was not the doctrine of pessimism, or the epistomology and ethics, but solely the brilliant language of the aphorisms, the cutting irony with which he attacked the professorial science of his time, the ruthless criticism and acid polemical style of that witty philosopher. That was the limit of Hitler's contact with the world of the intellect.

He proclaimed a new *weltanschauung*—but scarcely ever deigned to mention the great thinkers of mankind from Plato to Kant and Goethe. The loftiest truths, the greatest wisdom, the sum of human intellectual labors for centuries, simply did not exist for Hitler unless they happened to fall into line with his nationalistic ideology.

He built temples of art—but despised the cathedral of the spirit! For all his emphasis upon culture and fondness for art, he had not the slightest feeling for spiritual values or ethics. Instead he claimed to have a sixth sense for the highest good of his people and an inner receiving apparatus which kept him abreast of the highest racial ideals.

Hitler's frequent stays in Bayreuth were an indication of his love for classical music. He was an enthusiastic Wagnerian and in peacetime regularly attended the festivals for two weeks. There was no doubt that he was extremely musical, for he was able to reproduce the *Meistersinger*, for example, completely from memory, humming or whistling all the motifs. That particular opera he must have heard over a hundred times. In addition to Wagner he favored Beethoven's and Bruckner's symphonies. For a change he would also listen with pleasure to Italian opera and the classical Viennese operettas. As an oddity I may mention that within a six-month period he saw a particularly good production of *The Merry Widow* no less than six times. Modern atonal music he did not like.

Hitler did a great deal for the German theater, which he vigorously supported in line with his own ideas. His regular public receptions for actors in Berlin, Munich, and Bayreuth helped to give them social prominence. Once the war began, however, Hitler attended the theater only once. At Bayreuth in July 1940 he heard the last opera of his life. It was—what a fateful symbol!—Richard Wagner's *Götterdämmerung*!

In Bayreuth Hitler stayed at Wahnfried as the guest of Frau Winifred Wagner, with whose family he was on terms of friendship. He had known the four grandchildren of Richard Wagner since their childhood, and after the death of their father Siegfried he took an almost paternal interest in them. These four, when they were grown men and women, were among the very few persons who used the familiar pronoun *du* in addressing Hitler. He would take part in intimate dinners at the Wagner home, exactly like one of the family. He was greatly shocked when, some time before the war, the eldest daughter left house and home and from abroad came out publicly against him. It is well known that through the Wagner family Hitler met Houston Stewart Chamberlain, from whom he borrowed part of the intellectual basis of his anti-Semitism.

Bayreuth was also the seat of the National Socialist Teachers Association and the House of German Education. However, Hitler took little interest in the German educators; his attitude toward teachers had been one of hostility from childhood. By his own account, Hitler as a boy had been wild and hard to control. He often spoke of his crazy pranks and his untamable, adventurous disposition. His conflicts with school and church had begun early.

He was once suspended from school for carrying his mischief too far. Attending a parochial school, he functioned for a while as a ministrant. However, at confession, out of sheer youthful devilry he asked the priest some very embarrassing questions. On that occasion his uncle (who was his guardian) had to intervene, persuade him to make an apology, and have him taken back. His teachers and neighbors called him a good-for-nothing. Since he felt immeasurably superior to these people, he found equally unflattering names for them. His prejudiced opinion of his teachers—with the exception of his history teacher—remained with him all his life and was later to produce some violent outbursts. He went so far as to declare that the teaching profession was basically unmanly, that actually only women should be permitted to go into the field of education. He intended later on to attempt to put this idea into practice.

The head of the National Socialist Teachers Association, Gauleiter Wächtler, speaking at a teachers' conference in Vienna, once commented upon the bad things former pupils have to say of their teachers. "The revenge of the last row, last seat," he called it. Hitler, hearing about this, merely made fun of the speech; he did not feel that he himself had been hit. I may mention as a fact which may or may not have any connection with this speech that in the last year of the war Hitler ordered Wächtler to be shot without trial on account of his alleged refusal to defend Bayreuth.

From his boyhood, Hitler had not the slightest positive relationship to family and school. Since his father died early and he found himself at sixteen thrown upon his own resources, this is to some extent natural. Later on his interest in the training of youth was restricted to their political education alone. Children were taken from parents and school at a very early age dubbed *Pimpfe* and *Jungmädel* (boys and girls under fourteen), and reared in conformity to Hitler's ideas. They would be henceforth kept to those patterns of thinking and conduct. There was no room in Hitler's mind for the traditional German schooling.

Hitler was fond of ideas with cosmic sweep. He spoke of human beings as "planetary bacilli" and was a passionate adherent of Hörbiger's Universal Ice Theory. His evolutionary views on natural selection and survival of the fittest coincided with the ideas of Darwin and Haeckel. Nevertheless, Hitler was no atheist. He professed a highly general, monotheistic faith. He believed in guidance from above and in the existence of a Supreme Being whose wisdom and will had created laws for the preservation and evolution of the human race. He believed that the highest aim of mankind was to survive for the achievement of progress and perfection. From this belief there was a sense of his own mission to be the Leader of the German people. He was acting, he believed, on the command of this Supreme Being; he had a fixed conception of this Being, which nothing could change. In his speeches he often mentioned the Almighty and Providence. But he personally was sharply hostile to Christianity and the churches, although the Party program came out for a "positive" Christianity. In private conversation he often remarked sarcastically, in reference to churches and priests, that there were some who "boasted of having a direct hook-up with God." Primitive Christianity, he declared, was the "first Jewish-Communistic cell." And he denied that the Christian churches, in the course of their evolution, had developed any genuine moral foundation. Having ordered trials of certain Catholic priests on charges of immorality, he used the findings of the courts as the basis for the broadest generalizations. He considered the Reformation Germany's greatest national misfortune because it "split the country and prevented its unification for centuries."

At the beginning of his reign he tried to promote a Protestant National Church which would be tied to the state. But he very quickly abandoned this project. At the time that he was thinking about Catholic matters, during the course of his negotiations with Rome, he had much to say about the impressive appearance of Catholic bishops and cardinals, and asserted that Catholicism had such a power over the masses because of its elaborate ceremony. His feeling about the Protestant ecclesiastical dignitaries is indicated by the following typical story:

A group of Protestant dignitaries called upon President von Hindenburg to complain about Hitler. Hitler himself was to attend the audience. Shortly before, he was brought a transcript, obtained by wire-tapping, of a private telephone conversation between some of the visitors. They had discussed, in rather disrespectful fashion, what approach they would use with Hindenburg. One of them had remarked over the telephone that in regard to Hitler they would try to give the "Old Man extreme unction." During the interview with Hindenburg Hitler audaciously took the transcript of the conversation from his pocket and held it under the noses of the heads of the Protestant Churches, in the presence of the embarrassed Hindenburg. This little gesture—so Hitler said—won the day for him.

In view of the highly complicated emotional problems involved, Hitler remained outwardly restrained toward the religious groups. He permitted the publication of Rosenberg's *Myth of the Twentieth Century* only upon the author's insistent urging. Hitler himself had grave doubts about the matter and stipulated that the doctrines therein must not be considered official. On the other hand he did not hold back the hotheads in the Party, Himmler and especially Bormann, who incessantly attacked the churches. On the contrary, he supported them and encouraged them by his private, violently anti-church remarks. In the early days he had to endure attacks on National Socialism by bishops and cardinals. He could take no measures against them without alienating some of his followers. But he threatened to take his revenge later on.

Considerable unofficial pressure was brought to bear upon functionaries to leave the churches. Hitler himself, for reasons of political strategy, never actually carried out his withdrawal from the Catholic church. He repeatedly took part in official Protestant and Catholic church ceremonies such as weddings, baptisms, and so on. Many National Socialists who had been urged to leave their own churches blamed him severely for this.

At one time Hitler was informed that the mother of the manager of the Party hotel in Nuremberg, the Deutscher Hof, had inserted in a Catholic family magazine an advertisement for chambermaids. The Führer flew into a rage entirely disproportionate to the importance of the matter; the manager was dismissed out of hand and professionally blacklisted. It was only due to my intervention that this man later succeeded in getting another job in the hotel business.

Another time the gauleiter of Northern Westphalia, Joseph Wagner, was accused of maintaining private relations with Catholic Action circles. At Bormann's instigation, Hitler took occasion during a gauleiters' meeting in Munich to make a scene and expel Wagner from Party leadership. The charges against the man were that his wife had attended a papal audience in Rome, and that this same wife had driven their daughter from the house for wishing to marry an SS officer who had withdrawn from the Catholic Church.

Hitler was convinced that Christianity was outmoded and dying. He thought he could speed its death by systematic education of German youth. Christianity would be replaced, he thought, by a new heroic, racial ideal of God.

Hitler's attitude toward Charles the Great [Charlemagne] can more easily be understood now, although in the past it puzzled many people. Charles had imposed Christianity upon the Germans with the sword. Because of his bloody struggle against the Saxon Widukind he was referred to by some German publicists as the "Butcher of the Saxons." Hitler imposed a strict ban upon the use of such epithets. He revered Charles as one of the very great figures in German history, the unifier of the Germans and the creator of the Reich. For the sake of this supreme national goal Hitler quite approved of his hero's having used ruthless force, as well as his introduction of Christianity—for it was clear that Charlemagne had used Christianity as a spiritual bond to insure national unification. Consequently, he would stand for no criticism of Charlemagne's bloody massacres; who could have suspected that he was already unconsciously seeking justifications for the monstrous mass extermination that he himself would order some years later? Who could have suspected that he was already looking for precedents for the annihilation of an entire race whom he called "ferments of decomposition"?

Yet he must have recognized that these inhumane crimes were inexcusable and unforgivable. He must have thought that after a victorious war he would be able to clear himself before the bar of history by virtue of might. And so he maintained absolute silence about them, never mentioning these matters to any of his associates. Toward the end of 1944 the first allegations about the crimes in Poland began appearing in the foreign press—although the stories were not nearly as terrible as the reality that was revealed later. I handed these reports to him and took occasion to ask him twice whether those assertions should be denied. Each time he replied indignantly that the reports were typical "propaganda lies and distortions of the enemy, intended to cover up their own crimes at Katyn Forest."

All the roads Hitler traveled between Munich and Berlin passed through Nuremberg. The city had a special significance in Hitler's life. Originally he had chosen the city for Party meetings because of its central location, its historical significance as the location of the imperial jewels, and its firm circle of old Party members, National Socialists of many years standing in the group around Julius Streicher. Founder of an anti-Semitic sectarian party, Streicher had early thrown in his lot with Hitler, bringing with him his entire group in a body. Hitler had always allowed Streicher to cultivate his fanatical anti-Semitism and had never censored Streicher's newspaper, *Der Stürmer.* Streicher's "primitive method," Hitler declared, was the most effective way to reach the "little man." In Nuremberg Hitler always found a group of credulous, highly suggestible people who hung upon his lips and listened worshipfully to his pronouncements. Of course he had such groups more or less everywhere in Germany; they fed his mania for speechmaking.

The first two Party Days in Nuremberg in 1927 and 1929 had proved eminently successful and suggested that the city was a fine place for holding mass demonstrations. After coming to power, Hitler decided to develop the open terrain on the outskirts of the city, and as the work proceeded, Hitler's megalomaniacal nature cast up more and more grandiose plans. Passionately given to lavish architecture, he began reveling in superlatives. The "greatest arena in the world," the "most gigantic hall of assembly," and the "most stupendous athletic stadium in the world" were to be built here. He himself sketched the first plans for Nuremberg, as he did for his superprojects almost everywhere else in the Reich. Professional architects had to work out the details.

There is no doubt that Hitler possessed a great talent for architecture. This was recognized when he was only seventeen by the Vienna Academy of Art where he failed the admission examination in painting but was told that his talents lay in the direction of architecture. He repeatedly said of himself that if he had not become the foremost politician of the Reich, he would have become its foremost architect. In Nuremberg he literally wanted to build for the millennia. Stone and building materials were selected especially for their durability. The overall plan was to link Old Nuremberg with the new world of towering steel and iron buildings—to link the First Reich with the Third—by means of a majestic concrete highway spanning the Nuremberg ponds. Watching the progress of this work, holding conferences with the local architects, and inspecting the models was endlessly fascinating to Hitler. It was his interest in the project that drew him so frequently to Nuremberg, in addition to the times he visited it for the Party meetings. In this city, even more than in Berlin and Munich, Hitler gave vent to his passion for architecture. But architecture was not only a passion; it was also his one real relaxation, the one thing which took him outside the realm of politics and theories in which he was otherwise steeped.

In early days he took frequent pleasure trips to visit the Bavarian royal palaces of Neuschwanstein, Hohenschwangau, and Herrenchiemsee, as well as Ludwig the Second's "Valhalla" at Regensburg. Hitler felt a spiritual closeness to Ludwig and believed firmly that the king had not committed suicide in Starnberger Lake in a moment of insanity, but had been done away with by his political enemies of the clerical party.

Wherever Hitler stopped, whatever he was busy with at the moment, all his other interests were dropped as soon as his architects appeared. His personal servant had to keep a drawing pencil and set of compasses ready at hand at all times, for at any moment the impulse might strike him to sketch monumental façades, victory columns, triumphal arches, theaters, models of tanks, concrete bunkers, or revolving turrets for warships. There was hardly a book on architecture that Hitler had not read, and he took the keenest interest in all new publications. In Nuremberg, Berlin, and Munich there were large halls filled with models of National Socialist buildings, and in peacetime he would spend several hours almost every day, or rather every night, looking over these things.

As is well known, Hitler favored a classicistic and monumental style. He always laid stress on the nordic origin of classical Hellenism's great cultural creativity. In conversation he was fond of describing with vivid detail the profound impression a few hundred Teutonic farmers' sons must have made, in gray antiquity, upon the frightened inhabitants of Greece and the Peloponnesus when they appeared at the Ismuth of Corinth in the course of their migration from north to south.

Hitler considered Professor Troost of Munich, the builder of the House of German Art and of the National Socialist Patty buildings on Königlicher Platz in Munich, as the great architectural genius of our age, whom he himself had discovered. Troost died comparatively young. At the laying of the cornerstone for the House of German Art, the hammer handle broke in Hitler's hand. This was seen to be an evil omen—and caused much talk among the people—not only in Munich. The story went that this unfortunate incident dealt Troost such a psychological shock that it hastened the progress of a disease from which he already suffered.

Architects were high in Hitler's favor. It was through architecture that Speer became so intimate with Hitler that the Führer later entrusted him—under his own direct supervision, of course—with a wide variety of the most important military and economic tasks; with, in fact, such a burden of work as can hardly be given to any one man without unfortunate results.

While inspecting the Storm Trooper Stadium which was being built in Nuremberg, and which he intended to be the largest stadium in the world, Hitler dropped a remark which was indicative of his narrowness, his attitude toward sports, and the split in his personality. That was the year of the Olympic Games in Garmisch and Berlin, which had gone off so brilliantly. Everybody except Hitler had hailed the spirit of the athletes and the international character of the Games. Hitler sneered at the "trembling old men" of the Olympic Committee; he had been expecting to meet hale and hearty, well-preserved former athletes. A few months later, standing in the vast area at Nuremberg where the colossal stadium was being built, I heard him say, "That was the last international Olympics in which Germany will take part. In the future we ourselves shall put on the finest sports program in the world and the biggest athletic competition that has ever taken place. We shall do it right here in Nuremberg, and we shall run the whole show." He refused to understand that international competition was the very essence of the Olympic Games and that the records made at these games were important precisely because they were world records.

Sports were quite alien to Hitler's nature. Great athletic feats meant little to him. He liked watching Sonia Henie and Maxi Herber perform on ice, but otherwise he cared about sports only because they helped produce national physical fitness. He forbade his close associates to go in for sports badges—because of the danger of accidents, so he said. At the Olympic Games he made an ostentatious fuss over the victors, in order to convey the impression that he was deeply concerned with sports, but in fact he was not so at all. He himself did not go in for any kind of game or physical exercise; the reason, he said, was that he could not permit himself to participate in any sport unless he could be superior to all competition. During the Olympics he attended a soccer game because he had been told that the German team was expected to win. When it lost, he was angry and scolded those who had persuaded him to come for having made him the involuntary witness of a German defeat. There was no room in his nationalistic narrowness for any conception of fair play.

Alongside dreamy, hoary old Nuremberg Hitler erected the colossal monuments of his volcanic nature, assembly points for monster National Socialist demonstrations. Had these demonstrations been prompted by a constructive international spirit, had they been designed to bring to the attention of the world new ideas for peaceful progress—as Hitler said of them when he gave audiences to guests of honor and foreign correspondents—they might have served a noble purpose. But the unrestrained drum-beating, the needless chest-thumping, and the superfluous military displays were not the symbol of new, peaceful, and progressive ways of life; they were the tangible expression of Hitler's lust for power and therefore a warning to all other nations to beware.

If we add up all Hitler's stops in Nuremberg, it is evident that he spent a considerable part of each year in that city. The Deutscher Hof hotel had a special suite reserved for him. In the evenings he liked to sit in its fine, spacious lobby and hob-nob with architects and theatrical people.

On the way from Nuremberg to Munich Hitler would pause at the old episcopal seat of Eichstätt in Franconia, and at Ingolstadt on the Danube. Or else he would drive through the Upper Palatinate by way of Neumarkt and Regensburg. Here he would often stay at the historic Rathaus where the German Emperors held their Diets and where special rooms were reserved for him. He was a special patron of the famous boys choir, the Regensburg Cathedral Sparrows, as they are called, and often attended their performances.

Whenever he stopped at the small town of Neumarkt in the Upper Palatinate he visited the grave of Dietrich Eckart, who had been born in that place. Eckart was the man who according to Hitler's own statement had had the greatest influence upon his career. He had been Hitler's best friend and may well be called Hitler's spiritual father. His fanatical racist patriotism and his radical anti-Semitism guided Hitler at the very start of his political career.

Eckart had distinguished himself as a writer, as editor of the magazine *Auf gut Deutsch* (Plain Words). He had done the German stage adaptation of Ibsen's fantastic nordic drama *Peer Gynt.* It was he who obtained financial support for Hitler in the early days when he was building up his party. Eckart was acquainted with a group of wealthy men to whom he had appealed for subsidies for his newspaper; he introduced Hitler to these men. They were the first backers who, out of general patriotic considerations, lent aid to Hitler. Hitler was fond of telling how Eckart used to introduce him with the words: "This is the man who will one day liberate Germany." Eckart also brought Hitler together with the Baltic German, Alfred Rosenberg. With Eckart, Hitler piled into an open sporting plane and flew off to Berlin in order to be on hand for the Kapp putsch. (This was Hitler's first flight.) Kapp had set up his headquarters in the lobby of the Hotel Adlon in Berlin. While waiting there Eckart and Hitler saw Kapp's newly-appointed press chief, Trebitsch-Lincoln, going up the stairs to Kapp's rooms. Trebitsch-Lincoln was reputed to be Jewish. Eckart promptly gripped Hitler's arm and drew him toward the door, saying, "Come on, Adolf, we have no further business here." Whereupon they left Berlin. Hitler often described this incident in conversation.

Eckart was a drug addict. Persecuted after the Munich putsch, he died soon afterwards in Berchtesgaden. It is worth noting that the pilot of Hitler's plane the day of that first flight to Berlin was Ritter von Greim who in the last days of the war—he was then a colonel general—Hitler appointed Göring's successor as Air Force commander-in-chief. In the dread days of April 1945, Greim flew to join Hitler in besieged Berlin and committed suicide at his master's side.

In Eichstätt Hitler also liked to visit a small outdoor restaurant located on the outskirts of the town, in the meadows along the Altmühl River. Here, sitting at one of the long garden tables, he often invited passing boys and girls, members of the Hitler Youth, to join him in coffee and cake. After such occasions he used to remark that, to judge by the biological specimens he had observed, the youth of Germany, at least in the last generation, had grown physically "taller and more beautiful." Hitler loved the German youth, but he did not regard them with the loving eye of a parent and the thoughtful responsibility of a family man. He judged them only in relation to the future of his nation and saw them as instruments for the furtherance of his ambitions in power politics.

Hitler's tours often took him into the western part of Germany. The places he preferred throw interesting sidelights upon his mode of life. When his fleet of automobiles started off from Munich toward West Germany, his first stop was Augsburg where he put up in the famous Fugger Hotel, the Drei Mohren. During the war he was greatly concerned about the bombing of the Augsburg Rathaus which he considered one of the finest monuments of German culture. He had many photographs taken of it, with a view to later rebuilding it.

From Augsburg Hitler proceeded either via Nördlingen and Rothenburg, where he stayed at the historic Hotel Eisenhuth, or else he went via Würzburg, through the Spessart Mountain Range made famous by the fantastic tales of Wilhelm Hauff. Or he might take the southern route passing by the Cathedral at Ulm and thence on to Stuttgart. At Stuttgart he always stayed at the Christian Hospice where—as he ironically remarked—the Bible was always to be found on his night table. From Solitude, the pleasure palace in Stuttgart, he often enjoyed the view over the fertile farmlands of Württemberg. In the vicinity of the Pforzheim he would regularly visit the

Monastery of Maulbronn, and walk in the famous old cloisters. When he rode on through the Neckar Valley to Heidelberg, he stopped at the former imperial manor at Wimpfen.

In Mannheim Hitler was interested in the Mercedes Works which he often inspected when he passed through that city. He was a devoted motorist. Before 1933 he could never resist urging his chauffeur to race and pass every car on the highway; he loved speed. Later, after a run of automobile accidents which took the lives of many leading personalities in the Reich, Hitler went to the opposite extreme and ordered speed limits of twenty-five miles per hour in all towns. Thereafter, even when he was proceeding at a snail's pace he refused to allow his cavalcade to pass any cars at all—which often resulted in troublesome traffic jams. When Frank, the Governor General of Poland, violated this order and passed Hitler's car on a Munich street, Hitler ordered Frank's automobile to be confiscated on the spot, and threatened to treat every other government and Party leader in the same way.

Hitler honored Daimler and Benz as the inventors of the automobile and was concerned for their world reputations. He considered the Mercedes the foremost German quality automobile; moreover, at the beginning of his political career the firm had obligingly permitted him to acquire his first automobile by installment payments. This sentimental factor may have prompted Hitler to drive nothing but Mercedes, and to prefer them to all other automobiles in the world. He would make a point of attending the annual German Automobile Show. At national and international automobile races he made no secret of his partiality. For reasons of national glory he wanted to improve the Mercedes cars more and more and establish the firm as the foremost automobile company in the world. On the other hand, he was guided by entirely different principles in his efforts to popularize the Volkswagen, the construction of which he personally directed down to the smallest details. If Hitler had devoted only a part of the effort he expended on automobiles to improving the quality and standardizing the production of airplanes, the war in the air might well have taken an entirely different course.

The numerous victories of German racing cars at the peacetime international auto races had, incidentally, a fateful and unfortunate aspect. From these victories, Hitler drew wrong conclusions about the state of technological development and industrial potential in the United States. Those "gladiatorial" successes of the German automobile industry, which had created specially boosted racing cars, seemed to him to prove the clear superiority of German industry over American industry. With pride and satisfaction he decided that Germany was far ahead of America. Some persons who were familiar with the true state of affairs tried to warn him. He replied that he would not believe "typical American exaggerations, propaganda, and bluff"—until, during the war, he was confronted with the facts in all their enormity. Shortly before the war I was present at a private motion picture showing in the Chancellery. There was a view of New York as seen from the air. Hitler was visibly impressed by the enormous vitality and power radiated by those buildings which, by European standards, are truly colossal. Afterwards Hitler made remarks ostensibly intended to correct the statements of others, but in reality directed at himself. Later on he repeated several times the conclusions he had come to under the impact of these new impressions. But in the floodtide of events this too-brief insight was soon forgotten. It may have been this which made him try to keep the United States out of the war.

Magnificent specimens of Mercedes automobiles were Hitler's standard gifts to chiefs of state and crowned heads. His fleets of automobiles, of which he kept several stationed in Munich, Berlin, and other cities, consisted of six or eight of these elegant, open black monsters. Hitler himself usually sat up front beside the driver; only when accompanied by very important guests would he sit in the rear, to their left. His valet usually sat directly behind him to hand him anything he might need during the ride, and beside the valet his chief adjutant, along with anybody else he had invited to join him in the car. Directly behind the Führer's automobile came a car filled with men of his SS bodyguard, and behind that the police; then came a car reserved for adjutants, his doctor, and other companions, including the head of the Party Chancellery, representatives of Göring, the Supreme Command, Ribbentrop, and so on. Hitler also had a special radio car for press agency representatives, and one or two of his stenographers, so that during the drive he was always prepared to work. On longer trips another car carried provisions.

In late years Hitler's seat in the front of the car was protected by armored walls and bulletproof glass. Several more armored limousines were built and Hitler insisted that these be used by his high officials, including Göring, Himmler, and Goebbels. However, no attempt was ever made on Hitler's life while he was out driving. On a ride through the Berlin Woods to Schorfheide, where Göring lived, some object the size of a bullet once pierced the then unprotected windscreen; but whether it was a shot or just a pebble thrown up by the wheels could not be determined. I assumed the latter, since nothing more was heard of the matter. Aside from the attacks of November 8, 1939 in the Munich Bürgerbräukeller, and of July 20, 1944 in Hitler's headquarters, there were no assassination attempts, although in the course of his journeys (until the last years of the war, when he avoided showing himself to the people) he was often so closely surrounded by huge crowds that he seemed in danger of being crushed.

In peacetime I witnessed dramatic scenes of this sort during Hitler's automobile trips. The crowds were thickest when he drove along main throughways which ran through the centers of towns. Then the people in the towns and villages along the road would telephone ahead to inform others of his coming. That was the case on the mountain road which he liked to use when coming from Heidelberg, or on the narrow Rhine Drive from Mainz to Cologne, wine-growing country sprinkled with many villages. In Darmstadt and the vicinity, where tens of thousands of people blocked the streets, there was once a near catastrophe which Hitler averted only by standing up in his car and driving for hours at a walking pace, calming the fanatical crowds and warning people away from the wheels of his car. By the time we arrived at the Hotel Rose in Wiesbaden late that night, having proceeded by side roads and literally sneaking into the town, Hitler was completely exhausted.

At Bad Godesberg, to which Hitler often proceeded by Rhine steamer from Mainz or Coblenz on fine summer days, the Hotel Dreesen was his regular headquarters. Rudolf Hess, who had gone to school here in the Siebengebirge, had recommended this hotel to him, and in the early years of his struggle for power he had often stayed there. Later he kept to this habit. His rooms looked out over the Rhine, and at coffee time in the afternoons he often drove out to the Petersberg. At the peak of Petersberg hill is a hotel with the finest view in western Germany. Chamberlain stayed here during his meetings with Hitler. The hotel had been closed at the time, but on Hitler's orders it was made ready for Chamberlain within a few hours.

Hitler had been at Godesberg in the winter of 1932 when he left for Cologne to hold his first secret, decisive conference with von Papen at the home of the banker von Schroeder. He left his entourage waiting for two hours on the highway to Düsseldorf; no one knew where Hitler had gone. That same year he went to Düsseldorf to attend the famous conference of industrialists at the Park Hotel; he made a speech to these leaders of German industry and won their support. In the West German industrial area Hitler addressed captains of industry for the first time in 1926 in my home town of Essen. It may be of interest for me to tell what I know about his relations with heavy industry.

It all stemmed from Hitler's friendship with Emil Kirdorf, senior head of the Ruhr Coal Syndicate. Kirdorf was already retired; in 1927 and 1929 he was present as an interested onlooker at the Party Days in Nuremberg. Hitler was a frequent guest at his house in Mühlheim-Saarn near Duisberg. His connection with Kirdorf enabled Hitler to address a sizable group of leaders of industry at the Saalbau in Essen and to attempt to win them to his cause. But as far as I know this presentation of ideas led to no material support worth mentioning. The key men in industry were politically cool and restrained; they preferred to wait and see. Hitler's propaganda affected the masses and his comrades in the Party; they were the ones who made the necessary financial sacrifices. For a long time he was dependent upon Party contributions and the collections at mass meetings. Not until 1932, after Göring had established close ties with Fritz Thyssen, the leader of the Stahlhelm [the German equivalent of the American Legion], who then openly came out for Hitler at a meeting of Düsseldorf industrialists, was the ice broken. Sympathy among the participants at that meeting was aroused, and a fund was collected at the door. But the contributions, though well-meant, were insignificant in amount. Beyond that, there was no question of any significant subsidizing of Hitler's political efforts at that time by "heavy industry," although undoubtedly local Party Organizations may have obtained smaller or larger contributions from individual sympathetic industrialists. Hitler's large-scale propaganda tours in the decisive year of 1932 were financed solely by the entrance fees at the gigantic mass demonstrations at which fantastic prices were often paid for seats in the first rows. Assertions have often been made that Hitler came to power on money from heavy industry. On this question I can contribute the following personal details.

Up to August 1931 I had been working as an editor in Essen. When I shifted to Munich and became "Chief of the Press Bureau in the National Headquarters of the National Socialist Party," opposition newspapers wrote that I was the "liaison man of

Rhineland heavy industry," that I had previously negotiated the support and financing of Hitler by the "coal barons," and had now been called by him to Munich in order to establish even closer links between himself and the industrialists. In reality my only income at that time, as an editor and publishing house employee, was my salary of between 600 and 800 marks a month—and my employers were often in arrears about paying it. I did not even have a bank account, let alone a fortune. I had nothing whatsoever to do with heavy industry. Hitler had contacted me at the suggestion of Hess and I offered to serve the Party without pay if I were able to earn my living in Munich by resuming my former work as a correspondent for foreign newspapers. Hitler would not hear of this arrangement on principle; he asked me to devote all my time to Party work in return for compensation equal to what I had been earning. I mention this unimportant personal matter only because it was the sole financial problem I ever discussed in my life with Hitler.

The true facts emerge even more clearly from a small incident that took place during the election campaign in Lippe in December 1932. At that time I accompanied Hitler as press reporter to the public meetings and could therefore watch the process by which, from one meeting to the next, he literally scraped up the money to cover his traveling expenses. Just seven weeks before he came to power Hitler was spending the night at the Grevenburg near Detmold when his chief adjutant came to me and in great embarrassment asked whether I could advance him 2,000 marks since Hitler had not got another pfennig and the local Party organization had been unable to pay the rental for the hall where the next day's demonstration was slated to be held. How could such a financial predicament at such a decisive moment be conceivable if Hitler had been receiving money from industry!

In Berlin Hitler often put up for weeks, with his entire staff, at the Hotel Kaiserhof—which cost sizable sums. Several times he raised the money for the hotel bill only by granting exclusive copyrighted interviews to American news agencies or newspapers, for which he received several thousand dollars.

Naturally conditions changed fundamentally once Hitler became head of the government. For a brief transition period government orders had a pump-priming effect on the nation's industry, which then ran on at full speed under its own impetus. In 1934 I heard that "business" had voluntarily donated to Hitler—in gratitude, so to speak, for the boost he had given to the economy—a fund of several million marks annually which was to be at his personal disposal, to use as he saw fit. Hitler himself in no way requested these funds and so far as I know never himself directed the spending of them. Under the name of the Adolf Hitler Industrial Fund the sum was administered by Rudolf Hess, then chief of staff, and later Party secretary, Martin Bormann. Bormann, acting as trustee, used the money for Hitler's personal projects. I shall return to this subject in connection with the building of the Berchtesgaden eyrie, a project which Hitler demurred at for a long time.

Looking back and seeing the thing as a whole, I believe I am justified in saying that, granting everything else that may he said against him, Hitler never allowed financial considerations to affect his decisions. The industrial barons did not buy him and bend him to their will. Far from it. On the contrary, he slowly but surely imposed his will upon "business." He fitted business into a planned economy and placed it under absolute government control which in the long run could only smother all economic initiative and which culminated in a total war economy.

What was his general attitude toward economic questions? I think he felt that in the course of its evolution society had already outgrown the traditional form of autonomous, private capitalism, and that reason demanded a new and more functional economic order, in other words a planned economy. The economic System he had in mind might be termed as follows: private enterprise on principles of common welfare under government control. But the hypernationalism with which he imbued everything, the haste and excessiveness that he displayed in everything, led here as in politics to an effect opposite from what he intended. Hitler was aware that we are living in a transitional period between two ages. He recognized the economic problem history has posed. But he saw it in a warped political perspective as a German problem, not as a universal problem calling for broad readjustments. His was the outmoded, narrow point of view of extreme nationalist, racist autarchy. And in a progressive era like the present, autarchy cannot any longer be fruitful.

In Essen Hitler stayed at the Evangelischer Vereinshaus (Protestant Hostel) in the early years, and later on at the Hotel Kaiserhof. After he became chancellor he was a frequent guest at Villa Hügel, Krupp's residence. The day before the Röhm purge in 1934 Hitler was in Essen for the wedding of Gauleiter Terboven, and attended both the civil and the religious ceremonies. He had a high opinion of Terboven's bride, who had formerly been Goebbels's private secretary; she had taken confidential dictation for Hitler during the negotiations in Berlin which led to his taking over the government. The real reason for his much-publicized presence at this wedding in the Catholic Cathedral at Essen, however, was his desire to cover up his plans. No one could suspect that the attack on Röhm was already on his schedule. That same evening he drove to Godesberg and then to the airfield of Hangelaar near Bonn. His destination was Munich. We who were in his party had no idea what was up until his adjutant told us, while we were sitting in the plane, that we had better release the safety catches on our guns.

Hitler's capable chauffeur, Kempka, who served him for so many years, came from Oberhausen near Essen. Kempka was one of sixteen children of a miner's family. Seated before the wheel of Hitler's many Mercedes, he could not have guessed that on April 30, 1945 he would perform a last service for the Führer—carrying Hitler's body, wrapped in a carpet, out of the bunker of the Chancellery in order to consign it to the flames in the garden.

During the early years of his struggle Hitler had met the former German women's swimming champion, Anni Rehborn. She spent her vacation at Berchtesgaden one year and Hitler invited her to visit the Berghof. She brought along her fiancé, Dr. Brandt, who was at that time a resident physician under Professor Magnus at the Welfare Hospital in Bochum. Hitler kept Brandt at his side, appointing him his permanent personal physician and later, during the war, making him civilian head in charge of the military medical corps.

One of the basic ideas in Hitler's national economic system was the manipulation of demand to drain off the surplus purchasing power of the masses. For when the country itself could not produce sufficient necessities and luxuries, surplus purchasing power constituted a permanent threat to the price structure and the stability of the currency. That, along with social-welfare considerations, was one of the most important reasons for the enormous build-up of the Strength Through Joy organization. Hitler wanted to divert the masses of wage earners and salaried employees from the markets; instead of offering them material goods, instead of providing more bread, butter, and meat, which could not be obtained without foreign exchange, he persuaded the people to buy intangibles—entertainment, travel, art, and knowledge—at prices they could afford. Thus social welfare was combined with practical economic aims. The best theaters and concert halls were rented; big ships were built, and huge beach developments to provide swimming for the masses were projected. During the years of peace Hitler twice took a North Sea cruise on one of the big Strength Through Joy boats. He visited the islands of Helgoland and Borkum, shared in the common life of the Strength Through Joy travelers, and entered into their evening entertainments aboard the ships. These were among the very few occasions when he came into contact, privately and on an easy basis, with life outside the peculiar circle which he had created for himself. He had become acquainted with the North Sea coast before 1933; he used to spend several days at a time at Horumersiel, staying at the inn on the dike run by "Father Tjark," a famous skipper of life-saving craft. There he met Leni Riefenstahl, with whom he maintained a warm platonic friendship for many years. Hitler also saw the Norwegian fjords, though only from the sea; he went on a battleship which was cruising along the Norwegian coast in order to obtain an impression of the landscape. A Norwegian pilot who was taken on board reported meeting Hitler, and the story was published in a foreign newspaper.

On board his dispatch boat, the *Grille* (Whimsy), from which he witnessed the naval maneuvers near Skagen, Hitler set sail for Copenhagen and studied the silhouette of the city through his binoculars. He drove frequently to Wilhelmshaven, Hamburg, and Kiel to inspect ships and attended launchings. In Hamburg, where he stayed frequently, his quarters were always in the Hotel Atlantik on the Alster; he was particularly fond of the tea for which this hotel was famous. When in Hamburg he usually invited the family of Bismarck's grandson to be his guests. For Hamburg Hitler was planning a gigantic steel bridge across the Elbe. Incidentally, while at Hamburg he discovered in the storeroom of the Town Hall a colossal painting by one of his favorites, the Viennese painter Mackart. This painting, the *Entrance of Charles V into Antwerp*, he promptly had placed in a prominent position in a gallery.

During a flight from Königsberg to Kiel in 1932 in a Junkers 52, I went through a dramatic adventure with Hitler. Flying blind, the pilot took a wrong bearing and instead of following the coast of Jutland turned north and headed far out into the open sea. Fuel was running low; we were flying under a dense bank of clouds only a hundred and fifty feet above the surging waves. We had no way of knowing our whereabouts. At this point Hitler went up to the cockpit and instinctively ordered the pilot to head south. He had acted just in the nick of time. We reached the German Baltic coast near Wismar with just half a gallon of gasoline left in the tank.

Hitler twice spent a few days at the bathing resort of Heiligendamm on the Baltic coast. There his then foreign press chief, "Putzi" Hanfstaengl (in whose villa on Staffel Lake Hitler had been arrested after the 1923 Munich putsch), introduced him to Fräulein von Laffert, for whom he felt a friendly affection for many years. He wished to see her married to some member of his entourage, but she chose otherwise.

Dramatic events of fateful significance link Hitler's life with East Prussia. When this Austrian German visited the region in the spring of 1932, the German frontier population hailed him as their veritable champion. How different it was a decade later, when Hitler returned to this same land of many lakes. This time he lived in bunkers and wooden barracks in the heart of the mysterious forest, cut off from all contact with the population. Under such conditions he spent more than three full years, the most depressing and wearing years of his life.

In Königsberg in 1932, when he was still only the leader of the National Socialist Party, Hitler established personal contact with the generals of the tiny German army which had been permitted under the Versailles Treaty. At the East Prussian estate of a former World War I general, von Litzmann, he met Colonel von Reichenau, and through the latter he was introduced to the District Commander in Königsberg, General von Brauchitsch. Under his regime both were promoted to general field marshals, the one as commander of the blitzkrieg army, the other as the conqueror of Warsaw—until Hitler himself replaced von Brauchitsch.

During Hindenburg's lifetime Hitler was frequently the old president's guest at Neudeck. He also paid visits to Danzig, Elbing and Marienburg. One of his favorite stopping places in East Germany was Finckenstein Palace. If he happened to be traveling in the vicinity, he made a point of staying there for a few days. A Prussian general and war minister named Finckenstein had built the elegant, spacious palace in the heart of the woods and lakes of West Prussia, with money given him by his king. On his way to Russia in 1812 Napoleon stayed there for several weeks, living with the Polish Countess Walewska. It is said that when the Emperor first caught sight of the palace he exclaimed: "*Enfin un chateau!*" Hitler enjoyed the spaciousness of the palace, which breathed refined culture and historic atmosphere. He spent many pleasant hours there in 1932 as a guest of the family of Count Dohna-Finckenstein. But even in these relaxing surroundings his talk was not free of the excitable political note so characteristic of him.

Hitler's favorite city in Saxony was Dresden. He loved the drive across the Elbe bridge into the beautiful quarter around the palace. He always put up at the Hotel Bellevue, and invariably visited the opera and the Zwinger [the Museum of Natural History]. Through Dresden's rich artistic life Hitler was brought into touch with the more private and human sides of life.

Then there was Austria, his homeland, to which he would return as conqueror in 1938. After the Anschluss he frequently visited the places where he had spent his childhood: Braunau on the Inn, where the local newspaper still had in its files the original birth notice sent in by his father, an Austrian customs official—refutation of the spiteful rumor that his birth was illegitimate. He saw again the monastery school at Lambach where he had been a pupil, and Leonding; where his parents were buried. Graz, Klagenfurt, Salzburg, and Innsbruck were other favorite cities of his in his native land. He was also very fond of Vienna. He stored up happy impressions of that city in the form of pleasant days spent in the royal suite at the Hotel Imperial, receptions at Prince Eugen's Belvedere, drives around the Ring, outings with groups of artists to the Kahlenberg, the Burgtheater, and the Opera. The great cultural and architectural wealth of the old imperial city exercised a great fascination upon him. Hitler did much for the city of Vienna, architecturally and otherwise. But never did he altogether overcome his prejudices, the provincial Austrian's more or less justified dislike for traditional Viennese centralism. Even in his youth he had hated this centralism, and in his later political measures he always favored the Austrian states as against the capital. His policy in the new Greater Germany was aimed at tying the new "provinces of the *Ostmark*" to the Reich rather than to Vienna.

Toward Linz, the city of his young manhood, he felt special obligations. He himself drafted a new city plan, providing for a new bridge over the Danube and sending his own architects to the city. He established the gigantic Hermann Göring Steel Works at Linz, and made a personal gift to the city of a picture gallery of German Romantic painters, including the finest Spitzwegs in the world. Hitler said he wanted this gallery to be unique of its kind, the equal to any metropolitan gallery and a place of pilgrimage for all lovers of Romantic painting.

Hitler was able to extend such generous patronage to German art and artists by means of a "cultural fund" which Postal Minister Ohnesorge had on his own initiative set up. With Hitler's permission Ohnesorge had printed a special stamp for collectors bearing a picture of Hitler. This stamp could be bought at all post offices in the Reich; the sale of it yielded several million marks which Ohnesorge turned over to Hitler for his own use every year.

Munich was Hitler's chosen home, the city he loved above all others and which he held to be the pearl of Germany. He had come from Vienna to Munich as a member of the artistic proletariat, so to speak, an artist who virtually peddled his water-colors and drawings on the street and among the art dealers of the city. Here he lived the life of a lonely man going his own way; here in August 1914 he hailed the outbreak of the war which promised him an outlet for his morbidly intensified vanity. He returned from the war a corporal with the Iron Cross, First Class, and amid the turbulence of revolution he delivered patriotic lectures at barracks and demobilization camps as an "indoctrination officer." Here he discovered his gift for oratory and the power of his words over people. His instinctive, demonic will to dominate the masses fused with his genuine pride as a German and his obsession with racist ideas to create the conviction that he was fated to carry out a great political and national mission.

In the political atmosphere of Munich his star began to rise. But "nationalistic" Munich was not only the starting point of his fabulous political career. The city of art and culture on the Isar was also the soil in which the private and personal aspect of his life struck its few roots. There if anywhere was the fixed axis in Hitler's unstable life.

In Munich Hitler felt himself at home. Once they reached the door of his apartment on the Prinzregentenplatz, which he occupied for fifteen years, his adjutants and traveling companions took their leave and left him in the care of the good couple who managed his household, Frau Winter and her husband. Here Hitler would settle down in his rooms for at least a few hours during the day and arrange by telephone his schedule and private visits from among his circle of Munich acquaintances. While in Munich he would telephone me at my hotel and ask me to bring him the latest press items. When I arrived at his apartment I would often find him dining alone, whereas elsewhere he never deviated from his custom of taking his meals amid a sizable group.

Here in Munich he lived the life of a bachelor who did not care for any sort of family life. For example, on Christmas Eve he would give all his followers leave to visit their families; then he and his adjutant Brückner would go motoring through the countryside because he wished to escape the Christmas atmosphere, which he thoroughly disliked. No amount of talk could change his attitude in this matter.

In order to make Christmas festive for him, the custom arose of holding a Christmas dinner in his name at a beer hall in Munich. This afternoon affair was scheduled for December 24, and Hitler never failed to attend. After dining he would deliver a talk half political, half a tribute to comradeship. But his refusal to have a Christmas tree persisted even after he had assumed power, when his house would pile up with gifts and flowers sent to him with compliments of the season. On the other hand, Hitler was very attentive to his friends at Christmas as regards gifts. His Berlin household steward would spend weeks going through Hitler's gift list, which included his numerous political associates, the personnel of his household, his closer acquaintances, and many artists. One Christmas during the war years Hitler gave each person on his list a package of coffee from a shipload that a Near Eastern shah had sent to him as a personal present.

When I settled in Munich in 1931 Hitler's sister, Frau Raubal, was staying with him at his apartment on Prinzregentenplatz. Later she kept house for him on the Obersalzberg for several years. Also with him at this time was his stepniece Angelika, a young Viennese girl whom I myself never met. Hitler was extremely fond of her and she was almost always with him when he went to the theater, the cinema, or the coffee house. Whether his feelings toward her went beyond those of kinship, I do not know.

One morning in the fall of 1931 Hitler left his apartment bright and early to go on one of his automobile trips. On the way to Würzburg he was stopped at Ansbach; a telephone message had come through for him. It seemed that shortly after his departure from Munich Angelika had shot herself. She had used a revolver from the drawer of his night table to take her own life. Hitler was—his chauffeur told me—shaken to the core by this news; he turned back at once and throughout the entire three-and-a-half-hour return trip spoke not a single word. Hess, Gregor Strasser, and others were waiting for him at his apartment. When Strasser returned to the Brown House he reported that Hitler had declared that, in view of the scandal caused by this dreadful event, he must resign the presidency of the National Socialist Party. Strasser said he had had the greatest difficulty rousing Hitler from his severe depression. The explanation for the suicide which was heard at the time was that Angelika had been in a state of emotional disturbance because Hitler had forbidden her return to Vienna, where she had fastened her affections upon a young doctor. Hitler was granted a two-day entry permit by the Austrian government and went to Vienna for the funeral. Later on, whenever he was in the Austrian capital, he never failed to visit the cemetery and lay a wreath upon Angelika's grave.

The small group of personal acquaintances with whom Hitler regularly associated while in Munich was really limited to the family of Heinrich Hoffmann, the photographer, whom he visited almost every day. Hoffmann had been close to Hitler since the earliest days of his struggle and for almost two decades had enjoyed a monopoly on the right to photograph Hitler. Before he met Hitler he had made a specialty of sensational news photographs, a branch of photography which he had learned in London. One of his most famous pictures was the shot he had succeeded in taking, back in 1905, of Czar Nicholas II with Kaiser Wilhelm when the two were hunting together in the park at Fürstenberg Palace in Donaueschingen. Before 1923 no pictures at all had been taken of that new political revolutionary, Adolf Hitler. In order to protect himself against the political police, Hitler had systematically avoided photographs. Hoffmann lay in wait for him one day and snapped a picture of him in the doorway of the Party business office in Munich. The plate was promptly taken from him by Hitler's companions. Some time afterwards Dietrich Eckart recommended Hoffmann to Hitler, who promised the photographer the "privilege of the first picture." That privilege Hitler allowed him to retain for many years after the days of struggle lay in the past.

To Hitler's great concern, Hoffmann fell seriously ill in 1936. Hitler expressed his sorrow that Hoffmann, who had been at his side during the hardest period of the struggle, might not live to experience with him "the decade of Germany's rise." When Hoffmann's physician, Doctor Morell, restored the photographer to health, Hitler was so impressed that he appointed Doctor Morell his own permanent personal physician. The same Hoffmann who had snapped Czar Nicholas in Germany, and published the photograph against the Czar's will, accompanied Ribbentrop to Russia and secured a picture of Marshal Stalin at table in the Kremlin. However, Stalin asked that the picture should not be published, with which wish Hoffmann complied.

Many old adherents of the Party lived in Munich. Among them were supporters of the Movement to whom Hitler paid visits from a sense of deep obligation. With such persons he would occasionally stay to tea. Among these was the wife of the publisher Brückmann, in whose salon I first met Hess. There were also the Hanfstaengls, whom he visited frequently in the early days, and the home of Gauleiter Wagner where in later years he enjoyed meeting artists, whose company he found relaxing.

He was a constant visitor, however, at Hoffmann's home. Almost every afternoon and evening during his stays in Munich would find him there. He prized Hoffmann's conversational gifts and his knowledge of painting. Hoffmann lived for a time in Schwabing and later in Bogenhausen, in the immediate vicinity of Hitler's home. Hitler would drop in there whenever he could no longer stand being alone in his apartment on Prinzregentenplatz. Long before 1933 he had met in Hoffmann's studio the latter's assistant, Eva Braun. She was the daughter of a respected secondary school master, a good-looking girl, vivacious, interested in culture, and altogether nonpolitical—a trait Hitler appreciated highly in women.

It was only natural that the bachelor Hitler should take pleasure in Fräulein Braun's company while at the Hoffmann's. But the deeper emotions he later felt for her sprang from an attempt at suicide on her part. Believing herself rejected by him, the young woman attempted to cut open the arteries of her wrists. I heard about this incident and about the shaking effect it had had upon Hitler from his own lips in the course of a private talk with him. From that time on Hitler spent more of his time with Fräulein Braun, who later moved with her sister into a small house near his, across the street from Hoffmann's. He invited her out on automobile trips and, with growing frequency, to his house on the Obersalzberg above Berchtesgaden. In Munich, however, she was never seen publicly in Hitler's company.

Munich was the one city in the Reich where Hitler, even after he became chief of state, could openly visit restaurants and coffee houses as a private person, without being besieged by the curious. Naturally certain police precautions were necessary in order to guard him against surprises. Incidentally, I have never found out why for fifteen years, up to the very first months of his reign, Hitler always carried a dog-whip in his hand wherever he went; it was fastened to his wrist by a strap. Once he himself recounted, he had used it to threaten and fend off some quarrelsome members of a Munich student *Korps*. Hitler, his secretary, Rudolph Hess, and some ladies had been sitting at a Munich café when these young men had come along and made nuisances of themselves by molesting the ladies of the company. Hess had angrily ordered them to stop and they had retaliated by demanding satisfaction. It was on this occasion that the dog-whip came in handy. Hitler was firmly opposed to dueling; when he came to power he fought the lingering tradition for it in Germany and issued general orders banning it.

Hitler's daily program in Munich in peacetime was as follows: He rose around noon. Toward one o'clock he regularly went to Troost's studio where the architects were awaiting him with the latest models of projected buildings. He was passionately ambitious to see a still more brilliant Munich arise, expressing all the force of the Third Reich. To that end he had many structures torn down which the people of Munich loved, but which interfered with his plans. His projects for rebuilding the heart of Munich absorbed him constantly, and he paid no attention to the feelings of the citizens.

From the studio he went to lunch at the Osteria Bavaria, located on the same street. There his usual table companions would be waiting for him. The cooks at this modest eating-place had learned in the course of years to cater to his vegetarian tastes. A table was always reserved for him in the idyllic little garden of the tavern.

After lunch Hitler paid official or private visits. He would drop in at his home briefly and later in the afternoon go either to the Carlton Tearoom opposite the Café Luitpold on Brienner Strasse or the outdoor café of the House of German Art. Or else he would visit Gauleiter Wagner at his home on Kalbachstrasse. It may be noted incidentally that in 1943 there was considerable ill feeling in Munich when Hitler personally ordered that Wagner's residence, which had been hit in the bombings, be given priority for rebuilding.

Hitler's afternoon "coffee" session usually lasted for several hours. Unless he chose to spend his evening at home—an exceptional thing for him—he dined at the Hoffmann's, or at the House of Artists on Lembachplatz, or more rarely at the restaurant in the House of German Art, if not at the Osteria Bavaria. In earlier years he also frequently ate in the small basement canteen at the Brown House, later on in the comfortable casino of the new Führer's Building. On the traditional holidays of the Party he regularly went to the Café Heck for the evening. On Sunday afternoons and regular holidays Hitler customarily went for a drive out to Tegernsee with the Hoffmann family and their friends. There he was warmly welcomed by a number of Party friends—who formed almost a colony out there, all living in wooden houses built in the charming Upper Bavarian style. The latter part of the evening was usually spent at Hoffmann's house.

Throughout such a day as this the business of government was not neglected, any more than it was during his travels. Conferences or audiences which he thought important were fitted into the schedule and held either at his home or amid the luxurious surroundings of the "Führer's Building." Important messages and questions were delivered to him constantly and often answered by him in the presence of others; similarly, he might issue orders at table. This casual and somewhat sketchy way of conducting the government—the Cabinet in Berlin had simply been placed on ice—is indicative of the peculiar nature of Hitler's dictatorial rule.

The permanent atmosphere of unreal, forced, self-deceiving sociability with which he surrounded himself, was an elaborate precaution against serious, hard-and-fast, uncomfortable discussions. He was thus enabled to take up only such matters as suited him and to pretend not to know about and brush aside those matters which were inconvenient. He exaggerated or belittled, boasted of all his successes but changed the subject or cast blame on someone else when things went wrong. His administration was a peculiar compound of political seriousness and private casualness, of hard, authoritarian sternness, artistic slackness, and personal irresponsibility. Surrounded by external distractions but with his gaze always turned inward, Hitler often made his decisions purely on impulse, in large matters as well as in small.

Just one example. Sitting one day at table in the Osteria Bavaria, he spontaneously ordered Bormann to stop publication of the *Frankfurter Zeitung*. He paid no attention to the remonstrances of the specialists on press matters who were present. The reason for this order was a complaint by the wife of Troost, the architect, who had taken offense at something in a column of that newspaper.

At this same table in the Osteria Bavaria Hitler made the acquaintance of the Englishwoman Unity Mitford, daughter of Lord Redesdale, a member of the British House of Lords. Unity Mitford was an enthusiastic follower of the British fascist leader Sir Oswald Mosley and a fervent admirer of Hitler. She had many private conversations about Anglo-German relationships with Hitler, whose secret itineraries she usually guessed with great acuteness. Over the years Hitler frequently included her among the guests who accompanied him on his travels. She introduced Hitler to her father, Lord Redesdale, and her brother, when the two were passing through Munich. Her elder sister, who had been the wife of the British industrialist Guinness, was divorced and later married Sir Oswald

Mosley. The informal wedding party of Mosley and his bride was held in Hitler's apartment in Berlin, Hitler and his close associates being guests. On September 3, 1939, the day of England's declaration of war against Germany, Unity Mitford sat down upon a bench in a Munich park and put a bullet through her temple. The suicide attempt failed. After a long, slow recovery she was returned to her family in England, Hitler arranging the matter through neutral diplomats.

Hitler's relationship to art was, on the whole, perhaps the least ambiguous side of his character. Culture and art, of which Munich was to be the shining symbol visible throughout Germany, were to Hitler a particularly important factor in the life of the nation. In 1934, after returning from a visit to Hess's newly decorated home in the Isar Valley near Munich, he mentioned that he could not make Hess his successor as Führer because the latter's house betrayed such a lack of feeling for art and culture. Göring, whom he respected for his broad grasp of the political significance of art, was shortly afterwards appointed Hitler's successor.

Hitler's fierce stand against "degeneracy" in the plastic arts was certainly sincere in intent. It was a reaction to the excesses of the age. But it was also rooted in a highly questionable conception of what art is.

Hitler certainly possessed aesthetic sensibility. But he raised his own ideal of beauty into a dogma everyone had to follow. He wanted to issue commands, even in a field where personal taste and individual sensitivity are what count. Consequently, he did not limit himself to merely guiding popular taste. The state, if it wishes to throw the realm of art open to the masses of the people, is entitled to curb certain obvious excesses. But that is as far as art policy ought to go. Hitler, however, as in so many other fields, showed no moderation at all. In his radical intolerance he went far beyond the measures needed to accomplish his purpose. He smashed images like the iconoclasts of old and threw out the baby with the bath water. Architecture and sculpture were stimulated by the scale and lavishness of his support, and in these fields every unbiased observer must admit that he was able to awaken certain impulses in the artists. But with painting he had no such success; do what he might after his "purge," he was unable to set creative forces in motion. Aside from a few isolated specimens, the level of painting remained low. Among his intimates he resignedly admitted the fact—though this opinion of his was jealously guarded from the ears of the public.

Hitler had made the "Great German Art Exhibition" in Munich the showcase for German plastic art. It was to open the way to public recognition for the German artist. Hitler personally was the jury; professional artists must be rigorously excluded from juries, he declared, so that they would not be able to exercise a deciding vote in their own affairs. Only the masses, insofar as they were interested at all in art, and the public of art buyers and patrons, should decide who deserved the honor of having his work shown. Hitler considered himself the representative of all art-lovers.

In practice the selection of paintings and sculptures took place as follows.

Every year Hitler appointed Heinrich Hoffmann as his preliminary examiner. All the works submitted were left in the basement of the museum where Hoffmann sifted through them and made a first selection. The works he considered worthy to be looked upon by the Führer were then taken upstairs to the exhibition rooms and provisionally hung so that Hitler himself could judge them. It always affected me most unpleasantly when Hitler, going the rounds for hours, would let fall one personal opinion after the next upon the paintings, thereby deciding the fate of the artists. Hitler's inspection sometimes took place only a few days before the opening, though usually he would get around to it several weeks before. He had in effect nominated himself the pope of art. The things he liked would be exhibited; what he rejected was second-rate, and therefore the artist was also second-rate. The works that were not shown to Hitler at all were not even considered art.

Gradually, this state of affairs aroused widespread dissatisfaction among the artists. When Hitler heard of this, he flared up. Those artists who had said they would no longer send work to the show were no longer to be mentioned at all in the press or over the radio, he ordered.

Hitler's judgment of art was not guided fundamentally by aesthetic principles, but by his nationalistic and racial feelings. The national character of the observer is, of course, the soil out of which his ideas and feelings spring and will therefore always play a part in his reaction to a work of art. But Hitler as supreme judge of art was so entirely convinced that all cultural creativity sprang from nordic-Germanic roots alone—he traced the great flowering of classical Greek and Italian art to the same roots—that this racial fanaticism blinded him to all other possible standards. I realized the extent of his aesthetic blindness when I witnessed his complete rejection of the modern Italian art show at Venice, which he attended in the course of his first meeting with Mussolini. His reaction to a Japanese art show held in Berlin a few years later was equally incomprehensible. Incomprehension might be forgivable. But he went further, denying that the work had any of the qualities of art—simply because he felt no personal associations with the objects represented or the Japanese landscape, culture, and way of life. We may concede to any ordinary citizen the right to hold such a view. But the man who claims supreme authority in the world of art should not be so limited.

Hitler regarded art only from the point of view of the spectator, never from that of the artist. From the spectator's point of view he rightly demanded that a work of art must have beauty of form and that the object depicted must be one of inherent beauty. But he overlooked the fact that the artist can create such beauty only according to his own inner laws. Hitler's complete indifference to all the more human aspects of people is the key to his denseness in the realm of aesthetics. His policy was directed toward arousing interest in art among the people. In line with this he demanded fine craftsmanship and technical ability from painters. He also insisted that they deal with popular subjects. This was supposed to create a kind of art which would appeal to the masses, with their natural, unspoiled feeling for beauty. But this dictatorial conception of art utterly ignored those elements which go beyond the representation of nature and which are peculiar to the creative artist. It is the presence of these elements which marks all genuine art. For the real value of a work of art inheres not in the external image of the form it reproduces, but in the essence it radiates from within the object and communicates to the spectator. A truly good painting, for example, reveals the special quality of a landscape; a truly good portrait exposes the inner nature of a person—as distinguished from a photograph which is usually only the mirror image of his outward appearance. It is no accident that all but one of the portraits of Hitler were copied from photographs. He sat for a portrait to only one painter, Professor Knirr, who came and stayed at Berchtesgaden for that purpose. Beauty lives within a work of art only to the extent that the artist, out of his own intuitive perception, has breathed that beauty into it. But Hitler considered the essence of art to be grounded in national character. His ideal of beauty, which was to be binding upon all, was the aesthetic embodiment of Rosenberg's indefinable "racial soul." Since Hitler had no sensitivity whatsoever to the human aspects of aesthetics, all he could do for the artists who followed him was to crown them with outward prestige; he could not inspire them with any creative impulses. In his arrogance Hitler had wanted to be master of art and to use it for his ends. But the divinity which is in art would not bend to his will!

It is about a hundred miles by automobile from Munich to Berchtesgaden. Along this entire stretch there is a clear view of the greater part of the German Alps. I do not know how many hundreds of times Hitler drove along this road in an open car, nor what he felt at the sight of those majestic mountains. But it may surely be said that those rides, taken together over two decades, were an important part of his private life.

The small group of Munich guests whom he regularly invited to his home on the Obersalzberg usually waited for him on the highway just outside the environs of Munich and there joined his column of automobiles. The panorama along this drive extends from the Zugspitze massif to the Watzmann. In the distance the Wetterstein and the Karwendel, the Rotwand and Wendelstein mountains can be seen; along the highway are the Wilder Kaiser and the Kampenwand. Soon the unfathomable gray-blue of Chiemsee is reached, that strangely moody lake which exercised a great attraction upon Hitler. For many years he regularly made a stop at the Lambach inn on the north shore of the lake, where a *Stammtisch* was reserved for him and his guests—a table which in the course of time gathered more and more associations. Hitler was sitting at this table in 1932 when the message came to confer at once with President von Hindenburg. Six miles away along the lake Hitler planned to build the first of his mammoth universities; he wanted to move university life out of the great cities and plant these new universities in the heart of the open country. They were to be provided with the most modern technical and athletic equipment. The execution of this interesting idea he left to Rosenberg, and in Rosenberg's mind they vanished in the ideological fog of his "myth."

When Hitler built the Reich's first autobahn, from Munich to Reichenhall, he made it run along the southern shore of the Chiemsee. Halfway along the route a huge hotel, the *Gasthaus am Chiemsee*, was put up. It was provided with a pavilion-like Führer's room, but after visiting it twice Hitler never went there again because the room had glass walls and he did not like the public looking in on him while he dined. This highway is also graced by a monument to the ground-breaking ceremony. At the time of the building of the autobahn, all Hitler's thoughts were turned upon the program of peaceful construction which won him a place in the hearts of the people. Five years later the autobahn was extended to Salzburg. By then Hitler was already caught up in the intoxication of power, and as his road went beyond the borders of the Reich he himself was already gazing with his inward eye to more distant, more alluring, but ruinous goals.

Beyond Chiemsee the German Alpine Highway branches off from the autobahn to the south, entering the mountains near Inzell. This road was the product of Hitler's dream of opening the beautiful German Alps to tourist traffic by constructing a splendid system of highways. A cross-alpine highway from Lindau to Berchtesgaden was begun but died a premature death when the war began.

According to Hitler's own account, it was Dietrich Eckart who introduced him to the mountain near Berchtesgaden known as the Obersalzberg. Eckart himself hid out there after the failure of the Munich putsch. The Bechstein family owned a mountain villa nearby. In those days the Bechsteins called Hitler by the name of "Wolf," for which reason he later gave his headquarters the names "Wolf's Bastion" and "Wolf's Ravine." In an idyllic situation some three hundred feet above the Bechstein villa, on a steep sloping meadow, was the small wooden house called Wachenfeld. Hitler liked it so well that he rented it, and several years later bought it. In memory of the early years he later retained the fireplace and veranda of this house, though otherwise it was entirely rebuilt. After 1933 he added to it and made alterations several times, until it attained the form of the Berghof, as it was later called. Fourteen days before the end of the war the Berghof was smashed within ten minutes by the concentrated bombing of a hundred special enemy planes.

Hitler paid for the Berghof out of the income from his book, *Mein Kampf.* This raises the question of his habits and ideas with regard to money, capital, and private property—a subject that has been much discussed. Actually it may be said that money meant nothing to Hitler. He never had a bank account. He did not use a wallet. Whenever he needed ready cash for contributions to the Winter Relief or for some similar purpose, it was slipped to him by his adjutant, or else he reached for loose change in his trousers pocket. The administrator of his property and his money was Max Amann in his capacity of director of the Eher Verlag, which published *Mein Kampf.* Once or twice a year Amann would drop in on Hitler to present his accounts. At such times he would always bring up his wishes with regard to newspapers and book publishing and would ask Hitler for authority in various matters. He was seldom or never refused. Whether his unassailable position with Hitler was due more to his capacity as the Führer's business agent or to his having been the sergeant of Hitler's company during the First World War, was a subject much discussed among Hitler's intimates. In financial matters Hitler was ignorant, but generous. As a private person he did not know how to handle his own money, and as head of state he could not manage the government budget.

Other funds were used to extend Hitler's private domain on the Obersalzberg beyond the actual Berghof property and to build up that mysterious cordoned-off area on the mountain. This work was tied up with Martin Bormann's rise to the point of becoming one of Hitler's closest intimates. I have mentioned earlier that as chief of staff for Rudolf Hess, Bormann was in charge of the Adolf Hitler Industrial Fund. Bormann had formerly been administrator of the SA Relief Fund. Using the millions of the Industrial Fund to enlarge Hitler's private holdings around the Berghof, Bormann skillfully wheedled his way into Hitler's favor. He established himself so securely that Hitler more and more came to consider him indispensable. As a result the brainless Bormann won more and more political influence. Hitler trusted him right down to the end, recognizing in Bormann a blindly obedient instrument who would pass on and execute his commands without the slightest deviation. In Hitler's will, which bears Bormann's signature as a witness, Hitler recommended him to posterity as his "most loyal Party comrade."

In 1936 Bormann came to Berchtesgaden armed with money from the Industrial Fund. He bought parcel after parcel of land around

Hitler's house and began literally to bore holes into the mountain. Hitler watched these proceedings with some initial doubts, but after a while he let Bormann have his head. He would often pun on the name, saying Bormann was certainly a man for boring.

The changes in the landscape around the mountain which started in 1936, and which certainly did not improve its appearance, had their parallel in the change in Hitler's mode of life and inward attitude which began coming into evidence at about that time. The peace of the remote mountain was replaced by noisy bustle. The farmers of the area were bought off and had to leave their lands. The village of Obersalzberg vanished; it was leveled to the ground. In its place there grew up barracks housing an entire SS guard battalion. The peaceful idyllic paths through the meadows were transformed into wide driveways and concrete roads. Where teams of oxen had moved along at their meditative pace, huge trucks now rattled by. Flowery mountain pastures were transformed into monstrous dumps; the woods were cut down to build camps. The silence of the mountainside was shattered by the rumble of dynamite explosions. After a while Hitler directed Bormann not to undertake any blasting before noon, so that he would not be awakened from his sleep. The pace of the work, the gigantic earth-moving projects, increased rather than diminished with the years. For as the work progressed Bormann's importance to Hitler increased. It will give some idea of the extent of the undertaking to consider that no less than five thousand workers, most of them foreign laborers, were employed well into the war years on the Obersalzberg, that industrial oasis in the heart of the mountains.

What was the result of all the tremendous effort? The area around Hitler's house which had been a lovely bit of nature was transformed into an artificial park with driveways and gravel paths. The whole was hermetically enclosed within a huge cordoned-off area ringed by many barbed-wire fences and dozens of guarded gates. Until 1937 anyone had had the right to move freely in this area, and from 1933 to 1937, whenever Hitler was staying at the Berghof, thousands of people from far and near daily climbed the mountain in the hope of being able to greet him in the afternoon, when he used to take short walks on the road in front of his house. At such times he would be photographed playing with children. He would personally accept letters and petitions from people. He would invite groups of girls and boys to join him on his terrace. He was also in the habit of going for walks in the vicinity, with just a few people for company. The reconstruction project put an end to these contacts with the public. Bormann had built Hitler a golden cage, and Hitler never went outside it again.

Hitler sought out isolation and laid more stress on his uniqueness as The Leader as he became conscious of his almost uncanny influence upon the masses, his unlimited power over people, and his growing military strength—which he himself considered invincible. This change in inward attitude was reflected in many outward symbols. Inside the fences of his mountain residence, a good quarter of a hour's walk from the Berghof, a small tea pavilion was erected. On clear days, Salzburg could be seen from here. If no urgent business detained him, Hitler would visit this pavilion with his guests almost every day. Nearby a set of farm buildings was erected—at an altitude of 3,300 feet. It was intended to be Hitler's model farm—but Hitler himself was not particularly interested in it. He was more pleased with the extensive hothouses which were built some three hundred feet above his house and which, summer and winter, supplied fresh vegetables for his vegetarian diet. A handsome building with a wonderful view had stood near Hitler's house and had served as a privately run rest-home for sailors. It was removed, and the plans called for building in its place a gigantic, unique mountain hotel which would attract tourists from all over the world. But when the outlines of the new hotel were painted on a gigantic screen, Bormann discovered that viewed from the valley the projected building would far outshine Hitler's own residence, the Berghof. Construction was stopped at once and for years nothing but rubble heaps remained. In place of the suspended hotel, the nearby "Platterhof" where Dietrich Eckart had once lived was bought and built up.

In 1939 I was present when Hitler was the recipient of a "surprise"—a "tea house" built for him on the peak known as the Kehlstein, some 6,600 feet high. For more than two years the most difficult imaginable of roads had been blasted out of the rock of the mountain. One day Bormann invited Hitler to inspect and take possession of this rocky eyrie, as intimate as it was grandiose. Situated on the peak of the Kehlstein, it was visible for a great distance. The way up from the Berghof wound along a broad asphalt road with a magnificent view of the Alps, past steep precipices, and through many tunnels, to a spacious parking area at an altitude of nearly six thousand feet. This road ended abruptly in front of a huge, heavy brass door set into the living rock. The door opened upon a brilliantly illuminated corridor five hundred feet long leading into the heart of the mountain. At the end there was a second door belonging to a huge elevator which carried us swiftly up through the rock to the vestibule of an original, striking, and quite pretty stone tea house. It was furnished in choicest taste. There was a dining room, a sun terrace, and precisely upon the peak of the mountain a huge circular hall with fireplace. Numerous big windows let into massive stone walls gave a magnificent view out over the beautiful mountainous landscape on all sides.

Before the war Hitler visited this "tea house" only two or three times, taking guests up there for brief stays. François Poncet, who was for many years French ambassador to Berlin, was invited to tea there for a farewell audience. This was a sign of special favor; Hitler thought highly of Poncet's elegant and witty conversation. Poncet has written about his visit to the tea house. The last time Hitler visited his unique and beautiful eyrie he was accompanied by the British journalist Ward Price, who published a sensational article in the *Daily Mail* describing the place. Hitler refused to permit stories about it to be published in the German press.

The five thousand workers in the huge construction camp on the mountain also built a sizable network of private roads deep into the mountains. Some of these were never completed. Roads were, however, finished to Eckernsattel, Goellhaus, and Rossfeld, and during the war anti-aircraft batteries were posted in these places. As a final gigantic project I heard of a road which was to lead past the Jenner and Gotzenalm peaks, high above the Königssee, to what is known as the Stone Sea (Steinernes Meer). Hitler would sometimes say that he intended at some future date to open these roads to the public.

During the last years of the war there were many rumors abroad about huge underground military installations being built at the "mountain fortress of Obersalzberg." There was no truth to these stories. In 1944, directly behind the Berghof, living quarters were cut into the rock. These were intended simply as air-raid shelters, and special rooms were provided for Hitler. However, he never moved into them.

No less striking than the external transformations in the landscape were the changes in the domestic routine of the Berghof during those later years. In the days when the small house called Wachenfeld on the slope had been a quiet, modest place designed for family living, Hitler's sister kept house for him there; she had moved from the house on Prinzregentenplatz in Munich after her niece Angelika's suicide. Hitler praised her conscientiousness and her Viennese pastries. As the number of guests in the enormously enlarged house continued to swell, and as Hitler's future wife, Eva Braun, gradually began assuming the direction of things, a housekeeper and steward were added to the household. Hitler's sister returned to Vienna and a few years afterward married a Dresden doctor. Bormann had meanwhile settled down in a house of his own a few hundred yards away. Subsequently the Hoher Göll Inn, the Bechstein house—where Mussolini later stayed—and various local tearooms were made into adjuncts of the growing Berghof, since quarters were needed for a sizable squad of guards. Bormann then assumed economic and financial direction of the entire "household of the Führer." He was especially attentive to the lady of the house, anticipating her every wish and skillfully helping her with the often rather complicated arrangements for social and state functions. This was all the more necessary since she herself tactfully kept in the background as much as possible. Bormann's adroitness in this matter undoubtedly strengthened his unassailable position of trust with Hitler, who was extraordinarily sensitive about Eva Braun.

During this period Hitler's habits of life, hitherto so informal and unconstrained, took on strict conventional forms. For every private noon and evening meal in his house the seating order was fixed according to his instructions, and written down. Before every meal Hitler regularly asked his adjutant to show him the seating plan, so that he could check it over once more. The guests gathered in the small room with the traditional chimney-corner. When all were present, this fact was reported to Hitler. For lunch, which was at about three o'clock, after Hitler had finished his "morning" conferences, there were generally more than ten and less than twenty persons. The composition of the luncheon party emphasized the private nature of Hitler's life at Berchtesgaden, for there were more women than men present. Here at Berchtesgaden Hitler deliberately sought feminine company for relaxation; the masculine guests were more or less subsidiary.

The virtually permanent house guests at the Berghof consisted actually of the small group from Munich who had gathered around Eva Braun. They included her younger sister, one of her schoolgirl friends, and one or two married women of her acquaintance. In addition there was the Hoffmann family, including Hoffmann's daughter, whom Hitler had known as a child and who was now married to the youth leader Baldur von Schirach. Hoffmann frequently brought Hermann Esser and his wife. Also regularly included in the circle of guests who dined with Hitler were Bormann, the two physicians who lived at the Berghof, Hitler's adjutants (who lived in adjoining buildings), and the wives of these men. There were also his secretaries and a few of Hitler's official associates, including myself. When Hitler was at the Berghof I stayed at the hotel in Berchtesgaden. Speer, who had his house and architect's office nearby, frequently came with his wife and sometimes brought with him Arno Breker and Josef Thorak, two sculptors who were friends of his. Goebbels, who was not particularly fond of the Munich atmosphere, preferring to see Hitler in private or among the circle of artists in Berlin, would come for only brief visits. He always brought his wife, whom Hitler liked. Robert Ley (the Minister of Labor) and his wife, with whom Hitler was also extremely friendly, were frequently invited. Although as far back as 1933 Hermann Göring had built a house in the immediate vicinity, upon a ridge which he baptized the "Adolf Hitler Peak," he never was one of the restricted circle of dinner guests. Hess remained to dine only when he came on official business. The same was true of Ribbentrop, who regularly set up his headquarters hear the Fuschlsee in the Salzburg area whenever Hitler stayed at Berchtesgaden.

Such was in general the composition of the group whom Hitler asked to table at the Berghof when his servant reported to him that all was ready. The gentlemen would then offer their arms to the ladies and follow Hitler down the broad colonnaded corridor to the dining room, which was paneled in natural wood. Each time they went in to dinner, Hitler would give his arm to another of the ladies, who would then have the privilege of sitting on his right. Another lady was always placed opposite him, unless a special guest were honored with this place. Eva Braun always sat on his left; her partner at table was invariably Bormann. In this circle dominated by the fair sex Hitler was a charming host. The ladies always had to be served first; the smallest breaches of this rule would stir Hitler to angry reproofs of his servants. With the ladies he made a point of conversing about nonpolitical matters. Since they were in awe of him and hence a bit abashed, and since he felt a certain social embarrassment, the conversation sometimes sounded forced and halting. But often, when he found a suitable subject, it went along smoothly and interestingly.

Hitler was a complete vegetarian; he never ate meat or fish. He lived almost entirely on vegetables and certain cereals; even bread and butter would give him indigestion. Zwieback and knaekkebroed, honey, tomato ketchup, mushrooms, curds, and yogurt were for a long time the basic elements in his diet. In later years he could no longer stand coffee, and only limited amounts of milk. All his food was specially prepared; even his soups were not the same as those served to the other guests. In his last years he had a special Viennese dietetic cook who even at military headquarters would prepare the Führer's meals in a special small kitchen. Incidentally, in 1932 when Hitler was living at the Hotel Kaiserhof in Berlin and suspected a plot to poison him, Frau Goebbels used frequently to prepare his meals at her home and spirit them up to his hotel room.

I have often wondered how, given his austere diet and his insomnia, Hitler managed to summon up the strength and the tremendous force of will that he manifested for so many years. His energy verged on the abnormal. The only possible biological explanation for it was that he must have been consuming his physical reserves at a pace which would surely lead to premature bodily degeneration.

Hitler exerted no pressure upon his guests with regard to vegetarianism, although he often talked with them about it and teased them about their food habits, calling them "corpse eaters." Only a few persons followed his custom at table. Among these was Bormann—although everyone knew that at home Bormann would not turn down a good steak. Hitler provided his guests with a substantial but never luxurious cuisine, and of course observed the wartime one-dish meal. Even at the greatest state banquets he never permitted at his table more than one main course, along with soup or entrée, and a dessert. At one time his doctors recommended him to eat caviar for its nutritional value. It did him good, but after a while he stopped having it, saying it was "sinfully expensive." Hitler also despised alcohol, the taste of which was repugnant to him. On ceremonial occasions when he had to drink a toast, his glass was always filled with mineral water. But in this respect also he let his guests follow their own tastes. However, they were restrained in the use of alcohol at his table. His opposition to smoking was much stronger. He considered nicotine extremely harmful, saying he would offer cigars and cigarettes only to his worst enemies, never to his friends. He forbade smoking in his rooms. There were exceptions to this rule only at important official functions in Berlin or Munich, and then separate smoking rooms were provided, which Hitler gave a wide berth. At the entrance to his bunker Berlin there hung, toward the end of the war, a sign reading: "No Smoking."

I have already mentioned that Hitler restricted the conversation at table to nonpolitical topics. For this interlude at least he wanted to shake off the political and military problems with which his mind incessantly toiled. If serious matters were brought up, he curtly and angrily evaded them. If one had to listen to the table conversation fairly often, it soon became rather dull, revolving around a number of fixed topics to which he would always refer. He spoke a great deal about food and diet—an obvious subject at any dinner table; about the differences in foods and their preparation in various parts of the country; and about vitamins and calorific content. At this point Hitler would usually draw his doctors into the conversation, asking for expert opinions. He himself would argue in favor of a vegetarian diet, saying it had been the primeval diet of the human race and was to be desired as the diet of the future because it was both wholesome and economical. One of his favorite subjects of conversation—to the distress of Göring—was his vigorous condemnation of hunting unless it involved the hunter's actually risking his own life. He said he could never harm so beautiful an animal as a deer, and forbade all hunting on the Obersalzberg. He sneered at the amateur sportsmen, while he had words of praise for poachers, who at least killed for food. During the war he had poachers released from the prisons and placed in probationary battalions. During the last years of the war, irritated by some newspaper article, he suddenly forbade all mention of hunting in the press except for plain advertisements of game being sold for meat.

In peacetime he spoke often and intensely about the protection of animals and antivivisection. He vigorously opposed vivisection—which won him much applause from the ladies—unless experiments with animals served some military purpose. To animals he ascribed the ability to think, and for them he felt sympathy—not for human beings. He was sensitive to the sufferings of animals and expressed his sympathy in the most decided terms. But he never wasted a word on humanitarianism except, on one occasion, to characterize it as a mixture of cowardice, stupidity, and intellectual conceit. And that indeed was his fundamental view of it. He studiously avoided the subject of the concentration camps.

Hitler would brighten up the conversation by telling stories about his life and his experiences while traveling. Insofar as I had been present at some of these incidents he described, I noted his distinct tendency to exaggerate; he often adorned his tales with extravagant imagination. Music, the cinema, the theater, painting, and architecture were also topics of conversation, or rather afforded him the chance to express his purely personal views. Such conversations, however, were seldom very fruitful, since there were strict limits to how far his interlocutors dared go in replying to him. Hitler made an effort to be humorous. Some of the guests, Hoffmann in particular, had natural gifts for light, witty conversation; as long as Hitler spoke with them, all went well. However Hitler's wit was distinctly artificial, more often the product of his sarcastic disposition than of genuine humor. He would taunt certain persons at table, go out of his way to find barbed gibes, and since he kept up this banter with some obstinacy, and it was impossible to pay him back in the same coin, the result was often great embarrassment on all sides.

Hitler would rise from the table and kiss the hands of the ladies on either side of him to signify the end of the meal. He would leave the dining room after the last of the ladies, but before all the men. Immediately afterwards he would go out to the yard to feed his German police dog himself. Later he took this dog with him to his field headquarters in East Prussia and the Ukraine.

Hitler never took a nap after lunch, although this might have been expected, since he slept so little at night. During the last years of the war, when he was already very much on the decline physically, he would take a rest at the rather unusual hour of nine to ten at night.

When at the Berghof, Hitler would usually hold a few brief administrative conferences after lunch. He might, for example, discuss Party matters with Bormann, with his chief of the Reich Chancellery, Lammers—who maintained a branch office of the Berlin Chancellery at Berchtesgaden—or have a talk with Ribbentrop, who would drive up from the Fuschlsee in response to a telephoned summons.

In the afternoon, often shortly after lunch, Hitler took his one walk of the day to the small tea pavilion, about fifteen minutes away at a leisurely strolling pace. In order to combine business with pleasure, Hitler usually took his stroll in the company of some official visitor who happened to be present. A short distance behind him followed the ladies and gentlemen of the private circle. The tail of this odd "procession," as it was often jokingly called, was formed by his bodyguard.

The party would remain for an hour or two in the pavilion. The conversation in this unvarying circle would often be on the dull side, and Hitler would frequently doze off in his chair by the big round table in front of the fireplace. As a rule an automobile would bring the party back the short distance to the Berghof. Thereafter Hitler, unless he had some special visits or conferences, would withdraw to his two private rooms on the first floor of the house—a master's sitting room with fireplace and balcony, and a bedroom. He would remain in these rooms until around 8:30 in the evening, when the same circle of guests would assemble for dinner. A new set of seating arrangements would meanwhile have been drawn up. The ladies dressed for dinner.

Fräulein Braun owned a pair of droll little Scotch terriers, one of which was named "Negus." When dinner was delayed, Hitler was fond of playing with this amusing but snappy little beast which would respond only to its mistress's orders.

During the war Hitler sometimes stayed at the Berghof when state receptions at Klessheim Castle near Salzburg or Party affairs at Munich were being held. At such times the headquarters of the Wehrmacht also followed him to Berchtesgaden. It was housed in a barracks, and in the Berchtesgaden annex of the Chancellery. The members of the Oberkommando der Wehrmacht would come up to the Berghof at noon and late in the evening for the regular situation conferences with Hitler. Hitler had accordingly issued instructions that from noon until about two o'clock, when the conference was over and the generals had left, the ladies were to remain in their rooms. In the evenings it was so arranged that the members of the OKW arrived at the Berghof while Hitler was dining with his private guests. The adjutant would then report that the generals were all assembled in the main salon. After dinner Hitler would go to them while the ladies waited in the dining room until the end of the conference or, if they were regular residents, went to their rooms on the first floor. The heart of the house was the main salon. It had red marble steps and a huge sliding picture window which brought the whole landscape into the room like a tremendous painting. There, beside an outsize globe, Hitler worked standing at the large table by the window. There he signed papers, corrected drafts, scanned memoranda; on that desk he unfolded architects' plans and military maps. At that table stood Stauffenberg a few days before his attempt of July 20, 1944 to assassinate Hitler. In that salon Hitler had received the visits of Mussolini, King Carol and his son, and many others of the crowned and uncrowned heads of Europe. In it Schuschnigg was received and Austria's fate decided. There on New Year's Eve at the end of 1940 Hitler raised his glass, for once filled with champagne, to toast victory, which he thought would certainly be his in 1941. There, in May of that year, he unsuspectingly opened a letter that struck him like a blow in the face—Hess's letter announcing his flight to England. There, among his guests, he sat through that terrible night which I shall never forget when the proud *Bismarck,* after sinking the *Hood,* drifted rudderless at sea, sending Hitler one radio message after the next. There was nothing he could do for those thousand brave sailors who were looking death in the eye, no way he could help them in their heroic struggle; he could only send them a last greeting. There he also heard the first news of the great Allied invasion of France, which marked the beginning of the end. And there too he received the dreadful news of the irrevocable collapse of the German Eastern Front at the Baranov bridgehead—though during the first three days of the Russian breakthrough he did not consider the situation of the German army serious enough to warrant his flying back at once to his field headquarters in East Prussia.

Over the years much else took place in that imposing room. It was the silent witness of Hitler's transports of joy at times of success, and his outbursts of rage when luck went against him.

A great deal has been written about Hitler's rages, and they were always much talked about. I witnessed them often and felt the intensity of his fury directed against my own person. They represented the revolt of his demonic energies against the world of crude reality, this emotion being vented against some human object. They were the thunder of a hard will being shattered by the still harder reality of things. Hitler's mind stirred up his heart; his blood in turn inflamed his brain. The fury raged itself out in a hurricane of words that contradiction only lashed to greater intensity. At such times he would crush all objections simply by raising his voice.

Such scenes might be produced by little as well as big things. They occurred whenever events took a course different from that which Hitler had willed and predicted, whenever in his endless distrust he scented sabotage (he always preferred to hide his own defeats by charging sabotage), or whenever human inadequacy got on his nerves. When he was in such a state, trivial blunders and oversights would be branded damnable crimes. Death penalties or the concentration camp were as often the result of his uncontrollable rages as of his "ice-cold" reflection—to use his own phrase.

The most insignificant incidents could have a shattering effect upon his temper. During the war years, for example, the death of the opera singer Manowarda, of whom Hitler thought highly, was not recorded with banner headlines on the first pages of the newspapers. This omission threw Hitler into a frenzy of rage against the press. His fury lasted for hours and made him literally incapable of work for the rest of the day. Another time, at his house on the Obersalzberg, his police dog Blondi refused to come to heel when he called. I saw the blood rush to his head at this defiance of his command. There was a crowd of several thousand people around Hitler who was about to take his customary walk past these visitors. Two minutes later, when a woman handed him a petition, he suddenly screamed out at one of his closest associates, who happened to be standing behind him. Without giving any explanation, disregarding the amazement of the crowd, he gave the man a ferocious bawling out over nothing.

In none of these rages, however, did Hitler ever let himself be carried away to the point of inflicting physical abuse. The one exception to this was June 30, 1934 at the Ministry of the Interior in Munich. There I saw him rip epaulets and war decorations from the uniforms of the top SA leaders with his own hands. The story that in his rages Hitler would throw himself on the floor and bite the rug is an invention which is no truer for having been repeated so frequently.

It is hard to imagine a greater contrast in one and the same person than that between the frenzied splenetic and the Hitler whose pleasant and likable traits emerged in conversation or on public occasions. This man, so often brutal, inflexible, senselessly furious, would appear as a deeply sympathetic, artistically sensitive being, the kindly father of his people, ever ready to extend a helping hand to those in trouble. People who had known him only in the second phase could not possibly imagine what the other Hitler was like.

Over the years there was a great deal of public speculation about Hitler's being a sick man. On the basis of much observation of his life and of my constant association with his doctors I do not believe that his states of violent agitation were the symptoms or the consequence of some acute physical illness. On the contrary, these outbursts of emotion were the cause of his frequent physical distress; they were his disease. Those explosive blasts of an overcharged brain, which left him in a state of exhaustion, affected the nerves of his stomach, and deranged his digestive system. Then the physical disability exerted a reciprocal effect, intensifying his tendency to outbursts of rage.

Hitler's physical health was extraordinarily unstable. He was sick as often as he was well. Almost invariably his complaint was indigestion. In 1937, on the advice of Doctor Morell, he underwent a "mutaflor" cure for several months, taking pills to renew his destroyed intestinal flora. Afterwards he said he felt "reborn" and for several years was able to eat many foods that had previously made him ill. Later, as a result of the excitements and spiritual trials of the war years, his condition deteriorated again. He was given vitamin injections but by no means relied on intravenous feeding, as rumor had it. On the contrary, he did well on the food prepared for him by his Viennese diet cook. The rapid physical degeneration which brought him to the verge of collapse during the last year of the war was the result of his obstinately overstraining himself, and of the constant agitation which followed the attempt upon his life of July 20, 1944. One day early in 1945 his doctor was suddenly called to his bunker at the headquarters in the Forest of Rastenburg. From a remark later dropped by the doctor I gathered that Hitler had recovered from a very light cerebral stroke. Hitler himself once said in my presence that he had restrained himself during a violent dressing-down of a "criminally incompetent" general only because he feared he would bring a stroke on himself. For a considerable time his close associates suspected that Hitler was suffering from cancer of the larynx. A stubborn growth had made it impossible for him to talk loudly. This fear, however, proved unfounded. The well-known Berlin specialist, Doctor Eicken, who operated on Hitler for this condition, told me during a train ride from the headquarters to Berlin that the growth had been benign, a typical polypus of the larynx; he had, he said, over the years twice performed relatively simple operations upon this growth and had been able to prove it completely.

The evil in Hitler's life was not the outcome of any serious physical disease. The fatal dynamism of his whole existence was conditioned by his very nature; it was a psychological phenomenon. In the end his demonic will consumed his body as well as everything else it touched. Hitler's whole mode of life was unhealthy, virtually suicidal, and he would not listen to his doctors' advice. The burden of work which he carried, and which he increased by insisting upon making all decisions himself, was not so great that it need have crushed his health. His "service to the race and the nation" need not have kept him from living reasonably. If he had only understood how to organize his time, if only he had set aside for rest and recuperation a fraction of the days and nights he wasted in boring, artificial "sociability," his physical condition would never have deteriorated as it did. During the more than ten years that I sat at his table, Hitler took his meals with grotesque irregularity, often not lunching before four or five o'clock in the afternoon, not dining before midnight. It was only under pressure from his associates that he reluctantly and very gradually began keeping to a somewhat more even schedule in the conduct of his life.

Every evening after dinner Hitler would see one or two movies. In the Chancellery in Berlin there was a motion picture room; at the Berghof the main salon would be used. In a sense, movies provided contact with normal life in the world outside, which otherwise he never encountered. Occasionally it was proposed that he should disguise himself and go about among the public, seeing Berlin unattended, as a private citizen. He would not hear of it. He never had a double, as rumors abroad persistently maintained; the idea never even entered his head.

During the war Hitler deliberately gave up this pleasure. During all those years he saw only a single motion picture. That was one evening at the Berghof when Mussolini was visiting. If I remember rightly the movie was the successful comedy *Napoleon is to Blame for Everything.* Instead of films he preferred recorded concerts of classical works or grand opera. He also frequently called in a first-rate amateur conjuror to put on a performance. These performances so captivated him that he issued a strict ban forbidding the newspapers from disillusioning the masses about the art of magic by publishing "explanatory" articles.

Around midnight—seldom earlier and often later—there began Hitler's nightly gathering around the fireplace. During the last peacetime years this would take place after the movies had been shown; during the war, after the end of the military conference. Some fifteen to twenty persons, those I have already described, would assemble round him on the fireplace side of the main salon, in the circle of light cast by the flaming logs. The walls around the room glowed with the rich colors of classical paintings by German and Italian masters. Over the mantelpiece a madonna by an unknown Italian looked down upon the company. On the left was Feuerbach's *Nana* and a portrait of King Henry, the "founder of cities," holding compass and rule; on the right a female nude by Botticelli and the sea-nymphs from Böcklin's *Play of the Waves*. In the dark background of the room the bronze bust of Richard Wagner seemed to come to life.

In the muted semidarkness it was again Hitler who held the floor, as he had done all day long; the rest of the company were largely listeners, there only to give him an excuse for talking. Yet I often had the impression that his mind was absent while he spoke, that his thoughts were elsewhere. Now and then, when the conversation lagged, Hitler would request reports from the OKW, the foreign office, or the press. He would then retire briefly to an adjoining room with one of his adjutants, if he thought it necessary to issue orders.

He seldom violated his basic principle that conversation here among the ladies must remain on the lighter side. This obviously feigned insouciance was a difficult attitude for many of the others to maintain during the grave crises of the latter years of the war. As a result some of them accepted invitations to the Berghof only when they were issued as express requests from Hitler, virtually command appearances. His adjutants were kept busy trying to fill the gaps in the dinner company and the fireplace gatherings whenever the ranks began to thin. Although these sessions often dragged on until dawn, Hitler never asked whether any of those present felt tired and wished to retire. This was his one failure in courtesy and consideration toward the ladies. Their time was their own only when Hitler rose and took his leave. To listen to him and stay by him until he thought he could sleep was the tribute which he unsparingly exacted of his guests.

Hitler certainly had innumerable opportunities for conversation with important and interesting people. I have never understood why he never made use of these opportunities. Instead, for years he abstained from anything which might have added to his personal experience. He remained perpetually in the same company, among the same faces, in the same atmosphere, and, I may almost say, in the same state of monotony and boredom, producing eternally the same speeches and declarations. Only the abnormality of his disposition can explain this.

Sometimes, at a very late hour, Hitler would turn his attention solely to the ladies who sat close by him and would engage them alone in a quiet, intimate conversation. The other persons in the room would talk in whispers in order not to disturb him. At such times a note of real human warmth would enter his voice. Aside from Eva Braun, this favored feminine circle included Frau Goebbels and Frau Ley. Fräulein von Laffert, who was part of his group in Berlin, and Unity Mitford, whom Hitler saw frequently in Munich, did not enter the Berghof circle.

Since Hitler's death a great deal has been written about his alleged amours with actresses, dancers, and other women. If we wish to stick to the sober facts, these tales must be relegated to the realm of fable. Those so-called mistresses—whether in Berlin, Berchtesgaden, Munich, or elsewhere—were ladies who happened to attend the Führer's evening parties whose pattern I have just described. There was no possibility for an affair under these conditions. Except for the time he spent with the woman whom he later married, there was hardly an hour in Hitler's life when he was not surrounded with people. As for his intimacy with Eva Braun, this most personal of human relationships even the chronicler must respect; there his obligation to history stops.

In peacetime Hitler held an annual grand reception for the artists of the Reich, either in his apartment in the Chancellery in Berlin, or in the Führer's Building in Munich. Only practicing artists were invited, not their wives or husbands. In addition, he frequently paid more or less private visits, accompanied only by a small entourage, to the building dedicated to the "comradeship of German artists" on Victoriastrasse in Berlin, and to the Künstlerhaus (Artists' House) on Lembachplatz in Munich. At these places he would engage in free and easy conversation with women artists, and often men as well. At home he was usually glad to see artists who came to him to talk over professional or personal matters. In Berlin he frequently had afternoon tea with Leni Riefenstahl by his fireside, and would advise her about her film problems. He had the greatest respect for Maria Müller, Madame Ursuleac, and other great singers; he admired Henny Porten, considering her a splendid motion picture actress. When Brigitte Helm faced manslaughter charges for a fatal automobile accident, Hitler saw to it that the case was dropped. At Goebbels' house he met Olga Tschechowa, Jenny Jugo, and many other actresses. Gossips whispered that he had intimate relations with all these women. The stories are utterly false.

Out of respect for them as genuine artists, Hitler furthered the interests of dancers and variety stars. For example, he had a law passed forbidding tightrope performances without a net. He wished to see ballet dancers elevated in the social scale and made a decree to this effect. He made Dinah Grace and other dancers perform specially for him at his home in Berlin. But in all these relationships he never overstepped the bounds of polite social behavior toward ladies. We cannot be so bigoted as to maintain that a chief of state has not as much right to the company of ladies as any ordinary citizen.

There is no doubt that Hitler had a weakness for women, but not in any morally reprehensible sense. He was gallant toward them, but restrained; an admirer but not a lover. As vegetarian and teetotaler Hitler was little inclined toward tête-à-têtes or dinners for two. The magnitude of his goals shut out the small pleasures of life—as his will to power excluded pettier vulgar aims. It must be said, however, that his relationship toward women had a dual aspect, like everything else in his life. He shunned publicity in regard to his private life; in the interests of the state and of his reputation, he kept his private life invisible. In public life—which was for him another plane—he put women into the uniform of the League of German Girls and the National Socialist Women's Organization; he ordered them to stick to *Kinder* and *Küche.* But in private life he did not inquire into their political views; he liked to see women dress beautifully and expensively. Nevertheless, he was no Don Juan; rather, he was a queer sort of monk who rather enjoyed being suspected of many amours—although no one in his immediate circle ever noticed signs of such intimacies.

Whatever charges may be leveled against Hitler as man and politician, in the sphere of morality and in his personal relations with women no one can throw a stone at him. Hitler had a great many ardent followers among women. As a bachelor he received many fantastic love-letters, usually from somewhat elderly ladies. These letters, which often passed the bounds of discretion and good taste, were tactfully taken care of by his secretaries. He himself often said half jokingly, half seriously: "I cannot afford to marry; if I did I would lose half of my best and most loyal adherents."

In the summer of 1944 the wedding of Eva Braun's sister to Himmler's liaison officer with Hitler, was celebrated at Salzburg and Berchtesgaden. Pictures taken from Hoffmann's private collection have since been published in the newspapers. Taken together, they give the impression of a riotous revel. The facts about this affair are as follows.

Eva Braun had never fully reconciled herself to Hitler's decision not to marry. Since she could never have a wedding of her own, she asked Hitler's permission to arrange for a sizable celebration of her sister's wedding. Hitler gave his assent, but he himself did not take part in the celebration. Instead, he only invited the couple to a simple lunch at his table, at which occasion he tendered his congratulations in a few suitable phrases. The ceremony itself was performed at Salzburg. The wedding party, to which a fair number of guests outside the immediate family were invited, was held at Bormann's house on the Obersalzberg, and in the tea house eyrie. This wedding was the one party which was ever given up there. Some of the guests from Munich, including the actor Handschuhmacher, were killed a few days later during an air raid on Munich.

It is hard to imagine a more contrasting pair than Adolf Hitler and Eva Braun. The ideal woman, according to Hitler's ideas, should be tall and blonde, although he did not prize extreme slimness. Eva Braun had a very well-proportioned figure, but she was petite rather than tall, and brunette. Hitler would frequently take her to task for her passion for high-heeled shoes. Hitler's mind was obsessed with weighty ideological problems; she, on the other hand, was a creature of pure emotion and *joie de vivre.* She always dressed becomingly and in the latest fashion, whereas he cared little about his outward appearance. Even in front of others she would frequently scold Hitler for his naturally ill-fitting uniforms and suits, and his drab ties. He always accepted such criticism with forebearing courtesy. Unlike Hitler, Eva Braun did not refrain from alcohol. She smoked heavily when he was not about and loved dancing, whereas he had a distinct aversion to social dancing and never set foot upon a dance floor. In spite of all these temperamental differences, the two apparently got along well; in the course of many years no serious disputes between them came to light. Eva Braun was not unintelligent. She belonged to no Party organizations—not actively, at any rate—and seldom or never said a word about politics. Undoubtedly she had an influence upon Hitler in social and cultural matters, especially in regard to the theater and the cinema, but none whatsoever in public and political life.

Nevertheless, I believe that Hitler paid a high price for not being married. He absolutely lacked any feeling about family life, his alienation from it extending even to the members of his own family. This went so far that, for example, his step-brother Alois Hitler, who ran a restaurant on Wittenbergplatz in Berlin, could never even be mentioned in Hitler's presence. This absence of family ties severed him from the general run of mankind, for he could have no inner sympathy with the way normal people live. If he had been married, the influence of a wife, the raising of children, and the duties and cares attendant upon family life, might have provided him with a natural counterpoise to his one-sided political fanaticism. Participation in the natural and human aspects of life might have affected his work for the national community and guided his public activities into more moderate and fruitful channels. As it was, the violent impulsiveness of his will ranged on unchecked to the final catastrophe. He chose to remain single throughout life and married only on the point of death. That act rounded out the profound human tragedy which comprehended even his personal relations with women. Of the six women who stood in a close human relationship to him in his life, five died by suicide, or had attempted suicide.

As chief of state Hitler had to appear at state functions. These were the responsibility of his *Staatssekretär* and later *Staatsminister* Meissner. Meissner was assisted by a Chief of Protocol who was formally subordinate to the Minister of Foreign Affairs.

In peacetime the most important of these functions was the New Year reception for the Diplomatic Corps. It was regularly held in Berlin in the marble rooms of the New Chancellery, which were as grand in scale as they were handsome in their appointments. They had been designed by Speer especially for such official functions. For Hitler's receptions as leader of the Party there was a set of rooms which duplicated those designed by Professor Troost in the Führer's Building on Königlicher Platz in Munich. Since Hitler almost always spent the New Year holiday in the mountains, where the Berchtesgaden farmers fired cannon-salutes for him at midnight, he shifted the New Year reception for the diplomats from January 1 to January 10. The foreign ambassadors and ministers were happy about this change, since they preferred to have the New Year holiday free for personal trips. Hitler never thought these formal gatherings, with their prepared speeches, very fruitful politically. Afterwards he would often mention that some representatives of other Powers had attempted, while shaking hands with him, to bring up particular matters, but that he himself had either answered according to whim and the way the political winds were blowing at the moment, or had passed over the matter in silence.

Such formal receptions for heads of state and delegations considerably increased in frequency during the war as the result of the Anti-Comintern Pact and the Three Powers Pact. When the Axis was initially "forged" and put into energetic operation, ceremonial receptions were held in Vienna at the Palais Belvedere, that gay and beautiful summer palace built by the famous Austrian general Prince Eugene. Later on, since Hitler preferred staying in Berchtesgaden, he had Klessheim Palace near Salzburg furnished specially for that purpose. He did not consider his private house at Berchtesgaden the right place for large official functions.

Klessheim Palace could be reached from Berchtesgaden in half an hour by automobile. Situated just a few miles outside of Salzburg, it had been built by Fischer von Erlach as a pleasure palace for the prince-bishops of Salzburg, who had a penchant for the lighter sides of life. With its splendid park and the panoramic mountain views from its many terraces and lawns, it inspired all visitors with admiration for this beautiful corner of the world. The palace had last been a possession of the House of Hapsburg. A feeble-minded archduke had been confined there; he had died only a few years before Hitler took it over. Neo-Renaissance in style, the edifice had been planned for impressiveness. There was an imposing entrance drive and a grand stairway that dominated the facade. The reception hall on the first floor was a tremendous oval reaching up into the open vault of the roof. The living quarters, on the other hand, were so limited that when Hitler had guests only the chiefs of state themselves could be sheltered in the palace. Delegations and entourage lived in a somewhat distant outbuilding which had been equipped with all conveniences. Also built in the days of the prince-bishops was a charming little ladies' pavilion in the shape of a four-leafed clover, tucked away in a quiet corner of the gardens. It was restored, and the first person to stay in it was the Italian ambassador Alfieri who enjoyed the reputation of being a great man for the ladies.

The state suite on the first floor of the palace—a suite containing only a salon and a bedroom—was at various times occupied by Mussolini, Horthy, King Boris, and others. Basking in the warm glow of political sunshine, taking their ease amid the sparkling circlet of mountains, it is no wonder that they felt optimistic when Hitler lectured them on the military situation in the small room behind the oblong dining hall, inspiring them with his own conviction of victory. But on other, later visits to the palace, they lay awake in that same state bedroom, while outside the tempests of the Salzburg mountains raged, through nights of evil premonitions and profound depression. For when the situation grew critical, the Supreme Commander of the Wehrmacht would have summoned them only to conjure up for them the darkest prospects and demand ultimate efforts and sacrifices from their nations.

At table at Klessheim Palace I saw the Italian Duce. How well I remembered the southern emotionalism of his conversation with Hitler ten years before in Venice. Now he sat silent and hunched, a broken Caesar, letting Hitler's torrent of words roll over his head. Here at the Palace I listened over afternoon coffee to the merry talk of the likable Bulgarian king. Boris was fond of driving locomotives, or taking the stick from the pilot of Hitler's plane when it was sent to Sofia for him. He would jokingly speak of Hitler as "my Führer." Here also I met the melancholy Norwegian Quisling and the slow-moving Tiso. On the afternoon of the first day of the Allied invasion I heard Göring, surrounded by the tense faces of men from many of the countries of Europe, expound for almost an hour on the hopeful prospects—a mobile German armored division was going to save the situation. Goebbels, meanwhile, stood in the circle with a look half of relief, half of doubt. And in the main hall of the palace I saw the seventy-year-old Admiral Horthy, ordinarily so charming and light-hearted, come from his apartment in a mood of deadly earnest. Resisting Hitler's demands, he ordered his special train to be made ready for departure. The train was delayed on account of "technical difficulties"; it did not leave until many eventful hours later, when Horthy declared his willingness to recognize the situation for what it was and act accordingly.

A separate railroad station had been built for this palace, so that the special trains could come directly to it. Guests who came by plane landed at the Salzburg airfield. Before the annexation of Austria Hitler had built the airport of Ainring near Freilassing for his own use when he wished to come by plane to Berchtesgaden. It also served a military purpose. Unless there were compelling reasons for leaving at a particular time, Hitler made a great point of flying only in perfect weather. He would not take off until reports had come in of uniformly favorable weather along his entire route. His last plane was a four-motored Focke-Wulff Condor specially built for him; under his seat was a trapdoor for parachute jumps, and the window wall could be opened by a special, patented handle. Before this plane, he had used a Junkers 52 for ten years; he considered it the most reliable commercial plane in the world until his pilot talked him into discarding "that old crate."

During the last years of the war there was much talk that Hitler was preparing to escape by plane to Japan or Spain. Was there anything to these stories? Only persons completely ignorant of Hitler's nature can imagine him guilty of personal cowardice. As for having any intentions to flee, as long as I was a member of his entourage, which was until March 30, 1945, that shameful idea never entered his mind, let alone crossed his lips. His pilot was at his disposal in Berlin up to the very last day. Hitler did not require his services; he never considered fleeing from Berlin.

When Hitler was at Berchtesgaden with the Oberkommando der Wehrmacht, the army chief of staff would remain behind at his field headquarters. As soon as the military situation demanded, the chief of staff would request his return. Then Hitler and the generals would take off from Salzburg airport to fly back to the field headquarters. For security reasons Hitler never announced beforehand the time of his departure from Berchtesgaden, not even in peacetime. It always took place suddenly, a wild flurry that was over within two hours. Hitler's special train, which he used far more frequently than the plane, always stood ready and under steam at the railroad station in Berchtesgaden or in some hidden spot nearby. Usually Hitler's private guests used this train to return from the Berghof to Munich, and sometimes went right along with him to Berlin. In that case the customary nightly tea and conversation at the fireplace would be held or continued in his saloon car.

This special train comprised some ten or twelve specially outfitted cars. Behind the locomotive and bringing up the rear of the train were two anti-aircraft cars armed with 2 cm. cannon. They never had occasion to go into action while Hitler was aboard the train. Hitler's living quarters consisted of a saloon paneled in walnut, with twelve seats around a table, a sleeping compartment, and an adjoining bath compartment. Sleeping compartments for adjutants and servants filled out the rest of this car. Adjoining it was the military car which contained a large room for the situation conferences, and compartments for radio communications and teletypes. Behind this were four or five large sleeping cars and two dining cars in which were housed the OKW, all Hitler's permanent companions and co-workers, and his temporary guests. During the last years, when the OKW was aboard this train for months, a special bathing car with baths and showers was added. At the tail end, before the service car, was a special car equipped with more radios and teletypes so that press messages could be received without interruption. In order to camouflage Hitler's movements, these press reports were continuously sent out from Berlin on a special wave length even when Hitler had not been on the train for months.

When this special train made a halt somewhere, it was often housed in railroad tunnels for protection against planes. Hitler used the train for his headquarters throughout the Polish campaign and the Balkan war of 1941. In it he rode all across France to Montoire, where he met with Pétain; he traveled in it as far as the Pyrenees and the Bridge at Irun, where he had conversations with Franco in the latter's own special train. During the battle for Berlin it was placed in a forest near Rosenheim in Bavaria. There, early in May 1945, after having been bombed heavily by low-flying planes, it fell into the hands of American troops.

Berlin had been the first city in North Germany that Hitler visited; it was also to be the city in which he spent his last moments. In 1917, after having lost his Austrian citizenship by entering the German army, he was at his own request given a furlough to Berlin; when he made out his leave certificate, he claimed no family relationships. He wanted to see the metropolis of the Reich, the city of his heart, the city that he had already chosen as the field of battle where his ideas were to win victory. For while it is generally believed that Hitler's interest turned to politics only during the Revolution of 1918, this was not the case. In June 1940, when Hitler revisited his old frontline positions and resting areas in the vicinity of Lille, where he had been posted in 1915, several comrades from his old company pointed out to me the garden arbor of a certain house where the eccentric young soldier had spouted his ideas to them, ideas which he later so forcefully developed to a larger public. As if in confirmation of their story the modest living room of that same French home displayed a photograph of Hitler in uniform taken in 1915.

On his first visit to Berlin Hitler wandered through the museums and drank in the life of the city. But he was very much disappointed by its architectural qualities. Before he became master of the Reich in 1933 he seriously considered the possibilities of making Munich the capital of the Reich, or else building an entirely new seat of government somewhere in the heart of Germany. The pressing economic and political problems which were thrust upon him as soon as he took office frustrated these plans. But the architect in Hitler had long before conceived of a gigantic reconstruction of the metropolis, and from the first day of his government this vast new city plan became a major point in his cultural program.

A mighty north-south avenue starting at the Brandenburger Tor was to complement the existing east-west axis and form the focal point for the reshaping of Berlin. All railroads were to be diverted from the heart of the city and concentrated in a single central railroad terminal at the southern end of the new boulevard, where the new government quarter would also be built. Hitler also intended to enlarge the gauge of the German railroads from 1.4 to the enormous width of more than 3 meters. This change would, he believed, so increase speed, safety, and capacity that the efficiency of the railroads would at one stroke be multiplied many times over. Two-story passenger cars were to be built, and freight cars so enlarged that the contents of a single freight train would fill the holds of a 10,000 ton freight steamer.

In regard to his transformation of the capital, Hitler once remarked: "Ten years from now no one will be able to say he knows the wonders of the world unless he has seen our new Berlin." He never suspected, when he said these words, in what a sense they would come true. Megalomaniac that he was, he thought he could impose the wild schemes of his artistic imagination not only on the city of Berlin but upon the sober and dead-earnest sphere of military power-politics. His Berlin was going to be a city like no other. What prophetic words! As a result of the fantastic development of modern air warfare, Berlin was smashed into prodigious ruins which do not have their like anywhere on earth. This visionary statesman who thought himself blessed among men never saw as far as this.

In 1940 Hitler visited Paris for the one and only time in his life. He stayed just three hours. At six o'clock in the morning he drove through the almost deserted city, went to the tomb of Napoleon, and looked down upon the city from the Eiffel Tower. In his plane on the way back he remarked that he had been little impressed by the Champs Elysées, the Arc de Triomphe, and the Place de la Concorde; he had imagined them far grander and more magnificent. Later I heard that he immediately afterwards made some changes in the general city plan for Berlin, widening the grand boulevard from 40 to 120 meters.

Hitler's relationship to monarchy and the development of his attitude toward it is closely linked with his stays in Berlin. A number of hitherto unrecorded facts will throw light on that aspect of his thinking.

Born and raised in Austria, the son of an official, Hitler was early taught to think in terms of a Greater Germany. Nevertheless, he remained inwardly more or less rooted in tradition; his attitudes were conditioned by an underlying conservatism. In November 1918 he had been unable to endorse the overthrow of royal dynasties and princely houses which had played such a glorious part in German history. This was a point he often stressed. Nevertheless, for all his hatred of German Social Democracy, he unconditionally agreed with its liquidation of the petty states which had made a patchwork quilt of Germany. That was, in his mind, a significant historic act.

Before the first balloting for the presidential election in 1932 Hitler wavered for a long time trying to select the National Socialist candidate who would oppose Hindenburg. Suddenly the name of the German crown prince bobbed up. There was a first-class sensation when Gregor Strasser produced a cavalry captain who declared he had come from the former crown prince who wished to offer himself as a candidate. But the negotiations came to nothing because Hitler then decided to enter the arena and run himself.

During the election campaign in Mecklenburg in that same year, behind-the-scenes negotiations with Schleicher had progressed to such a point that Hitler was expected to take over the government at any moment. Late one night Hitler sat with Goebbels and a small group of other persons in the living room of the manor house at Severin Estate, his headquarters at this time. Exhausted by the many meetings that had been held during the day, Hitler dozed off. While the others were sitting in silence he suddenly started up, as if waking from a dream, and said abruptly in all seriousness to Goebbels: "But then I will not have you making me an emperor or king!" Goebbels, usually so glib-tongued, stammered a few embarrassed words, and the subject was dropped.

Prince August Wilhelm of the House of Hohenzollern was an active storm trooper. In 1932 Hitler was a guest at his house in Potsdam several times. He also met the prince's likable sixteen-year-old son Alexander. One evening when Hitler was returning from Potsdam to Berlin he informed us that he intended to make Prince Alexander the successor to Kaiser Wilhelm II. In the next few months he spoke of this idea several times as if it were an established plan. After he came to power in 1933 he never mentioned the matter again. Thereafter his relationship with Prince August Wilhelm cooled, in fact became distinctly unfriendly. He stopped addressing the prince as "Royal Highness," as he had formerly done, told others that the prince was too much of a pusher, no longer issued invitations to him, and forbade his adjutant to have anything to do with him. This rather irrational change in his conduct toward the prince was indicative of a sudden shift in his monarchist views. He began making more and more spiteful remarks against the prince and the nobility as soon as he felt sure of the power he now held. Earlier he had not disdained the help of such people; as soon as he felt that he had won the people's favor, he grew cold toward the nobility. There were other causes for his change of heart. He smarted from certain petty personal slights on the part of members of the House of Hohenzollern. In the political salon of a noble lady of his acquaintance he was one day unexpectedly introduced to the former Empress Hermine—and was thoroughly discomfited by the deep court curtseys made by all the ladies present. Then, shortly before he took power, he was invited to tea at the home of Crown Princess Cäcilie. Later a servant of the household let him know that after his departure the crown princess had ordered all the windows to be opened "so that the stench of those creatures will leave the house with them."

These personal experiences may have helped alter his attitude toward monarchy. The primary fact is, however, that immediately after taking power Hitler threw overboard all his political and social ballast. He changed from head to foot and adopted the guise which had meanwhile been made ready for him, that of tribune of the people. On his very first visit to Venice he expressed regret that Mussolini had not had the courage to throw out the House of Savoy. Royalty put all kinds of checks on his personal regime, Hitler said, and represented a latent peril to fascism.

During the crisis in the British royal family Hitler passionately sided with the Prince of Wales, reproaching him only for not fighting the thing through and, supported by the sympathetic working class, making the government and the traditions of the Royal House "bow to reason." However, he strictly forbade the German press to intervene in any way. With his characteristic extremism he even banned all news stories, in order to keep or win the sympathies of the British Government at a time when he himself was busy rearming Germany.

Hitler's aversion to crowned heads increased during the political developments that preceded the Balkan campaign, and developed into intense hatred when Italy deserted the cause. For King Boris of Bulgaria alone he felt sincere liking. King Boris died shortly after a visit to Hitler's headquarters, and it was rumored that Hitler had had him poisoned. In view of the harmony I observed between the two men during this last visit, and of the many cordial and friendly remarks Hitler made about the king after his departure, these stories are absurd. On the contrary, Hitler was much depressed by the news of Boris's death. In fact, he accused the "queen and her court clique" of having committed political assassination by poisoning.

The middle-class atmosphere of the city of Berlin always remained distasteful to Hitler. Completely at ease as he was in Munich, during all the time he held power he never went to public places of entertainment in Berlin, except for theaters and concert halls. In 1933 he did have tea several times in the lobby of the Hotel Kaiserhof, but then he was frightened off by the dubious tale someone told him that in his absence the chairs he had sat in were rented out to elderly spinsters. His private life in the capital centered almost entirely upon the home and family of Goebbels. Hitler was a witness at Goebbels's wedding and as early as 1932 was virtually a daily guest in the Goebbels's flat on the square later known as Adolf Hitler Platz, or at their summer cottage in Caputh. Later on he went with them to Kladow and Schwanenwerder. Cruises on Wannsee in Goebbels's small motor yacht were among the few purely personal recreations Hitler was capable of.

Goebbels put Hitler in touch with the theatrical and cinema set of Berlin, and people from this set often made up the party for the evening film showings and the fireplace gatherings in his apartment. Aside from a few obligatory visits to Göring at Karinhall and later on somewhat more frequent visits to Dr. Ley, Hitler had no other social life in Berlin.

Hitler's apartment in Berlin was at 71 Wilhelmstrasse, on the first and second floors of the old Chancellery. Hindenburg had lived there for a few months during the reconstruction of the presidential palace. When Hitler moved in, Hindenburg warned him to "tread carefully"; in the course of the years, the stairs had become distinctly rickety and the floors were beginning to give. Hitler used to become quite indignant over the fact that the Prussian kings had assigned as a residence for their premiers and later their chancellors the building which had been used for their royal stables. He himself promptly had Bismarck's apartment rebuilt, with no respect whatsoever for its historical associations. It was also newly furnished in a severe classicist style, with interesting color schemes by Munich interior decorators. Hitler himself made sketches for the new furniture. After the completion of the New Chancellery the reception room and study on the ground floor were converted into a large auditorium for movies. Toward the back a spacious glassed-in porch was built, and adjoining it, for state receptions, a huge and dramatic dining hall with mighty columns of red marble. In the Chancellery garden Hitler ruthlessly ordered the cutting-down of the venerable oaks and beeches which Bismarck had loved. The trees had grown infirm, but a great many people were sorry to see them go. In their place Hitler had a fountain and pool constructed in the middle of the lawn. On the other hand, he fed the squirrels which made their way over from the nearby Tiergarten and trustfully came almost to the door of the apartment. No Providence and no sixth sense warned him in those promising years of peace that only a few years later he himself would find his grave among the roots of those historic trees, roots churned up by bombs and shells.

Hitler's private apartment, consisting of a study, a library, a bedroom, and a guestroom, adjoined the historic hall where the Congress of Berlin had been held. During the war, when he had his headquarters in Berlin, he would go from this apartment at noon, as soon as he got up, to the Congress Hall where the maps were already spread out and the generals were awaiting him for the situation conference. In that hall during the winter of 1939–40 his first plans for the campaign in France took shape. Here, too, in all probability—since this was where he planned his strategy—the ideas for the Norwegian campaign, the Balkan war, and the ill-fated Russian adventure were first born in his mind. Today it seems like the hand of Fate that the first of the bombs which struck the Chancellery in 1944 fell upon this historic chamber and smashed it completely.

When Hitler first moved into Wilhelmstrasse in 1933, he went about his unaccustomed tasks with diligence and punctuality. As long as Hindenburg was virtually his neighbor—their offices were separated only by those of the Foreign Office—Hitler appeared at his desk every morning at ten o'clock. He regularly, though reluctantly, conducted cabinet meetings; at that time he did not yet have a majority in the cabinet and had to accept compromises, infuriating though these were to him. For that reason he later on called cabinet meetings more and more rarely, and after 1937 not at all. Before and during the entire war he scornfully referred to the cabinet as a "club of defeatists." During the first days of his government he also attended the meetings of the Reichsrat and made a speech to that body. But when the representative of Prussia committed the sin of raising an objection to something he had said, he never again allowed the Reichsrat to meet. In the Reichstag he engaged in one blazing verbal battle with the deputies of the various parties and bullied them into passing the *Ermächtigungsgesetz*, the Enabling Act giving his administration the power to pass legislation. Thereafter he no longer needed the Reichstag. The new Reichstag, whose election he ordered, was only a farce; Hitler personally drew up the list of candidates. Henceforth the Reichstag was to be merely a sounding board for his declarations on domestic and foreign policy.

He called the leaders of industry to the Chancellery for a conference in which they were to set forth their views. Afterwards he remarked that it had amused him to see how each of these supposed captains of industry had recommended something different—usually the opposite of what the previous speaker had proposed—as the only right economic policy. Amid this confusion, he said, it had been easy for him to put across his own opinion and his own authoritarian conception, and he had then sent the lot of them packing.

At the beginning of his administration he attended a press conference for the first and last time, accompanied by Funk, who was then his press chief. Feeling his position still insecure, he wanted to introduce himself to the press as the new chief of state, and to make a gesture of good will. But it never remotely occurred to him to establish anything like real contact with the press, such as President Roosevelt and other heads of government maintained on an almost daily basis, for the good of their country. He considered it beneath his dignity to explain the reasons for his acts to journalists, to argue or even to discuss anything before the public. In spite of many requests he could never be induced to hold any regular press conferences. He gave a few interviews, the subject matter of which was outlined beforehand, if he thought they would help his reputation. In Berlin and in Nuremberg during the Party Day he would briefly receive accredited representatives of the foreign press, and after repeated urgings he once invited German journalists to the Führer's Building in Munich. He ruthlessly demanded the utmost of the journalists, for they were supposed to rally the people to supreme fulfillment of their duties. But he never opened his mind to them or recognized that they had any kind of intellectual mission or responsibility.

At the end of 1933 Hindenburg, whose health was failing, retired to East Prussia. That was the end of Hitler's hard-working schedule. He once more returned to his habit of rising at noon and during the day entered his offices only for important receptions. All other work was taken care of in his apartment as he stalked about his rooms, dropping a word here and a word there, settling important matters in the most casual fashion.

I describe an incident from my own career because it is typical of Hitler's way of running a government. In September 1937, when Schacht resigned, Funk was promoted from press chief to minister of economics. News of this shift had not yet been made public. Before lunch, about 1:30 P.M., I entered Hitler's apartment in the Chancellery and passed the fireplace room on my way to another room. Hitler was standing at a big marble-topped table, pen in hand. He was signing papers. Seeing me passing, he gestured to me to come over to him. Without interrupting his work, he said abruptly to me—he had never sounded me on this question at all—"I have just appointed you *Staatssekretär.* Minister Goebbels has not yet signed the appointment, but he will sign, you can depend on that." Whereupon he shook hands with me and without another word went on signing the documents, while his adjutant blotted each signature.

This rather tart remark about Goebbels, who would have liked to block my appointment, requires explanation. At this particular time

Hitler was on bad terms with Goebbels because of Goebbels's family difficulties arising out of his involvement with the Czech movie actress Lida Baarova. Not wanting public scandal, he had forbidden Frau Goebbels to sue for divorce. Those few months were the only time during which Hitler's friendship with Goebbels was strained. At all other times Hitler praised Goebbels for his talents as an orator (he really had a great gift for demagogy), publicly hailed him as his greatest friend, and backed up his hysterical theatricality.

Hitler's personnel policies were as high-handed as this story indicates. The idea of anyone's "accepting" an office did not exist for him, any more than anyone could resign without his permission. Hitler recognized only unconditional submission to whatever he himself defined as duty to the nation.

Adjoining the room with fireplace and red plush carpets, which Hitler preferred for floor-covering in all his rooms, was his dining room. It too was the scene of historic table-talk, especially in times of peace. During the war years such non-official gatherings were transferred to the casino at Hitler's headquarters, wherever that happened to be at the moment. The dining room in the Chancellery was a plain, whitewashed room. It contained a long sideboard that Hitler himself had designed. One entire wall was covered by a colossal painting of Aurora, the Dawn, driving through the clouds in the heavenly chariot, accompanied by a large entourage. In the center of the room was a generous-sized round table which seated fifteen persons. Fifteen red armchairs would be drawn up to this table between four and six o'clock in the afternoon, and between eight and ten o'clock at night, these being the usual hours for meals. The members of this "Round Table" were almost entirely male, and changed frequently. Some persons were constantly present in their official capacities. Others were members of the government or the Party whom Hitler had had in for a conference. The casual visitors might be ministers, gauleiters, ambassadors, generals, artists, or economists. Göring seldom stayed; Goebbels came over from his ministry on Wilhelmsplatz almost every day. Not infrequently, guests, after waiting for Hitler for several hours, would take their leave before the meal simply because they were too hungry to wait any longer.

Here in the Chancellery—in contrast to the Berghof—the table-talk was political; it centered around current social, economic, cultural, or foreign affairs as often as around general subjects. But here too Hitler held the floor. It is difficult to define the peculiar quality of these gatherings. No other dinner parties or luncheon parties I have ever attended were like these meals in the Chancellery. No one at this table felt free. In the atmosphere that surrounded Hitler people who were naturally vital and interesting individuals were transformed into taciturn listeners. People were abashed and remained in their shells, while Hitler spoke and bound them with the words and gestures he had tried and tested a thousand times before. Habitués of the circle knew that the conditions of discussion were unfair; there was no question of equal rights between Hitler and his table companions. Consequently, Hitler's well-known views alone were aired; there was seldom a profitable exchange of ideas. The visitors let Hitler talk; they themselves contributed nothing. The exception was Goebbels. As Gauleiter of Berlin and propaganda minister he would toss cues to Hitler during the conversation, would take up Hitler's ideas, carry them still further, and take advantage of the opportunity to obtain oral decisions from Hitler on the most diverse matters. If Hitler did not speak and Goebbels did not put in his oar, there were often prolonged, embarrassed silences which the host expected to be broken by the interjection of jokes. The photographer Hoffmann would then tell South German jokes and Viennese anecdotes about "Count Bobby." Or Goebbels would repeat the latest political witticisms in Berlin jargon—though he made a point of picking only the innocuous stories and those that were about Göring and not himself. Göring was magnanimous and maintained a private collection of jokes about himself. The person of Hitler was always sacrosanct. During meals Hitler had a habit of chatting with his household steward, who was a typical Berlin "original"; this man had formerly worked at the well-known outdoor restaurant *Onkel Toms Hütte* (Uncle Tom's Cabin). The steward often provided humor and a kind of low-level entertainment that relaxed and amused his guests.

One day at this table I had the following experience. It was the birthday of one of the adjutants. Goebbels, wishing to embarrass me, whispered to Hitler that I should be asked to stand up and deliver a birthday speech. Hitler fell in with the idea; he wrote a few words on a place card and passed me a categorical written command to stand up and speak. But Goebbels was fooled. I improvised a fairly nice little speech and managed to come out of the affair tolerably well. Moreover I took my revenge by making the whole table stand up twice to toast the health of the adjutant. . . .*

Hitler's humor at table was forced, not to say savage. Other characteristics of his also came to the fore on these occasions. He would criticize judicial verdicts, from which he would then go on to vent his hatred of men of law. He also sometimes discussed his right of amnesty. There were certain crimes which he chose to think well of, especially those concerning women or poaching or other actions which he felt sprang from the "sound instincts of the people." In such cases he would intervene, and see that only petty punishments were meted out. But most of the time he was not in favor of leniency; rather, his harsh outlook emerged.

There was, for example, the case of a confidence man who claimed he could distill gasoline out of water and even sold his idea to several prominent personages. Then there was a chemist who claimed he could make gold out of lead. Hitler ordered these men to be imprisoned "until they can make gasoline and gold."

* Goebbels, being club-footed, was thus placed at a disadvantage.

The general conclusion Hitler invariably drew was: "What we as a nation need is not softness and sentimental weakness, but hardness and ruthlessness." "Praised be what makes us hard"—this was his thesis. He hoped to breed toughness in the German people, who, he maintained, had hitherto taken too passive an attitude in the battle of life.

Hitler's personal unpretentiousness, his exterior simplicity, have often been taken as the reflection of inner modesty. In fact he was far from modest in his estimate of himself. He made it abundantly clear that he considered himself one of the very great men of history and used to speak, though with a pretence of irony, about the monuments that would be erected to him. I once happened to make a remark about the advantages of a modest demeanor, and mentioned the aphorism attributed to Moltke, "Be more than you seem." Hitler promptly retorted that any such modesty in great men could only spring from an "inadequate consciousness of their own value" and an "unbecoming sense of inferiority." He also corrected me on a point of fact, saying that the phrase was not Moltke's, that it had been used by Schueffen in his memorial address on Moltke to characterize the deceased general. A check-up proved that Hitler was right.

An understanding of human beings has always been considered one of the prime requirements for the politician and statesman. In the course of years I observed a lack of such understanding in Hitler which was at least as great as his prodigious belief in his own penetration. Persons whom he had grown accustomed to over the years he would as a rule not allow to leave his side. He drew new members into his entourage only if they had been around him so much that they had gradually grown into his peculiar life. In general his judgments about people were purely arbitrary.

He had respect for creative achievements; at any rate he proclaimed that he had. But he hailed people with above-average talents as great geniuses just because they happened to be successful and lucky at the moment. And he prematurely condemned persons of merit because they had not achieved popularity and were not serving his ends of the moment. His attitude resembled Napoleon's in this respect. The story goes that an officer once wanted to enter Napoleon's service. Questioned about his military career, he explained that unfortunately he had had a good deal of bad luck in the past. Napoleon replied that he could not use officers with whom bad luck was a habit. Hitler had the greatest scorn for boasters on the side of his enemies, but he himself was an easy mark for such individuals, provided that they flattered him or seemed ready to do what he wanted.

Hitler's opinion of the capabilities of various persons would vacillate wildly over the years. Wind-bags and incompetents he would hail as men of remarkable ability, and heap them with honors. Years later, when these same people had shown of what poor stuff they were made, he would cry damnation upon them and discover that they were really just the opposite of what he'd earlier said. And on the other hand he would dismiss others, especially his opponents, as political charlatans, lily-livered rascals, and puffed-up nonentities. It would take years of grim experience to prove to him that they were nothing of the kind. When I think over the ideas he had about people, I can only say that the sure instinct which he so prided himself on failed him in nine cases out of ten.

A few words of explanation may be necessary. It is well known that Hitler's cult of personality, the great stress he laid upon individuals, was one of the most important branches of his philosophy. As a socialist Hitler made much of the idea of the "folk community." But for himself as an individual there was something far more vital than the community-feeling: the individuality of the *Herrenmensch*, the man born to be a master. Personality is rooted in individualism; community in sense of the group. To strike a balance between the two and join them in a creative unity was the great aim of Hitler's doctrine. But it also became the great problem of his life, and the one he failed to solve. In going into this matter we touch upon ultimates, upon the underlying character of Hitler.

Personality can be considered a social concept, for it operates effectively only in the community. (That is, a person is a personality only insofar as he has accomplished something for the community; prestige is, as it were, conferred by the community. Otherwise a man may be an original, an eccentric, a virtuoso, or something of the sort, but not a personality.) Suppose then, that a man's greatness has been acknowledged by the community. The man is still of the community and as such cannot place himself outside and above it. He cannot compel the community to serve as the object of his personal need for domination—even if he should disguise that compulsion in the mythical trappings of fervent nationalism. Hitler was incapable of subordinating the forces of his own ego to the community which he had created. He arrogated to himself the right to be sole master; all others were to serve. On the plane of daily life he proclaimed the principle of community: the common good comes before the good of the individual. But in the sphere of the highest leadership he placed his personal drive to dominate far above the welfare of the people. Therein was revealed the flaw in his system. In his own person the two worlds of individual and community collided, and since he was too domineering to recognize his obligations to the community, the two worlds broke against each other.

The problem of all philosophical knowledge is that of the relationship of subject to object—that is, the incapacity of human beings as parts of the universe to place themselves above this universe as knowing subjects. In the sphere of national order Hitler, too, faced this problem. He wanted the impossible, but not even he could jump over his own shadow. His imperious nature could not strike a compromise between the individual and the community. At the very bottom of his soul the dualism of his character could not be overcome, and its effects were radiated outward for all to see.

His egocentricity operated strikingly in his treatment of people around him. No one in the vicinity of Hitler stood a chance of developing into a personality in his own right. Passionate subjectivist that Hitler was, he had no understanding or sympathy for objectivity. Again and again he stressed that he wanted to cleanse the minds of the German people of all "objectivity nonsense" and educate them to subjective thinking. He was the purest subjectivist imaginable, for he evaluated people solely by the standard of their usefulness to his ends. That alone explains his disastrous misjudgments, and the wild ups-and-downs of his favors.

Göring, who during the First World War had been a good fighter pilot, and who later was not a bad politician, was hailed by Hitler as the greatest genius in military aviation. Ten years later, when Göring could no longer deliver victories, Hitler decided that he was the greatest failure on record. Ribbentrop, who was stupid and gauche, touchy and servile, and who went about like a miniature edition of his master, wearing the expression of a frustrated Caesar, was a favorite of Hitler's. His obstinacy was proverbial. Once he had determined on a course, however misguided, nothing could budge him.

Hitler always judged Goebbels accurately. He recognized him as a person with a unique talent for oratory, admired his "gift of gab," and made use of it to the end.

Ley was a garrulous dullard, the type of German much in evidence during the last ten years, who had not a thought of his own and did not want to have any, and who "worshipped" Hitler. Hitler called him his "greatest idealist."

Himmler toadied up to Hitler intellectually. From my observation of him, the man had distinct traces of insanity. Hitler had a ridiculously high opinion of him. Only at the very end, after Himmler had vainly tried his hand at being a soldier and had failed as organizer of the last resistance, did Hitler recognize him for what he was, a "blank and a disappointment."

Koch he called his best gauleiter and Speer his most competent minister. Bormann, his secretary and Party manager, the unseen organizer of his private life, the witness at his wedding, and at the last the director of his funeral, Hitler characterized as his "most loyal Party comrade."

His testament affords the clearest proof that he was wrong about people down to his last breath.

His grotesque verdicts upon his contemporaries and opponents in international affairs, verdicts which he would burst out with during table-talk, now have only historical interest.

He had Chamberlain labeled as the prototype of the hide-bound British conservative. He felt himself affronted because the British prime minister would not grant him hegemony on the continent and would not make a deal with him on a land-and-sea partnership between England and Germany. After Godesberg he was furious with Chamberlain, whose efforts to keep peace on the continent he denounced as betrayal and fraud. On the whole, however, he admired the British Tories and their skill at governing throughout the world. He never ceased to hope that British conservatism would eventually become his ally in Europe.

Churchill he hated as the greatest antagonist of his life, a man whose whole style of life was diametrically opposed to his own. Churchill's earlier life as a war correspondent, writer, and critic aroused antipathy and feelings of rivalry in Hitler, the orator, and he would rant against Churchill on this account. Oddly enough, he was enraged at the idea that Churchill sold his articles for large sums—although Hitler himself, when the "Movement" was in need, had accepted payments of several thousand dollars for his interviews with American journalists. Churchill, so fond of good living and good whisky, with his inevitable cigar in his mouth, was an offence in the eyes of Hitler, the anti-smoker and teetotaler. When he heard that Churchill was in the habit of dictating in the mornings from his bathroom, and when he saw a picture of

Churchill bent over a prayer-book, praying for victory, he became absolutely rabid.

I always handed him the texts as well as the summary of Churchill's stirring wartime speeches. Hitler read them carefully, and I gathered from his entirely superficial and irrelevant remarks that he secretly admired them. But he would never discuss them in any serious way. Since the majority of his associates showed they were impressed by these speeches, Hitler himself preserved an icy silence on the subject. He would only pick away violently at random weak points in the speeches. He could not bring himself to admit that Churchill had the qualities of a great man. Before the war Churchill had once received a gauleiter of Hitler's in his London studio and had said, "Your Führer will be the greatest statesman in Europe if he preserves the peace of the world." Peace had not been preserved. In the war with Germany the same Churchill who had hurled imprecations against Bolshevism formed an alliance with Stalin against Hitler. For this maneuver Hitler so detested Churchill that objective judgment was out of the question.

Roosevelt was, to Hitler's mind, merely the capitalistic tool of "international Judaism"—Bolshevist Moscow being the other, the proletarian end of this conspiracy. To expose and defeat this double-barreled international plot was, he felt, the mission of his life. With each presidential election in America, he hoped to see Roosevelt trounced. Sooner than provide Roosevelt with anything which would be useful to his cause, he forbade the German press and the German radio to attack Roosevelt during the election campaigns against Willkie and Dewey. Roosevelt's sudden death aroused in Hitler one of his last hopes, and to this he clung almost up to his own death.

With Stalin Hitler felt a certain sense of solidarity, although he appraised the Russian's personality differently depending on his own political direction of the moment. As the high priest of Marxism and the enemy of his own ideology, Stalin was someone to be hated. After the nonaggression pact, Hitler was full of praise for his ally. When

Stalin became his deadly foe again, he did not stop respecting him, but he refused to say a good word for him.

Mussolini was Hitler's great love in politics. He honored the Duce as a great friend, a man of his own stature. He called him a "genuine Roman Caesar," and considered their community of interest a pledge of loyal friendship. After 1934 when their relationship became an entirely cordial one, Hitler more and more drew Mussolini under the spell of his own demonic personality. His psychological hold over Mussolini was such that the Italian was a will-less tool in his hand. But in the international sphere I always considered Mussolini a moderating influence upon Hitler. During the Sudeten crisis Mussolini interceded at the eleventh hour; it was he who arranged the Munich conference. He tried to restrain Hitler in his conflict with Poland, and attempted to hold Hitler back before the campaign against France. Then he too was swept away by the Hitler successes. After his fall and his rescue by Hitler, he was nothing but a living wreck; he scarcely spoke a word at table and was utterly submissive to Hitler. Mussolini's terrible death in Milan was very much in Hitler's mind when he resolved to put an end to his own life.

Upon Victor Emmanuel, whose guest in the Quirinal he was at one time, Hitler concentrated all his dislike for kings.

Horthy he valued as a person, but could not really like because of his deep-seated prejudice against Hungarians.

Antonescu struck him as a great political figure. His subsequent disillusionment with the man was as great as his over-estimation had been.

After meeting Franco on the Spanish border in 1940, Hitler no longer thought very well of him.

Hitler had a place in his heart for the "old fighters" in his Party. He went on cherishing many of them long after there was any reason for him to do so. On the other hand, there were many instances in which he was altogether unjust and ungrateful. For example, he made an ugly scene about a trivial blunder in the service at table, jumped on his adjutant Brückner for it, and dismissed the man. Brückner had stood at his side day and night, through bad times and good, for more than ten years. Another time Hitler flew into a fury in Dessau because the Hitler Youth were marching in the wrong place in a parade. He turned upon his constant companion of twenty years, Schaub, who had the ill luck to be standing right behind him, and reduced his rank in the SS then and there in the presence of the crowd—although Schaub had nothing whatsoever to do with the incident.

One certainly had the feeling that Hitler was bothered by inferiority complexes. These would be revealed on social and diplomatic occasions. During his second visit to Italy, when he was invited to the Royal Palace in Naples, the chief court marshal made what Hitler thought was an international slip-up in the arrangements. Hitler had saluted the crowd in his ordinary street clothes. On his way to change for the evening reception, he was obliged to pass by the guests who had already arrived. Hitler made a veritable international incident out of his having been given no time to change his clothes, and demanded a formal apology. Before that, in Rome, he had made a similar fuss, this time out of solidarity with the Duce. In reviewing the parades from the platform, Mussolini was supposed to stand behind the female members of the Royal House, while Hitler was to be given a place of honor in front. Hitler declared that he would not accept this place of honor when Mussolini was given a subsidiary place. Mussolini had to stand beside Hitler himself or beside the king.

Early in March 1945 an American bomb destroyed Hitler's dining room. It struck the table toward noon, putting a definitive end to that "Round Table."

Directly behind the dining room a stairway led down to the underground bunker which Hitler had ordered built for himself. There in the months of March and April 1945 the last act of the drama was played.

Some fifteen to twenty narrow steps, with several interposing gastight doors, separated this bunker from the street level. It was an underground cavern in the truest sense of the word. There Hitler's collapse took place. In striking contrast to the large, colorful rooms which he loved, those in the bunker were small, boxlike chambers painted a chalky white. His private quarters, a living room and bedroom, were situated at the lowest spot in the shelter, directly underneath the marble columns of the opulent dining hall where he had spent so much of his time in the years of peace, flanked by the highest dignitaries of Germany and foreign countries.

The bunker contained a somewhat larger reception room, where Hitler conferred during those last weeks with the generals of the army and air force, the admirals and officers of the OKW, who had continued to meet in his splendid offices in the New Chancellery up to February. Now the maps were spread out on a simple table between those four austere white walls. Hitler himself received reports from individuals in a tiny square concrete box hardly large enough to hold six persons. It too could be closed by a gastight bulkhead, and was the last cubicle in the shelter-directly adjoining the small flight of steps which led to the garden of the Chancellery.

In the other direction this bunker beneath the old Chancellery was connected by a rough corridor with the large shelter which had been built beneath the New Chancellery in the course of its construction. This shelter was entered from Voss Strasse. From 1942–44 Hitler had turned it over to Berlin schoolchildren as a regular night shelter for them. There they were cared for by the NSV (National Socialist People's Welfare) and other welfare organizations.

During the last years of the war the building of bunkers had been Hitler's hobby. The bunkers at his headquarters were constantly being strengthened with new layers of concrete. He expected incessant air raids, for it would be only natural, he thought, for his enemies to make every effort to attack his headquarters and eliminate him. Many hundreds of workers of the Todt Organization spent years working on the big headquarters in the Forest of Rastenburg. Ultimately his bunkers there were covered, in the shape of a cone, with more than twenty-five feet of concrete.

In addition to this headquarters where Hitler lived, after his return from the West, until February 1945, there were several other headquarters being built up and extended. One of these, in Silesia, was being blasted into rocky cliffs. Whenever there was the slightest danger from the air, Hitler insisted on everyone's going to the bunkers. He himself spent many hours in poorly ventilated, dark, and unhealthy rooms. It was from such living conditions, it may well be said, that his health broke down.

I saw that breakdown approaching step-by-step. It was in the Ukraine in October 1942 that Nature gave her first sharp warning. German reverses in the Caucasus had taken a toll of Hitler's nervous system. He no longer felt up to the long conversations of the daily dinners at the casino. An argument with General Jodl provided him with the initial excuse for withdrawing from the company. Henceforth he dined alone in his room. When he wanted company he would ask one or another of his female secretaries to eat with him.

The twentieth of July, the day of the attempt to assassinate him at his headquarters in East Prussia, was the point of crisis. That the attempt did not take place in a bunker, where Hitler was spending most of his time those days, undoubtedly was his salvation. For once, the situation conference was being held in a lightly constructed barracks room; the floor was of wood, with an open space underneath, and in the adjoining room the windows were open. As a result, the explosion produced no blast pressure, merely a sudden sharp flame. Had the bomb gone off in a concrete bunker, none of those present would have escaped with their lives; the blast pressure would have torn them to pieces. This is what happened:

About ten minutes to one in the afternoon I was in my bunker, some hundred yards away from the room where the situation conference was being held. Suddenly I heard a violent explosion that seemed to shake the whole forest. I ran out and raced toward the conference room, from which I saw a huge cloud of black smoke rising vertically. General Field Marshal Keitel, his hair singed, emerged from the barracks and came toward me. I heard him saying, "It was not yet to be this time." General Jodl was making a big to-do to the effect that such a disaster could not possibly take place "on his own grounds." Injured men were being carried out on stretchers, and I helped out with the first-aid work. When Hitler's chief military adjutant was carried past me on a stretcher, I saw at a glance that he would not be long among the living.

I asked about Hitler. He had already been taken to his bunker next door. I went in to find out how he was. He was sitting on a chair in his small living room, and he seemed to me to be fairly composed. His legs were almost bare, his trousers ripped into ribbons and shreds. His left arm was injured; it had received a severe blow from the tabletop on which he had been leaning his elbow when the bomb went off under the table only five feet away from him. His ear drums had burst, and his face had been cut by flying splinters of wood. He was completely controlled while the doctor examined him. He was thinking the matter over and discussing what might have happened; the enormity of the incident was gradually beginning to dawn on us. Meanwhile Göring and Himmler had arrived.

When we went into the shambles of the map room to inspect the scene, we discovered under the big map table a circular hole about twenty inches in diameter. Apparently half of the force of the explosion had been expended in the hollow space under the floor. At first the workers in the headquarters area were suspected. But in the course of the afternoon the picture was clarified.

Colonel Stauffenburg had arrived by plane from Berlin during the morning and had been given an appointment with Hitler. Accompanied by Keitel, he entered the conference room at 12:30 P.M. He placed his briefcase under the map table, to Hitler's right.

While the army chief of staff was reporting, he busied himself for a moment with his briefcase. He then remarked that he had to make a telephone call. The telephone orderly observed him leaving the room. He went to his car which was parked a hundred and fifty yards from the barracks and waited there until the explosion went off. Then he drove quickly past the column of smoke to the exit from the camp. Although a cordon had meanwhile automatically sealed off the entire area, an officer of the guard intervened to let Stauffenberg through. He drove to the airfield some two miles away. On the way he threw his second bomb into the underbrush where it was found during the next day's search. His plane was waiting for him; he flew to Berlin bringing word that Hitler was dead. The rest of the story is well known.

For Hitler, the after-effect was more serious than the immediate shock. When his left arm was freed from the sling, he was left with a nervous quivering of his hand which did not go away and obviously hampered him. His whole posture lost its tautness; his knees were thereafter weak and somewhat sagging.

The effect upon his spirit, however, was the reverse; his reaction was a powerful rallying of the will. After he had seen to it that the conspirators were rooted out and sternly punished, he gathered up his resources for one last great military effort. He drafted the plans for the final offensive in the West, hoping to turn the tide of battle there. On December 12, 1944 he went to the headquarters he had picked in the Taunus Mountains, near Bad Nauheim. It was a place remote from the world, on the slope of a forested height, a small, well-camouflaged colony of modest blockhouses. After the failure of this offensive he then returned to East Prussia for a few weeks. Although this headquarters was already threatened by the Russian advance, he stayed on in order to provide a good example for the population and the defenders of East Prussia. Not until February, when the situation temporarily eased for a few days, did he move the headquarters back to Berlin. His new chief of staff, Guderian, who until then had devoted all his energies to defending the German eastern front, now began opposing Hitler repeatedly during the situation conferences. He plainly no longer shared Hitler's confidence, or rather outward show of confidence. In the middle of March Hitler dismissed him, replacing him by his closest associate, General Wenck, and later by Wenck's deputy, General Krebs, who remained with Hitler to the very end.

Hitler had taken a resolve to remain in Berlin and to stand or fall with the capital. No one could persuade him otherwise, although many persons tried. He wanted to provide an example of steadfastness, and sharply rebuked those who urged him to leave. Well into April he went on displaying an iron composure and apparently continued to believe that by the force of his own will he could yet bring about a turn in destiny. He refused to consider any other thought. In the arrogance of better times he had said he would never capitulate. He was not going back on his word. In Berlin he wanted to defy fate, and he really believed in a miracle.

In this desperate situation he now carried his old fighting methods to their extremity. With Goebbels he started the insane "werewolf" movement. He categorically ordered all bridges to be blown up, wherever the enemy was advancing, and woe to him who questioned the senseless destructiveness of such an order. The tension between existing conditions and the inflexibility of Hitler's will had become unbearable. The breaking-point was approaching.

After telephone communications broke down, Hitler sent a radio message ordering the arrest of Göring, who was in his home on the Obersalzberg. Göring, having received no word from Hitler for days, had inquired by telegram whether or not he should prepare to take over as his successor. During those last days Hitler also expelled Himmler from the Party because Himmler, on his own initiative, had commissioned Schellenberg in Stockholm to sound out the possibilities of peace. Finally he had Himmler's liaison officer executed. This was General of the Waffen-SS Fegelein, Hitler's own brother-in-law.*

Two days after his fifty-sixth birthday, on April 22, there came a report of a deep breakthrough by a Russian division to the north of the capital. All at once the spirit, which had been maintained so far only by superhuman forces of the will, gave way completely. Hitler now admitted that everything was lost and wanted to commit suicide. But the military men in his entourage urged him not to throw away his last card.

He had one last resurgence of his old powers. During the night he sketched out a final strategic plan, which was condemned to failure by his own obstinacy even before it could be put into action. This was the plan to deploy the armies outside Berlin in such a way as to defeat the Russians there and block their retreat.

On his orders the High Command left Berlin so that it could conduct the operation from the north. He himself, with only a few others, remained behind in the bunker of the Chancellery, obviously to prepare himself for the end. The group included Goebbels with his entire family; during all the last weeks Goebbels lived in two tiny rooms directly adjoining Hitler's private quarters.

Hitler's external appearance was that of a man on his last legs physically. His complexion was chalky white; the traces of sleeplessness were plain in the pallid swellings under his bloodshot eyes. He walked in stooped posture, his knees shaking, his left hand quivering.

Now that the dream of rule was almost over and the content of his life had fled, the people were no longer in his mind. He left them to their fate. They could no longer serve his adventurous ambitions. They had been ruined by his will to power. When his last hopes vanished, there vanished also his ideas of national existence as an exclusively heroic process. He turned to his own personal life, at its

* Technically, Fegelein was Eva Braun's brother-in-law, rather than Hitler's. By the time that Braun and Hitler were married, Fegelein was already dead.

most mortal and unheroic level. His last days were devoted to his departure from life.

Eva Braun had spent the last two months with him in the bunker in Berlin. She had come there of her own accord. Her human and spiritual relationship to him at this time deserves respect. Her attitude made these last days easier for him to bear. In order to dignify her in the eyes of posterity and to remove all cause for evil gossip, Hitler decided that their marriage should take place at last. Bormann, as always, made all the preparations for the ceremony; he fetched a civil official and was one of the witnesses to the marriage, Goebbels being the other. The wedding was conducted during the night of April 28–29, in the bunker. That same night Hitler dictated his testaments. As I know his habits, these documents were products of the mood of the moment, dictated directly to the typist. For days those around him had been expecting him to apply himself to this last task. Now he suddenly decided to set it down in one headlong rush, without careful consideration. The political section follows the pattern of all his speeches. There, in his "last will," the terrible, abnormal dichotomy of his nature is given full rein. The dark side of his split personality which had remained more or less hidden throughout his life, is fully revealed.

The testament takes no notice whatsoever of the terrible plight of the German people. It willfully ignores the realities of the situation. It orders further resistance in the face of a predicament so frightful that Hitler himself is preparing to take his own life to escape from it. Hitler had appointed himself the leader of a rising, victorious nation; he feels no concern for the eighty million defeated people whose ruler he has been. He can find no word of sympathy, of helpfulness, of counsel or encouragement for the Germans he is leaving behind in sorest straits. He has no thought of his own responsibility for the conditions that arose out of his own dictatorial course. On the contrary, his testament simply repeats the very doctrines he had preached to the people all his life—repeats them at a moment when

Hitler should surely have realized that these doctrines had brought doom to the German people.

He instructed Goebbels to set up a cabinet, although he knew full well that Goebbels had resolved to join him in taking leave of life. Even in the face of death he clung to his fantasies and closed his eyes to the grim realities. A victim of the psychosis of treason, he accused his most faithful followers; reviling them, he thrust them into the outer darkness. The purpose of that "delirium of betrayal," of which Goebbels speaks in his own testament, was to clear himself in the eyes of posterity.

Then, without fear or hesitation, he put an end to his own life. Bormann had already been ordered to burn his mortal remains in the garden of the Chancellery.

Postscript

I SAW HITLER the man, his life, his work, and his extinction, as I have described it all in the preceding pages. I began writing this book five months after Hitler's death. That is, perhaps, too short an interval between the events themselves and their treatment as history. But it has this merit: that the facts are all fresh in my memory, undistorted by the passage of time. I hope that my story will be useful to future historians as source material with which to work.

In conversation Hitler himself used often to berate those "scribblers of history" who twist and falsify history in retrospect in order to grind political axes. Preserving the facts as they are still vivid in the memories of contemporaries and eye-witnesses is not to make oneself a historian, but rather to lay the groundwork for the historian.

The candid camera shots of a writer who records life as it was lived and experienced cannot and are not intended to be a substitute for the artistic portrait which catches the essence of a human being as seen in the most various lights. The contemporaneous record resembles a moving picture film taken in slow motion. Historiography is something else again; it portrays a human being within the framework of his nation, and its evaluations are based on different and perhaps wider considerations.

When it comes to writing history which will be meaningful for the German people, one cannot help but take into account the feelings of hero-worship which are very much alive in that people. Such feelings are strongly rooted in traditional German thinking. The great German historians have always been in accord with this national tendency. Those feelings have, however, been expressed with perhaps the greatest force and conviction by the famous English historian Thomas Carlyle, whose work is so highly esteemed in Germany. In his book *Heroes and Hero-Worship* he says: "Universal History, the history of what man has accomplished in this world, is at bottom the History of the Great Men who have worked here. . . . It is the soul of the whole world's history. . . . No nobler feeling than this of admiration for one higher than himself dwells in the breast of man."

In the interests of clarity, it is essential to define the nature of heroism. The hero, says Carlyle, "is the victorious interpreter of the divine idea, who lives within the inner sphere of things, in the True and the Eternal which is always present beneath the commonplace, invisible though it is to most eyes. Therefore it is at all times difficult to recognize what a great man is."

Leaving aside the criterion of total achievement, the characteristics of heroism according to Carlyle are valor, sincerity, harmony with the moral law, and the "seeing eye," the power of true insight into the essential characteristics of things. Was Hitler endowed with these characteristics indispensable to historical greatness?

Hitler was without doubt a brave man. His courage impressed everybody. And in his aspirations for his people Hitler was also profoundly sincere. He believed heart and soul in a Teutonic mission of the German people, in their special gift for organization and their talent for government, in the call of the nordic race to provide spiritual leadership, and in the destiny of the German nation to be a creator of culture. And he believed that it was his own special task, his supreme vocation, to direct this mission of his people.

These beliefs were the motivations of his acts. But the "seeing eye," the "power of true insight" which Carlyle calls the mark of divine kinship which in all epochs has united a great man with other men—this Hitler did not possess. He did not see through the appearance of things to their essence; rather, he succumbed to error and the lure of false ideas.

There are certain historical parallels for this condition. Odin, the greatest of the Germanic heroes, saw himself as a god, but he was, says Carlyle, "not necessarily false; he was but mistaken, speaking the truest he knew." In action for his people he was successful. Hitler was not. Hitler did not live in the days of old, but in the present age, which is one of extreme modernity.

Hitler had no insight into the divine character of human existence, nor into the always miraculous life of nature. He had a false view of evolution and saw the events of the present with the outmoded concepts of the past. This is one of the two critical points on which Hitler is disqualified for the historical role of a true heroic figure.

We will have to admit that Hitler had great social ideas, but he had no sense of development, no eye for inner harmony, no feeling for the natural maturing of things. Above all he had no inner comprehension of the necessity of the moral law in contemporary human society. Bent on realizing the fantastic world of his imagination, ready to use any means which would speed this end, he lacked all ability to distinguish between good and evil, lacked all understanding of a moral imperative, of a Thou Shalt or Thou Shalt Not. This was the second critical flaw in Hitler's character, by which he fell short of true greatness. It was a flaw which negated the genuinely heroic aspects of Hitler, his courage and sincerity.

Because Hitler possessed a number of heroic traits, which won the people's reverence, but lacked two of the essential requirements that lead human greatness to success, namely insight and moral strength—because of his unfortunate character structure, his dynamic leadership brought tragedy upon the people who had believed in him. This explains the terrible moral predicament of the German people, a Gordian knot which could only be cut through by the sword of the victorious Allies. A strange combination of evil circumstances was at work here.

The dangerous man, writes Carlyle, is the man who follows his fancies and misunderstands the nature of the thing with which he is dealing; called to high position, such a man is indescribably dangerous. And precisely such a man was Hitler.

For Hitler, the rude power of natural evolution, not human reason, was the motive force of the divine world order. He did not recognize that evolution also affects human thought. His mind was medieval in a century of world-shaking discoveries.

The phenomenon that was Hitler is unparalleled in history. In the incessant swings of the pendulum from good to evil, in the hardness and demonism of his character, and the extent of his influence upon the world, he was unique among historical figures. We will find no likeness to the total configuration of his personality; we can see only certain parallel traits in other historic characters. Perhaps these analogies may clarify some of his essential features.

Voltaire, in his *History of Charles XII*, describes that adventurous Swedish king as follows: "He was perhaps the most extraordinary man who ever lived. In himself he united all the great traits of his forefathers; his sole fault and his sole misfortune was that he carried all these traits to excess. He possessed unconquerable obstinacy and an uncontrollable character. He exaggerated all heroic virtues to such a degree that they became as dangerous as the opposite vices. His firmness became inflexibility."

Napoleon called himself the "Son of Fortune." Metternich told him in Dresden in 1813: "Failures as well as successes drive you to war." Carlyle, passing judgment on Napoleon, wrote: "Faith in democracy carried Napoleon through all his great work. . . . But at this point, I think, the fatal charlatan-element got the upper hand. . . . Self and false ambition had now become his god."

The Italian neurologist, Lombroso, coined the phrase: "Genius is madness." Professor Ernst Kretschmar, in his book *Men of Genius*, points out the connection between creative genius and certain forms of psychopathy and mental disturbances: "The psychopathic element in the inherited disposition of men of genius is an indispensable part of the psychological whole which we call genius."

Physically, Hitler was in my judgment a splenetic. Mentally, he was afflicted with a mania for excess; psychologically he was a schizophrenic personality of unique intensity.

His sound mind produced a great national ideal. His morbid viewpoint totally misread the future course of human evolution. His inhuman and insatiable will shattered the edifice of contemporary life.

Our teachers of history have stressed the value of personality and held up to us as luminous examples the ideal of the heroic; to teach young people appreciation for the hero has been one of the goals of education. But this desirable attitude on the part of historiography and pedagogy also has its undesirable side-effects, which have perhaps not emerged often enough in our history to be recognized clearly. Our interpreters of history, in their laudable effort to see only the positive and not the negative aspect of things, have sometimes overstepped the boundaries of idealism and represented matters in a falsely glorious light. In former days both sides of the question were aired, and certain bounds were set upon hero-worship. Such sobriety has recently become unfashionable, and to be "a debunker of heroes" has been to incur disgrace.

One excess in the writing of history begets another. We are now experiencing the opposite tendency. Indiscriminate worship is being corrected by what I may call "compensatory injustice." Youth heretofore has been educated to an immoderate and uncritical worship of "great men." Now, in one sudden blow that has descended with the violence of a natural disaster, the hard realities of life have corrected and overcorrected that fault in education. Belief in human greatness and infallibility, reverence for certain historical personalities is first carried to excess, then countermanded. The undisputed heroes of today are the mediocrities of tomorrow.

The really great men, those who are recognized as such by the history of all nations, are unaffected by this process. But it must be said that this education of the German nation for centuries to blind faith, to exaggerated worship, to unconditional respect, and to a totally uncritical attitude toward flattering speeches and fine words, has laid the people open to grievous mistakes and to total catastrophe.

The premises of this education reveal certain logical errors. It has long been an accepted principle in the natural sciences that thought and knowledge are also subject to progressive evolution. New methods of research follow from new knowledge and new developments. The same would appear to be true for the liberal arts and for history.

In practical life the ultimate and decisive criterion for the greatness and genius of a man is, in general, what that man has done for his nation or for humanity—whether his achievement be material or immaterial in nature, whether its importance emerges immediately or after a time.

But there remains a possibility I have left aside, and one which I must consider, lest I be charged with prejudice. For Carlyle speaks of heroes who are not victorious, who bravely fought and fell. Such men were what he calls "heroic seekers."

Such men there have certainly been—great inventors and unrecognized geniuses whose contributions to the nation or to mankind became evident only after their deaths, became a blessing enjoyed by posterity. Was Hitler one of these? Can such a collapse, such wholesale annihilation of all we valued in Germany, ever turn out to have been for the good, so that future generations will look to Hitler as the father of a better world? Does this seem likely? This is a question I may safely leave to the reader to answer.

The German people saw in Hitler the symbol of their own life and destiny. They saw their reflection in his greatness and sunned themselves in his good fortune. They perceived themselves in the bravery, endurance, and will-power of this man, admired themselves in the bold products of his mind. But they also worshipped themselves in his autocratic nature, his overestimation of himself, his psychological obtuseness, his conceit, and his inadequate sense of reality. And so in the end they fell victim to a worship of their own magnified and distorted mirror-image.

If we Germans would draw any lesson from the almost incomprehensible events of recent years, so that we may have mental clarity enough to strike out on a new path, we must raise the question: guilt or destiny? Was it guilt or destiny which brought the German people to their present predicament? From my participation in German history during this fateful decade and from my first-hand view of political events, I can say out of deepest conviction: It was not ill will, not criminal desires, which brought the nation to its present pass and which won for Germans the base reputation of being politically amoral. This nation followed Hitler in good faith and, alas, all too credulously; the blame is not the nation's but his alone. A victim of the demonism of his own nature, Hitler was not only their leader, but their seducer!

I have described the circumstances under which the nation awarded Hitler unprecedented power. Hitler was to lead the German nation onward and upward. His mandate did not include the mandate to make war. The Germans did not want war; the years 1914–1918 taught them to hate war in all its grimness and senselessness. They were led into war without their consent and against their innermost desires. That today they must assume *in toto* all responsibility for Hitler's lost war weighs them down with an oppressive burden. But if this is a fact and as such unalterable, the nation nevertheless must under no circumstances cover up for Hitler, assume for him the blame for the monstrously inhuman and immoral deviations and the abuse of power which Hitler committed without the knowledge or the desire of the people. For so, it would seem, the nation would refuse to admit the truth about their late Leader. Should the people, in mistaken loyalty and with violation of the truth, continue to make a hero out of him, they would be taking his sins upon their own shoulders. Such self-incrimination would bring no good to the nation, but only more grief. It would not be fair to future generations of Germans to encumber them so with a guilt in no way their own. Rather, the people must face the unadorned truth about Hitler. They will then understand themselves. And other nations will realize that when the mysterious figure of Hitler took over the direction of Germany, a tragic, fated guilt descended upon the people. Hitler's diabolic qualities, his self-contradictory traits, the alluring power of his ideas, and his seductive words, the hypnotic force of his will, and the ugly offshoots of his inhuman political morality—all these entered into and could not be separated from Hitler's "life work." In submitting to his leadership, the people enthroned his demon.

For thirty years our present generation has led a life of suffering and sacrifice. Hitler has plunged it into misery and misfortune. How, then, can we ascribe any real greatness to him?

But if we draw from this experience conclusions which will further rationality, morality, and progress, it is possible that the unhappiness which descended upon our people along with the figure of Hitler may become a blessing for posterity. In which case Hitler will not have lived in vain for the German people, for he was obviously sent by Dark Powers as the executor of an unknown destiny.

Appendices

Appendix 1

Preface

Publisher's Note
The following is the author's preface to the original German edition, which was published in 1955.

THE MAJORITY of the German people had put their trust in a single man, had revered him like a saint and loved him like a father. This man then led them into the greatest catastrophe in their history. That is the naked, brutal, and shocking fact, and the German people, reeling from the terrible blows of the war, groping among the ruins of their past, must face it. Millions are now seeking reasons and explanations for this unexampled collapse. Their search, however, follows the line of their preconceptions.

I am convinced that only a thorough and uncompromising knowledge of Hitler's personality, of his innermost nature and his true character, can explain the inexplicable. We can reach an understanding of the truth, of the guilt and destiny of Germany, only by understanding the uncanny magnetism of Hitler's personality. The mystery of Hitler is the prism in which all the rays of tentative knowledge are broken up. Only when these have been reunited can we arrive at the historical truth of recent events. Only Hitler's innermost nature can reveal to us the hidden background; only a true portrait of this man can explain the tragedy of the German people.

This titan has been overthrown, but the German people still lack any clarity about Hitler. Such clarity is the indispensable prerequisite for any successful emergence from the débris-choked past into a better future. In all aspects of life real accomplishments can be achieved only if there is genuine concern and passionate devotion to a job. The German people will find the strength to rise again out of their tribulations and make their way into the community of peaceful nations only after they have overcome the past within themselves, out of their own deepest convictions. And to do that they need full knowledge of Hitler's character and works.

As fate would have it, I spent many years in a position which has enabled me to make a contribution to that necessary knowledge. For twelve years I was, as a publicity man, in Hitler's immediate entourage. I did not thrust myself forward to obtain this post. On January 30, 1933, when Hitler appointed Funk the new press chief of his government, he himself ordered me to remain in his personal following. Perhaps even then he thought of me as his future biographer. I came to esteem his likable traits and his efforts for the welfare of the people; but in the course of the years I also came to recognize how he had changed inwardly, and to hate his despotic nature. In spite of repeated attempts on my part to break free, he did not permit me to leave. I heard a great deal, but by no means learned everything; for things that were not meant for the public to know were kept from the ear of a newspaperman. Hitler knew how to keep silence. With rigid strictness he carried out the principle: "Nobody need know more about important matters than is absolutely necessary for the performance of his duties. If only two persons need know something, no third person is to hear of it."

I took no notes. But out of a thousand details of Hitler's public and private life during more than twelve years I absorbed the essence of the personality of this mysterious man—until that thirtieth of March 1945 when, in the small room of his concrete bunker under the Chancellery, he stripped me of my functions—after a violent dispute.

Hitler's stupendous achievements during six years of extraordinary peacetime successes obscured his weaknesses. Six year of warfare brought to the fore his equivocal character traits and the excesses of his demonic personality. He was the standard-bearer, and as long as some hope remained of fending off a dire fate, innumerable Germans believed it was their solemn duty not to desert the flag.

Up to the last moment his overwhelming, despotic authority aroused false hopes and deceived his people and his entourage. Only at the end, when I watched the inglorious collapse and the obstinacy of his final downfall, was I able suddenly to fit together the bits of mosaic I had been amassing for twelve years into a complete picture of his opaque and sphinxlike personality. Revelation of the bestialities in the concentration camps at home and in Poland opened my eyes, and showed me in firm outline the shifting contours of this man's character. When we study his portrait in retrospect, the lights and shades fall quite differently from the way we used to see them. Up to the end, we were looking at the portrait from an entirely different angle. The uncanny duality of his nature and the monstrousness of his true being suddenly become apparent.

I have spent much time in recent months considering whether I as a German ought to make public my analysis and my private knowledge of Hitler. My personal observations are neither completely comprehensive nor absolutely final. But I trust that they have some point insofar as they dispel the last shreds of glamor from the myth of Hitler—if that myth is still alive and still exerts some fascination for posterity. What I have to say will help consign his figure to the doleful shades. For this reason I have come to feel that my knowledge must not be withheld from the people—for the people's own sake. If my contemporaries, with their eyes fixed upon the past, fail to understand me, those who come after will surely profit from this account.

Facts are more powerful than theories. The course of world history has turned out very differently from what Hitler imagined. National Socialism was carried to excess; when it took off into the stratosphere of racist ideas, it lost touch with the solid ground of practical reality. Philosophical and psychological blinkers blinded it to the international aspects of man's recent history. It could not see that as progress and technology have increasingly overcome space and time and the peoples of the globe have moved closer to one another, the community within the borders of each separate nation has necessarily been tending toward a general community of all nations. For Hitler all human problems stopped at the very point where in modern times they truly begin. Today the significant and fateful questions of man's future progress will not be decided on the national plane, as Hitler thought, but on the international plane. This is an age of world-shaking—though possibly also world-wrecking—inventions. Universal cooperation has become an inescapable necessity, if the nations are not to exterminate one another. And democracy in the broadest sense has become the only viable political form for a rational humanity. Within its flexible framework personalities and creative achievements will continue to stamp their impress upon history as they have always done. But in the future no politically mature nation will ever commit itself unreservedly to the hand of a single man and of an authoritarian government. Henceforth the democratic rules alone will regulate the game upon the chessboard of world politics. That is now a fact which needs no discussion; events have made it so. Consequently, if the German people do not wish to shut themselves out for all time from the community of nations, if after this collapse they desire to rebuild their life upon a new basis so as to share with other nations the benefits of culture and civilization, they must abandon all thought of going back to an absolutist leader-state of the Hitler type. They must recognize any propaganda for such a state as the spawn of a reactionary imagination. To revert to authoritarianism would bring about the final political suicide of the German nation. The memory of how tragically they went astray in the recent past ought to serve the German people as a historical lesson for all times: never again to entrust a single man with power, thereby surrendering to him their destinies and their lives. For the human weaknesses of even the greatest of mortals can wreak woe on a nation if that one man holds sole power over life and death, war and peace. It was precisely such power Hitler held in his own hands. He came to power as a socialistic popular leader, as the creator of new ideas. Because he rescued them from a dire economic catastrophe, the people believed his promises, hailed him as a bearer of good fortune, favorite of destiny, and conferred upon him total power. In the course of the years, as his character and his aims changed, he used this power to ruin the nation.

He was not the greatest of mortals as he imagined himself to be. For all his genius, he had no moral greatness, and his strength was without blessing. He fell victim to the intoxication of power, was led into conflicts which he could not control and which sucked the entire nation into the whirlpool of destruction. The people were dazzled by his great triumphs in the field of social welfare and his nationalistic achievements. His outward show of likable personal traits deceived them in regard to his great but ruinous political tendencies. Hitler's development, his gradual transformation from a social-minded popular leader to a Herostratus in the realm of power politics, took place over the course of many years. The process was imperceptible; it is not possible to pick any given time and say, "He had changed." The steps were hard to define, but the changes were real. The true measure of his political genius is his completed work, as we see it before us in Germany; and the true measure of his human and moral stature can be seen in the kind of death he chose and the legacy he left.

The German people had a right to expect that Hitler would not leave them to face alone their utter wretchedness, or at least that he would not go without a word of justification for himself and exoneration for them. He had, after all, demanded blind obedience from them, and until the last he had continued to hold out the prospect of victory. But even in the face of his own death, and with the death-agony of his nation before his eyes, he refused in his obstinacy to listen to reason. His legacy in death was a judgment upon his life. He departed without having fulfilled this last obligation to his people, without any feeling for the sufferings of the people; he abandoned the nation in its hour of need, burdening it with all the crimes for which he should have answered.

I have tried to imagine how harshly, how ruthlessly Hitler would have judged anyone else who in his position acted as he did toward his own people. And I believe the people will understand if the truth about their former leader is revealed with equal harshness and ruthlessness.

I have a responsibility to myself as well as to the German people to draw this portrait as faithfully as I know how. As a publicist who believed in the Nazi cause I consistently presented the more decent and likable sides of Hitler to the people, thereby helping to bring him closer to the hearts of many Germans. At that time I sincerely believed that my task was in the best interests of the nation. But my pro-Hitler writings have since, due to the change in the times and the change in the man, become a heavy burden on my conscience. I therefore feel obliged to present the darker aspects of the man which were later revealed, to draw in the shadows in order to finish the picture. In 1933 I wrote a book entitled *With Hitler on the Road to Power,* in which I enthusiastically described Hitler's peaceful struggle for the soul of the German people. I presented National Socialism as imbued with the desire for peace. At that time I honestly believed this. Now I owe to the public the tragic sequel to that book, the second part of the drama, which alone explains Hitler's plunge into the abyss and the collapse of the German Reich. I shall write this tragic sequel with the same passion, with love of truth and a sense of obligation toward the justice of history.

Appendix 2

Publisher's Note

Readers of *The Hitler I Knew: The Memoirs of the Third Reich's Press Chief* may also enjoy Heinz Linge's *With Hitler to the End* (2009). The following extracts are taken from Linge's memoir.

THE next day, April 30 1945, I went to Hitler in the early morning. He was opening the door as I arrived. He had lain on the bed fully dressed and awake as he had done the night before. While Bormann, Krebs and Burgdorf kept loaded pistols within reach, safety catches off, and dozed on sofas near his door, and the female secretaries made themselves as comfortable as possible while awaiting the events that must soon come (at any moment the Russians could reach the bunker entrance), he signalled to me to accompany him, finger to his lips, indicating I should be careful not to disturb the sleeping figures. We went to the telephone exchange, where Hitler rang the commandant, who told him that the defense of Berlin had already collapsed. The ring that the Russians had laid around the city could no longer be penetrated, and there was now no hope of relief. Arthur Axmann did offer to "bring the Führer out of Berlin" using about 200 Hitler Youth volunteers and a panzer, but Hitler declined, murmuring quietly, "That is no longer an option, I am remaining here!"

The "hour of truth" had come. Firstly, however, there was a last midday meal to be taken together. Hitler delivered a monologue about the future. The immediate postwar world would not have a good word to say for him, he said: the enemy would savor its triumph, and the German people would face very difficult times. Even we, his intimate circle, would soon experience things that we could not imagine. But he trusted to "the later histories" to "treat him justly." They would recognize that he had only wanted the very best for Germany. Not until after my release from captivity did I understand what he meant when he said: "You will soon experience things" that "you cannot imagine."

*

Immediately after this Hitler and I went into the common room where Goebbels appeared and begged Hitler briefly to allow the Hitler Youth to take him out of Berlin. Hitler responded brusquely: "Doctor, you know my decision. There is no change! You can of course leave Berlin with your family." Goebbels, standing proudly, replied that he would not do so. Like the Führer he intended to stay in Berlin—and die there. At that Hitler gave Goebbels his hand and, leaning on me, returned to his room.

Immediately afterward followed the last personal goodbyes. My mouth was dry. Soon I would have to carry out my last duty. Anxiously I gazed at the man whom I had served devotedly for more than ten years. He stood stooped, the hank of hair, as always, across the pale forehead. He had become gray. He looked at me with tired eyes and said he would now retire. I asked for his orders for the last time. Outwardly calm and in a quiet voice, as if he were sending me into the garden to fetch something, he said: "Linge, I am going to shoot myself now. You know what you have to do. I have given the order for the break-out. Attach yourself to one of the groups and try to get through to the west." Hitler took two or three tired steps towards me and offered his hand. Then for the last time in his life he raised his right arm in the Hitler salute. A ghostly scene. I turned on my heel, closed the door and went to the bunker exit where the SS bodyguard was sitting around.

*

I opened the door and went in, Bormann following me. He turned white as chalk and stared at me helplessly. Adolf Hitler and Eva Braun were seated on the sofa. Both were dead. Hitler had shot himself in the right temple with his 7.65-mm pistol. This weapon, and his 6.35-mm pistol which he had kept in reserve in the event that the larger gun misfired, lay near his feet on the floor. His head was inclined a little towards the wall. Blood had spattered on the carpet near the sofa. To his right beside him sat his wife. She had drawn up her legs on the sofa. Her contorted face betrayed how she had died. Cyanide poisoning. Its "bite" was marked in her features. The small box in which the capsule had been kept lay on the table. I pushed it aside to give myself room.

*

I reached below Hitler's head, two officers from his SS bodyguard lifted the body, wrapped in a gray blanket, and we carried him out. Immediately in front of the bunker door, in the Reich Chancellery garden, his body was laid next to Eva's in a small depression where gasoline was poured over the cadavers and an attempt was made to set light to them. At first this proved impossible. As a result of the various fires in the parkland there was a fierce wind circulating which smothered our attempts to set the bodies alight from a few metres' distance. Because of the relentless Russian artillery fire we could not approach the bodies and ignite the petrol with a match. I returned to the bunker and made a thick spill from some signal papers. Bormann lit it and I threw it onto Hitler's petrol-soaked body, which caught fire immediately. Standing at the bunker entrance we, the last witnesses—Bormann, Goebbels, Stumpfegger, Günsche, Kempka and I—raised our hands for a last Hitler salute. Then we withdrew into the bunker.

*

For Dr Joseph Goebbels, the new Reich Chancellor, it was not apparent until now that he and his wife Magda would commit suicide in Berlin this same day. After the experiences of recent days and weeks hardly anything could shock us men any more, but the women, the female secretaries and chambermaids were "programmed" differently. They were fearful that the six beautiful Goebbels children would be killed beforehand. The parents had decided upon this course of action. Hitler's physician Dr Stumpfegger was to see to it. The imploring pleas of the women and some of the staff, who suggested to Frau Goebbels that they would bring the children—Helga, Holde, Hilde, Heide, Hedda and Helmut—out of the bunker and care for them, went unheard. Once there she sank down in an armchair. She did not enter the children's room, but waited nervously until the door opened and Dr Stumpfegger came out. Their eyes met, Magda Goebbels stood up, silent and trembling. When the SS doctor nodded emotionally without speaking, she collapsed. It was done. The children lay dead in their beds, poisoned with cyanide. Two men of the SS bodyguard standing near the entrance led Frau Goebbels to her room in the Führer-bunker. Two and a half hours later both she and her husband were dead. The last act had begun.

Index